W9-CLQ-986

INDIA'S CHANGING VILLAGES

INTERNATIONAL LIBRARY OF SOCIOLOGY AND SOCIAL RECONSTRUCTION

Founded by Karl Mannheim
Editor: W. J. H. Sprott

A catalogue of the books available in the INTERNATIONAL LIBRARY OF SOCIOLOGY AND SOCIAL RECONSTRUCTION, and new books in preparation for the Library will be found at the end of this volume.

INDIA'S CHANGING VILLAGES

Human Factors in Community Development

by

S. C. DUBE
Professor of Anthropology
University of Saugar

LONDON
ROUTLEDGE AND KEGAN PAUL LTD
[1958]

First published in 1958
by Routledge & Kegan Paul Ltd
Broadway House, 68-74 Carter Lane
London, E.C.4.

Second Impression 1960
Third Impression 1963

Printed in Great Britain
by Lowe & Brydone (Printers) Ltd.,
London

CONTENTS

LIST OF ILLUSTRATIONS

ACKNOWLEDGEMENTS

As a product of group research this volume owes much to co-workers and associates at the Cornell Field Station, in Western U.P., India. Leela Dube, Raghuraj Gupta, R. Prakash Rao, and Tuljaram Singh worked with me as a team on this project. Materials gathered by them, both independently and under my direction, have gone into the writing of this book. R. Prakash Rao and Tuljaram Singh continued to help me from the field while I was analysing the data in the United States. Leela Dube undertook the responsibility for research among women in the field, and was associated closely with the analysis of field notes and writing of this book. Umesh Joshi coded and tabulated some of the questionnaires. Without their collaboration this work could not have been completed.

For stimulation, friendship, and general help in planning and conducting this research acknowledgement is due to John and Patricia Hitchcock, John Gumperz, Michael and Pauline Mahar, Edward E. LeClair, Jr., and Leigh Minturn. Hari Sahai Saksena helped with research on the role of village councils, and Shyam Narain Singh gave some of his time to investigations on the 4-H Clubs.

For co-operation in the field we are grateful to the village people, many of whom were interviewed several times, and to the officials of the Community Development Project who freely gave us their time and co-operation. For practical reasons they must remain anonymous.

Special thanks are due to D. G. Karve and V. Nath of the Programme Evaluation Organization, Tarlok Singh of the Planning Commission, and D. P. Singh, of the Planning Research and Action Institute, U.P., for their interest in the researches partly analysed in this volume. They provided critical insights and stimulation, but are in no way responsible for the views expressed in this study.

The book was written at the Cornell campus, in a stimulating atmosphere of research and discussion. Thanks are due to colleagues and students in the Department of Sociology and Anthropology and the Department of Far Eastern Studies, for fruitful discussion and exchange of ideas. Baidya Nath Varma of Columbia University and Baij Nath Singh and Rudra Datta Singh of Cornell University read some parts of the manuscript and gave the benefit of their ideas and experience. The substance of Chapter V was presented in a seminar at the Center for International Studies, Massachusetts Institute of Technology, and Chapter VI was offered as a paper in the Panel on 'The South Asian Village', at the 1956 Annual Meeting of the Far Eastern Association at Philadelphia.

Joan Sears is to be thanked for her understanding and ungrudging secretarial assistance.

The map of India showing the Community Development Projects and the National Extension Service Blocks was prepared by Vinod Misra of the Department of Geography, University of Saugar.

Finally, I have to thank the India Program of Cornell University for sponsoring this research in India, and for providing excellent facilities of analysis and writing in the United States. Morris Edward Opler was associated with this work at every stage, and his interest, sympathy, and guidance have gone much beyond his formal obligations as the Director of the Program.

S. C. DUBE

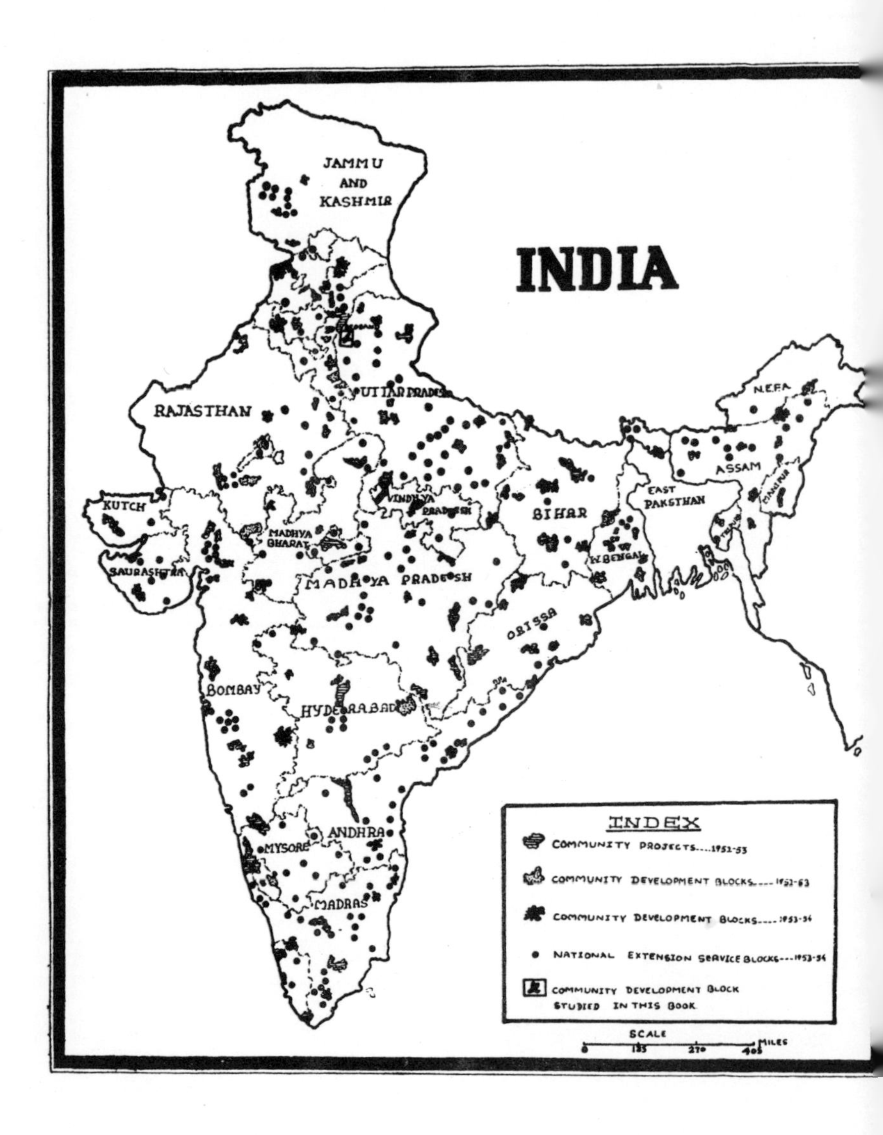

INDIA
JAMMU AND KASHMIR
RAJASTHAN
UTTAR PRADESH
KUTCH
SAURASHTRA
MADHYA BHARAT
VINDHYA PRADESH
MADHYA PRADESH
BIHAR
W. BENGAL
EAST PAKISTHAN
ASSAM
N.E.F.A.
MANIPUR
ORISSA
BOMBAY
HYDERABAD
ANDHRA
MYSORE
MADRAS
INDEX
COMMUNITY PROJECTS....1952-53
COMMUNITY DEVELOPMENT BLOCKS....1952-53
COMMUNITY DEVELOPMENT BLOCKS....1953-54
NATIONAL EXTENSION SERVICE BLOCKS---1953-54
COMMUNITY DEVELOPMENT BLOCK STUDIED IN THIS BOOK
SCALE
0 135 270 405 MILES

I

PLANNING FOR COMMUNITY DEVELOPMENT

1. Problems of Independent India

WHEN INDIA ATTAINED independence in 1947, she found herself faced with many vital problems of economic and social reconstruction. The political division of the country had left numerous tangled questions unsolved, caused considerable bloodshed and rioting, and brought into the country a large number of uprooted people. Its large and growing population of about 357 million people lived in more than 550 separate states. Of these only seventeen had constituted British India and had been ruled directly by Britain, the others belonged to the feudal order and had been ruled by native princes who paid a tribute of 5 per cent of their gross income for British protection. The consolidation of the Union of India and the integration of these princely states was one of the major tasks before the country. The antiquated land system, with several intermediary tax collectors between the peasant and the government, was crying for reform.

Even more serious than these matters of national unity and of other reforms in the economic structure, were a number of problems that demanded immediate attention. India's position in regard to food was precarious. Memories of the terrible famine in Bengal were still fresh in the minds of the people. Notwithstanding the government sponsored Grow More Food campaign, there were near-famine conditions in many parts of the country, and threats of famine were present in many more areas. In the last six decades of British rule the Indian population had grown over 50 per cent, but the increase in cultivated land was only 1·5 per cent. Shifts in agricultural production during war years, transfer of many important food producing areas to Pakistan as a result of partition, and a series of unprecedented natural calamities had aggravated the situation still further. Foreign food aid was welcome (and it did come in a fair measure when it was needed most), but the country could not count on it indefinitely and had to give serious thought to building up self sufficiency in food in the very near future.

In the industrial sphere, also, the picture was none too bright. Only 7·1 per cent of all gainfully employed people were in industry; competition of the factories had brought about a serious decline in rural cottage industries. The overall economic picture of the country, with a *per capita* yearly income of Rs255 and great differences in the incomes of the upper, middle, and lower classes, was distressing. Coupled with the problems of acute food shortage and general poverty of the masses were the problems of illiteracy and public health. Even in terms of a modest criterion of literacy, i.e. the ability to write and read one's name, only 14·4 per cent of the people could qualify. It was estimated that only 19 per cent of the children of school-going age were in schools, and only 50 per cent of these reached the fourth grade. There was an average life expectancy of twenty-nine years and the death rate was 19·7 per thousand. Among children the death rate was 146 per thousand. Taking the country's population as a whole there was one doctor per 6,300 of the population, but most of these were concentrated in urban centres; in village India, it was estimated, there was one doctor to 25,000 people. Low nutritional standards and unsanitary and unhygienic conditions of living exposed the rural areas to epidemics which took a heavy toll.

The social system also was in need of some modifications. The rise of social and political consciousness among the under-privileged groups and the reform movements started by Gandhi had initiated certain significant trends in the direction of the amelioration of the living conditions of these sections, but much more still needed to be done.

It was under conditions such as these that independent India launched her career as a welfare state. The Constitution of India, passed late in 1949, pledged to the people, '*Justice*, social economic, and political; *Liberty* of thought, expression, belief, faith and worship; *Equality* of status and opportunity; and to promote among them all *Fraternity* assuring the dignity of the individual and unity of the nation.' The directive principles of state policy defined some of the steps through which the goals of the welfare state were to be attained.

Contemporary planning and development activities in India are keyed to the objectives defined in the Constitution.

2. Planning in India

For the last few decades there has been considerable awareness of the importance of planning in India. In 1938 the Indian National Congress appointed a National Planning Committee to examine the resources of the nation and prepare plans for its reconstruction. During the last years of the Second World War there was considerable discussion of the problems of post-war reconstruction, and various departments of the government had undertaken important schemes for the welfare and development of the people. During these and the post-war years several plans, demonstrating varying approaches to the problem of the future reconstruction of India, were published and widely discussed. Among these special mention may be made of the Bombay Plan, the Gandhian Plan, and the People's Plan. The first Five Year Plan, framed by the Planning Commission, a draft outline of which was published in July 1951 and which went into action in a modified form in April 1951, represents the first massive effort on the part of the government in the direction of planned national development.

The National Planning Committee of the Indian National Congress had worked under the chairmanship of Jawaharlal Nehru for a number of years. Because of certain political developments and generally unsettled conditions in the country, it did not have an uninterrupted career. Although it could not come out with a comprehensive plan, it did much pioneering work by exploring the fundamental economic problems of the country and by examining the possibility of preparing a co-ordinated plan for national economic regeneration. In *Note for the Guidance of Sub-committees* (Handbook I), the concept of planning under a democratic system was defined as the technical co-ordination, by disinterested experts, of consumption, production, investment, trade, and income distribution, in accordance with social objectives set by bodies representing the nation, and was not only to be considered from the point of view of economics and the raising of the standard of living, but was to include cultural and spiritual values and the human side of life. The two major objectives of the Committee were to explore the means of attaining national self-sufficiency for the country as a whole without being involved as the result of such efforts in the whirlpool of economic imperialism, and of doubling of the present standard of living amongst the people of India, within a prescribed time limit, say, ten years. Standard of living, in this context, was broadly defined to include not only the provision of adequate food, shelter, and clothing, but also included such social services and civic amenities as are indispensable and integral part of modern civilized life and work. For the achievement of a minimum standard of living a set of ten norms were drawn up, which prescribed basic requirements in nutrition, clothing, housing, education, communication, etc.

As a *fact finding* body this Committee did very valuable work. Being a non-official body, and without any state support, it perhaps could not do more. However, its labour did not go in vain; in the formulation of the first Five Year Plan its findings were utilized to a considerable extent.

In the last years of the war as well as in early post-war years the Government of India, still under the British, was also aware of the necessity of planning for the country's development. Under its auspices a Planning Department was set up, which formulated certain plans with the major emphasis on industrial expansion. This department functioned as a co-ordinating agency, and was not in full control of initiative and execution in the matters of planning and development. In point of fact, each major department of the government had its separate division of planning. Lack of integration coupled with uncertainty regarding the complexion of the country's future government prevented this department from undertaking any ambitious ventures, but it did initiate a number of important projects. Creation of the Damodar Valley Project, the setting up of an important fertilizer plant, and initiation of several projects for industrial housing can be mentioned as its major achievements. Most of these projects, only partially completed at the time of British withdrawal from India, were later incorporated into the first Five Year Plan.

The Bombay Plan, sponsored by some of the leading industrialists of the country, attracted considerable public attention and was widely discussed in India. It called for a capital expenditure of Rs10,000 crores, and promised within fifteen years not only to double the present *per capita* income, but also to ensure for Indians a balanced diet of 2,800 calories *per capita* per day, 100 square feet of housing per person, and thirty yards of cloth per person per year.

The Gandhian Plan, prepared by one of Gandhi's associates, differed from the other plans in that it sought to make a self-sufficient village economy the basic foundation of the country's planned development. Under this Plan, with a capital expenditure of 3,500 crores, it was hoped to raise both the material and the cultural level of the Indian masses within a period of ten years. It provided for a balanced diet, sufficient clothing, adequate housing, health services, free and compulsory basic education, and recreational services. The Plan claimed to mitigate the evils both of capitalism and communism by visualizing a decentralized society as the ideal type of society for India. Under this social system land was to be nationalized and was to be given to the actual tillers on long-term tenancy. Decentralized cottage industries were to be encouraged, and where necessary they were to be supplemented by large-scale centralized industries.

The Peoples' Plan was also a non-official plan. Under the encouragement of the late M. N. Roy, it was prepared by a post-war committee of the Indian Federation of Labour. It provided for a capital expenditure of Rs15,000 crores, and hoped within ten years to raise the standard of living of the Indian people by 300 per cent. It advocated the nationalization of lands and mines with compensation to owners and gradual and voluntary collectivization of agriculture. According to the provisions of this plan all industries were to be state controlled or state owned; industries started under the plan were to be state owned.

These plans were widely discussed by the intelligentsia and the literate classes. Thus it can be seen that planning was very much in the air when India attained national independence. Indian leaders were greatly impressed by the results attained by some countries which had succeeded through their successive plans in transforming their backward and technologically under-developed economies. As soon as they came into positions of power and responsibility they had to apply themselves vigorously to the solution of the pressing problems of the country. Many of them felt that political freedom would remain a meaningless abstraction to the large masses of the Indian people unless it was accompanied by substantial welfare measures. They turned to national planning as an answer.

In March 1950, the Government of India set up the Planning Commission. The tasks delegated to it were these:

1. Make an assessment of the material, capital and human resources of the country, including technical personnel, and investigate the possibilities of augmenting such of these resources as are found to be deficient in relation to the nation's requirements;
2. formulate a Plan for the most effective and balanced utilization of the country's resources;
3. on a determination of priorities, define the stages in which the Plan should be carried out and propose the allocation of resources for the due completion of each stage;
4. indicate the factors which are tending to retard economic development, and determine the conditions which, in view of the current social and political situation, should be established for the successful execution of the Plan;
5. determine the nature of the machinery which will be necessary for securing the successful implementation of each stage of the Plan in all its aspects;
6. appraise from time to time the progress achieved in the execution of each stage of the Plan and recommend the adjustments of policy and measures that such appraisal may show to be necessary; and

7. make such interim or ancillary recommendations as appear to it to be appropriate either for facilitating the discharge of the duties assigned to it; or, on a consideration of the prevailing economic conditions, current policies, measures and development programmes, or on an examination of such specific problems as may be referred to it for advice by Central or State Governments.[1]

The Planning Commission published the draft outline of a national plan of development to cover a period of five years from April 1951 to March 1956. The members viewed planning in a democratic state as 'a social process in which, in some part, every citizen should have the opportunity to participate'. 'To set the patterns of future development', they added, 'is a task of such magnitude and significance that it should embody the impact of public opinion and the needs of the community.'[2] The draft outline was intended for the widest possible public discussion, and was indeed examined and commented upon by official and non-official bodies representing a large variety of interests and orientation. Officials from governments of the centre and the states, legislators, representatives of various interests, and university leaders were prominent among those who analysed the draft outline and communicated their reactions to the Commission. It received great publicity in the national Press. On the basis of the suggestions received, and to a considerable extent on the basis of independent study and research conducted under the auspices of the Commission, some of the provisions in the draft outline were modified and revised. The first Five Year Plan was published in its final form in December 1952. It included all development projects that were already in the process of implementation as well as several new ones.

It will perhaps be of some interest to compare the tentative allocations and priorities in the draft outline with those made in the Plan itself.

The Plan included projects which could be regarded as national as well as those which were regional or local in nature. The irrigation and power projects, on which 27·2 per cent of the total outlay in the first Plan was to be spent, were devised with three main aims in view: on completion they were expected to provide irrigation to 8,553,000 acres of agricultural land; they were to provide 1,082,000 kilowatt hours of electric power; and it was also hoped that they would be a great help in flood-control. Other physical developments provided

[1]Planning Commission (Government of India), *The First Five Year Plan, A Summary*, New Delhi (1952), p. iii.

[2]Planning Commission (Government of India), *Five Year Plan, A Draft Outline*, New Delhi (1951), p. 5.

for in the Plan were mainly in the field of transport and communications, on which 24 per cent of the total outlay was to be spent. The most vital part of the Plan, perhaps, was the one devoted to agriculture and rural community development. Although only 17·4 per cent of the total outlay of the Plan was to be spent under this head, this part was expected to make the first direct impact on the lives of a large number of people.

	Outlay during 1951–1956		Percentage of total outlay	
	Five Year Plan	Draft Outline	Five Year Plan	Draft Outline
Agriculture and Community Development	Rs 360·43 crore[1]	Rs 191·69 crore	17·4	12·8
Irrigation and Power	Rs 561·41 crore	Rs 450·36 crore	27·2	30·0
Transport and Communications	Rs 497·10 crore	Rs 388·12 crore	24·0	26·1
Industry	Rs 173·04 crore	Rs 100·99 crore	8·4	6·7
Social Services	Rs 339·81 crore	Rs 254·22 crore	16·64	17·0
Rehabilitation	Rs 85·00 crore	Rs 79·00 crore	4·1	5·3
Miscellaneous	Rs 51·00 crore	Rs 28·54 crore	2·5	1·9
	Rs. 2068·78 crore	Rs. 1492·92 crore	100·0	100·0

3. The Community Development Programme

In India 295,004,251 people, forming 82·7 per cent of the country's population, are village dwellers. They live in about 558,000 scattered village settlements. Out of a total population of 357 million, according to the 1951 census, 249 million fall into 'agricultural classes', and of these, 240 million or 96 per cent live in villages. In 1947, it was estimated, 73 per cent of all gainfully employed people were engaged in agriculture; 18 per cent of these being landless labourers. Agriculture in the country is mostly subsistence farming; 83·5 per cent of all agricultural production being foodstuffs. Besides the agricultural classes, the rest of the village population consists mainly of artisan and occupational castes whose economy and lives are largely integrated with the economic and socio-religious life of the peasant communities. In general, the village presents a picture of poverty, malnutrition, poor standards of public health, and illiteracy. In view of these problems it is easy to understand the importance of agriculture and rural community development for India's progress as a nation.

[1]One crore is equal to 10 million.

Planning for Community Development

The basic aims of the Community Development Movement in India under the first Five Year Plan in terms of its *immediate* and *ultimate* goals may be summarized, as:

1. To provide for a substantial increase in the country's agricultural production, and for improvements in the system of communications, in rural health and hygiene, and in village education.
2. To initiate and direct a process of integrated culture change aimed at transforming the social and economic life of the villages.

The inspiration for this movement was provided by similar experiments in other parts of the world, particularly by the agricultural extension service in the United States. It was, however, realized that foreign experience could not be transplanted to the Indian soil, for the sociocultural factors operating in village India are remarkably different from those in other parts of the world. Fortunately India did not lack in indigenous experiments and experience. Under British rule welfare and nation-building departments of state governments had functioned on the village level, and in the planning of the rural development projects valuable lessons could be drawn from their successes and failures. There had also been several small-scale, non-official experiments in this field, from which the planners could learn a good deal. Rural welfare work around Sevagram under the inspiration of Gandhi and in Sriniketan, a sister institution of Shantiniketan, under the influence of Tagore, deserve special mention. Immediate guidance in this direction, however, came from some of the larger experimental projects. Four of these provided models as well as some of the working principles for the rural community projects.

Late in 1947, S. K. Dey, formerly an electrical and mechanical engineer and later the Community Project Administrator for India, took charge of a small refugee resettlement centre which eventually grew into the now famous Nilokheri Project. On a marshy jungle near the village of Nilokheri, in the Karnal district of the Punjab, S. K. Dey built a more or less self-sufficient colony of 6,000 uprooted people. Eighty families in this colony took up agriculture; others organized small-scale workers' co-operatives and started manufacturing, among other things, hand-loom cloth, hosiery, soap, shoes and leather-goods, and ready-made clothes.

A similar project, perhaps somewhat broader in scope, was the refugee rehabilitation scheme at Faridabad near Delhi. When Sudhir Ghosh took charge of the project some 30,000 refugees from the North-west Frontier Province were living in the Faridabad camp. Ghosh undertook to transform the disorderly camp into a modern and practically self-sufficient industrial township. With small government loans, which were repayable in twenty years, the refugees undertook the construction work themselves. In a few years Faridabad was producing about half of its food requirements, and had many modern educational and health facilities. The uprooted people resettled in the colony have practically full employment.

Excellent by themselves as these experiments were, they could not provide a model for the national rural community development movement. They demonstrated what the co-operative endeavour of the people themselves, with technical guidance and modest financial aid provided by the government, could achieve, but they were not integrated with the economy of neighbouring village communities, as originally intended, and could consequently give little guidance for the development of stable rural communities.

The Etawah Project, originally conceived of by Albert Mayer (an American town-planner who was in India during the war) and executed under his guidance by a carefully selected Indian and American staff, provided not only a model but also some valuable experience for the guidance of the rural community development workers. This experiment was tried in ninety-seven villages of the Etawah district in the State of Uttar Pradesh. The plan was relatively simple and inexpensive. Realizing the need of co-ordination in the different types of welfare and development activities, the planners of the Etawah Project evolved the concept of a multi-purpose extension agent called the Village Level Worker. The VLWs, as they have come to be called, were the chief field workers operating on the village level. They had technical guidance from experts in different branches who functioned as Deputy Development Officers. The Project itself was under a Planning Officer. A systematic evaluation of this project has not been undertaken, but its major achievements are well known. The Project popularized improved seeds, chemical fertilizers, and green manuring. Under its guidance the people adopted several improved agricultural practices and techniques. As a result of these innovations, it is estimated, average yield per acre in the project area increased 50 to 60 per cent. The benefits of its activities were not restricted to the field of agricultural improvement; there was a marked improvement in health conditions, literacy, and means of communication. As a pioneer venture, Etawah had a good deal to offer to the nation: its successes as well as its failures had much in them to guide the future of the rural community development movement in India. The concept of a multi-purpose village level worker, a new pattern of administrative organization of the individual development projects, and development of some effective methods of approach are some of the important contributions of Etawah to community development in India.

Another important experiment of this nature was the *Firka Development Scheme*, now known as the Rural Welfare Scheme, of the government of Madras. Inspired by the constructive programme of Gandhi, the purpose of this scheme was 'to organize the villagers for a happier, fuller, and more prosperous life in which the individual villager will have the opportunity to develop both as an individual and as a member of a well-integrated society.'[1] This objective was to be realized by 'using local initiative and local resources to the utmost extent possible in the economic, political and social fields of reconstruction on co-operative lines'.[2] It was hoped that a 'self-reliant, self-dependent and properly organized life' would emerge in the villages as a result of these efforts. The *firka*[3] (an administrative unit consisting of twenty-five to thirty villages and covering an area of approximately forty to fifty square miles) was to be utilized as the unit of development. Intensive work was started in thirty-four *firkas* in the last quarter of 1946. Fifty more *firkas* were brought under the Scheme in 1950. In October 1951, the work was extended to twenty-five other *firkas*. On the State level the department had a Director and two Deputy Directors who were to implement the programmes and policies formulated by the Provincial Firka Development Board (now known as the Rural Development Board) consisting of the heads of development departments in the State as well as prominent constructive workers. On the district level the Collector (head of the district administration) was in overall charge of the development activities, and was advised by a District Rural Welfare Board consisting of the heads of various development departments in the district and important civic leaders. A Firka Development Officer (now District Welfare Officer) was placed in charge of two to four *firkas*. He was assisted by a technical staff, and a number of general village workers called *Grama Sevak* ('village servants'). Each *firka* was divided into three to five groups; each group consisting of five to ten villages. Each group was under a *Grama Sevak*. These officials were advised by a Firka Development Committee made up of officials, as well as representatives of villages and of non-official social service agencies working in the area. Two features of this programme deserve special notice: first, it laid great emphasis on educative propaganda; and, second, rather than render direct service to the village people it worked mostly through local agencies and institutions to which

[1]Belshaw, H., and Grant, John B. *Report of the Mission on Community Organization and Development in South and South-east Asia*, United Nations (1953), p. 118.

[2]*Ibid*., p. 118.

[3]Each 'district' in the State of Madras is divided into 'taluqas', which are in turn sub-divided into 'firkas'. A taluqa consisted of 5–6 firkas.

grants-in-aid were given for approved projects in the fields of agriculture, sanitation, improvement of communication, adult education, and cottage industries. This programme also provided a model for Community Development Projects, especially in respect to administrative organization and some operational principles.

Brief mention has already been made of the basic short term and long term objectives of the rural development projects. While the extension of welfare services was regarded as necessary and desirable, the educational aspect of the programme was viewed as the most important part of the movement. It was essentially a programme of mobilizing manpower and of developing local human and natural resources. It was not a programme of outside charity and aid, but one of village self-help. According to the first Five Year Plan the aim of this movement was 'to create in the rural population a burning desire for a higher standard of living, and the will to live better. . . .'[1] In the words of Jawaharlal Nehru people were to be 'invested with a sense of intimate partnership' in this national effort, and with this aim in view they were to be associated not only with the execution of the plans but also with their formulation. As its share in this effort, the government was to provide technical aid and modest financial assistance, but the people were ultimately expected to recognize their needs, and to evolve adequate leadership for their own welfare and progress. After an initial period of government aid and direction it was hoped that the movement would direct and support itself.

The programme was started with the assumption that, in general, 'village people are eager and ready to improve their way of life'.[2] What they needed most, it was felt, was an opportunity to see what they could accomplish through their own efforts. They were reluctant to accept the new unless they were convinced that it was better than what they already had. It was therefore necessary to translate development ideology into the language and symbols of the people. This raised the question of relating planning to the *felt needs* of the people, and also that of evolving an agency that could understand the village mind and interpret the programme to the village people in a language which they could understand.

Two valuable lessons were drawn from past experience in development work in rural areas. One was that the confusing multiplicity of welfare services, offered by the field agents of a number of separate government departments often bewildered the village people. The other was that the *extensive* type of welfare work attempted by

[1]Planning Commission (Government of India), *Five Year Plan, A Draft Outline*, New Delhi (1951), p. 82.

[2]Community Projects Administration (Government of India), *Manual for Village Level Workers*, New Delhi (n.d.), p. 2.

government departments touched only the surface of village problems; it was neither sufficiently sustained nor penetrating enough to leave any permanent impression on the lives of the people. The Community Development Programme under the Plan, therefore, was to be integrated and intensive, rather than diversified and extensive. Through this approach it was hoped that it would leave a lasting effect on village India.

With the full recognition of the assumptions and problems which have been outlined, the Planning Commission launched its community development programme. As the first step, early in 1952, fifteen Pilot Projects were started in different states of the Union. The second step was to establish fifty-five Community Development Projects, which started functioning on 2 October 1952. The third phase of the movement opened with the initiation of the National Extension Service in October 1953. It was stipulated that by the end of 1956 these programmes would cover approximately one-fourth of the entire rural population of the country.

The Pilot Projects were started with a view to examining the suitability of the programme which the planners had in view for a nation-wide community development movement. For this reason they were situated in different parts of the country. The major emphasis in these projects was on agricultural improvement and increased food production, though they were to give attention also to social education, rural health, and public works. Each of these projects was to extend to a block of about 100 villages with a population of approximately 50,000 people. The chief 'action' men in these projects were to be the specially trained multi-purpose extension agents and social workers designated as Village Level Workers. To equip them for this new type of work special training programmes were initiated.

The more ambitious community development programme was started on a nation-wide basis without awaiting the results of the Pilot Projects. The central government justified its decision by referring to the great pressure from the states to launch such a movement and the general popular enthusiasm which supported it. Another factor influencing this course was the Point 4 aid from the United States in support of these projects. Each Project under this programme was to consist of three development blocks, each block consisting of about 100 villages and covering an area of 450 to 500 square miles and a population of 200,000 to 300,000 people. At the outset the target was to start fifty-five such Projects. These came into existence in October 1952. Availability of additional financial aid and the enthusiastic reception accorded to the Pilot Project started in April 1952, led to an increase in the area covered by the Community Projects. In December 1952, it was decided to add fifty-five more Development Blocks to the programme. Most of these Blocks were added on 2 October 1953. There were already 165 Blocks under the fifty-five larger Projects comprising three blocks each. With the addition of these fifty-five one-block Projects, the total number of development blocks increased to 220. These affected approximately 21·5 million people living in 23,650 villages. By the end of 1956 a total of 700 blocks were to be brought under these Projects—some as three-block Community Project units, others as individual Community Development Blocks.

The Community Development Projects were more comprehensive in scope than the Pilot Projects. They offered a co-ordinated programme of many-sided rural development. A three-block Community Project had approximately fifteen times greater resources than those of a one-block Pilot Project. Besides emphasizing agricultural extension, they were to offer balanced programmes in the fields of village sanitation and public health, education and youth welfare, irrigation and public works, and women's welfare. In order to ensure smooth functioning of the Projects some significant administrative innovations were introduced. In the Central Government a separate Community Projects Administration was created under the Planning Commission. It was decided that at the state level responsibility for the implementation of the development programme should be vested in a Development Commissioner. On the Project level it was proposed to have a full-time officer to co-ordinate the activities and implement the programme.

In April 1953, the government took the decision to organize the National Extension Service. It was to begin work in 200 blocks of 100 villages each, from 2 October 1953. Activities under this programme were to be less intensive than those sponsored by the Community Projects, but the multi-purpose approach to rural problems was adopted for this programme also. The primary emphasis was to be on agricultural improvement and irrigation, but, on a lesser scale, attention was to be given also to education and health. The administrative structure of the National Extension Service was similar to that of the Community Projects: both were under the Community Projects Administration of the Centre, and the Development Commissioners of the States. It was planned that 500 blocks of the National Extension Service should be set up by the end of 1956.

The magnitude of these undertakings can well be imagined by a glance at the targets set under the first Five Year Plan. By the end of 1956, a total of 74 million people living in 120,000 villages were to benefit by the Community Projects and the National Extension Service.

4. Administrative Organization

The administrative organization of the various agencies of rural community development can now be outlined.

On the national level, under the Ministry of Planning and the Planning Commission, there was a separate Community Projects Administration. This agency had been created to provide a unified and co-ordinated direction of the community development activities all over the country. The Community Projects Administrator was the head of this organization, and functioned under the general supervision of a Central Committee, designated by the Government of India, which laid down broad policies. The Administrator was assisted by technical experts in the fields of finance, personnel and training, and planning, as well as by specialists in various areas of project operations such as agriculture, irrigation, health, education, industries, housing and community facilities. The Administrator had to work in consultation with appropriate state authorities. He was in overall charge of the development projects throughout the country, and his main responsibility was to ensure co-ordinated direction of projects on a nation-wide basis. The Community Projects Administration has now been replaced by a Ministry of Community Development.

At the state level, there is a Development Commissioner in general charge of development work within the state. Broad policies are framed by a Board or Committee of the state government. This body supervises the Development Commissioner's implementation of the plans. The organization and official titles of this body differ slightly in the different states of India. For example, in Uttar Pradesh there is a State Planning Board consisting of non-official experts and the members of the State Planning Committee. The Board functions under the chairmanship of the Chief Minister. The State Planning Committee consists of the Secretaries of all development departments of the government. The Chief Secretary functions as its chairman, and the Development Commissioner is the secretary of this committee. Technical guidance to the Development Commissioner is provided by a Board of Advisers, which consists of all the heads of development departments in the state government.

The same pattern applies to the District and Project levels also. The Collector or Deputy Commissioner of the district, actively assisted by a District Planning Officer or District Development Officer, is in general charge of development activities within the district. There is a District Planning Committee, consisting of official and non-official members, which fixes priorities and policies for the district. The Collector (or Deputy Commissioner) presides over this Committee, and the District Planning (or Development) Officer functions as its Secretary.

Finally, at the project level, each Community Development Project has a Project Executive Officer, and a National Extension Service Block has a Block Development Officer. There is a Project Advisory Committee for each of the projects, consisting of non-official as well as official members. The officers in charge of the individual projects are assisted by a group of technical men specializing in the different areas of project activities. The work in the villages is carried out by multi-purpose action men who are the field agents of the project.

Some significant characteristics of this administrative organization deserve to be noted.

First, in recognition of the necessity of unified and co-ordinated direction of development activities, final responsibility on all the four different levels has been vested in one individual and not in a multiplicity of specialists. Provision, however, has been made for technical consultation and guidance of experts on all the levels.

Second, in recognition of the necessity of associating non-officials with programme planning, and to a certain extent with programme execution, provision has been made for consultative and supervisory committees to be associated with appropriate officers on all levels.

Third, in order to cut down red tape and maintain an efficient supply line from the central and state headquarters to the individual projects, sufficiently important officers have been appointed at different levels, and direct channels of communication from the highest (centre) to the lowest (project) levels have been established. The principle of teamwork at different levels has also been emphasized.

Fourth, in view of the very special nature of the work to be undertaken, provisions have been made to organize orientation and training courses for officers on the two lower levels, and for frequent exchanges of views and consultation between officers on the two upper levels.

Fifth, in order to secure popular participation on the widest possible basis, it was decided to utilize all existing local agencies in the implementation of the development programme. Where such agencies did not exist or were not adequately developed, it was decided to create them.

Sixth, in recognition of the two important principles of modern public administration—namely, of research and progress—an independent Programme Evaluation Organization has been set up to evaluate the existing organization and methods of community development. The findings of this body are expected to lead to desirable modification and changes in the organizational set-up and methods of approach.

The last four characteristics need further comment. Earlier experience with the workings of welfare and nation-building departments had amply shown that unco-ordinated work often led to waste and duplication. Absence of proper communication between different levels of administration involved confusion and frequent delays. Decisions could not be arrived at quickly and the supply-line was often obstructed to a point that what was called for often reached the village level too late to be of any use. Certain specific projects requiring inter-departmental co-operation were wrecked by the indifference and mutual suspicion of those who were to collaborate. In appointing a Community Project Administrator with sufficient authority, and in recommending the appointment of a senior and experienced civil service officer (preferably with the status of Additional Chief Secretary to the state government) the priority and prestige of development work were stressed. Placing the Collector (also known in some districts as the Deputy Commissioner) in charge of planning and development work within the district was also a step calculated to achieve the same end. The projects themselves were placed under the charge of responsible and specially trained officers. The active association of the chief administrator of the district and of a high ranking officer at the state level was calculated to minimize red tape. This, together with the energetic supervision and guidance of the Community Project Administration, was also intended to ensure the maintenance of a steady and smooth flow of communication and supplies. It has been pointed out earlier that the desirability of co-ordinated teamwork at all levels was greatly emphasized.

It was recognized in the very early stages of the development of this movement that rural welfare workers would need special orientation and training. To make the projects a success the officers needed a new outlook: they were to function not as mercenaries, but as devoted servants of the nation. It was felt that the old bureaucratic ways and the 'official mentality' of the former régime would not suit the temper of New India. Understanding of the rural mind and a grasp of methods of extension work were regarded as indispensable qualifications for those who were to administer the projects. An executive level training programme was initiated in 1954 by the Community Projects Administration to train Project Executive Officers and Block Development Officers. Short six-week courses were designed to re-orient officials' attitudes, and to acquaint the trainees with modern methods of extension work. Training programmes were later developed to prepare subject-matter specialists who were to work under these officers. Provision for in-service training had been made in the form of periodic seminars, conferences, and workshops of the officers. With these even the higher central and state officers were associated.

More important than the training of officers was the training of the field agents of the development programme. The concept of a multi-purpose Village Level Worker had been adopted, and it was necessary to train a large number of people to man the increasing number of projects all over the country. The task was by no means easy. The training had two important aspects: it was necessary to give the trainees a reasonable grounding in the subject-matter of their multi-purpose activities, and they had to be trained in modern methods of extension-work and the vital problems in the area of human relations associated with it. As the Village Level Worker's field of operations covered such diverse subjects as agriculture, horticulture, irrigation, co-operatives, animal husbandry, public works, social education, youth welfare, and many more, it was not easy to devise a practical and workable curriculum. The training in the classroom had to be integrated with practical experience in the field. And to confuse the situation still further the steadily increasing number of projects in the country demanded a quick supply of trained personnel.

With the decision to launch fifteen Pilot Projects, five training centres for multi-purpose Village Level Workers were set up. Later, when it was decided to start an intensive community development programme in a much wider area, the number of these centres was increased to thirty-four. By the middle of 1952 most of these centres had started functioning. Finally, nine more centres were added to meet the requirements of the National Extension Service. According to a report of the Ford Foundation, which substantially financed these centres, this training programme had a threefold purpose: (i) instilling in the future village workers a clear understanding of the nature of rural community development; (ii) developing in the trainees a spirit of service to the people, and (iii) providing all the trainees with first-hand experience in applying principles and methods they study in the classroom to meeting the day-to-day problems of a village worker. As personnel completed their six-month training period they were assigned to the projects. Programmes were later initiated to train social education organizers, rural health workers, and women extension workers.

Because the rural development programme was viewed as *an expression of democracy*, the necessity of popular participation at different levels—both in planning and implementation—was emphasized. In accordance with the ideal of village self-help, it was decided to associate all existing agencies such as village councils (*panchayats*), co-operative societies, schools, and other voluntary organizations with development work in rural areas and to utilize their services in the implementation of the projects. Representatives of the people were given places on the different advisory committees. In some states special *ad hoc* bodies were created on the village level. For example, in Madhya Pradesh the government constituted Village Development Councils, with separate committees for agriculture, revenue, health, education, co-operation, animal husbandry, etc., to ensure direct and intimate association of the village people with the projects.

As there was general agreement on the experimental nature of the projects under the first Five Year Plan, it was realized that a continuing evaluation of their progress and methods would be invaluable both to the present and the future projects. Such evaluation was necessary to determine the progress of the projects in both quantitative and qualitative terms. It could provide guidance by measuring the degree of acceptance or rejection of project programmes, and by analysing the socio-cultural and value factors involved in such acceptance or rejection. Finally, it could provide a measurement of concrete achievements and determine if the projects were achieving the objectives for which they were set up. The Programme Evaluation Organization of the Planning Commission was established with this aim in view. It has published valuable annual evaluation reports, and also a few other studies on the different areas of planning and community development. Realizing the necessity of research and experimentation in the field of planning the government of Uttar Pradesh has established a Planning Research and Action Institute.

5. Programme and Methods

The rural community development projects, both of the intensive Community Projects type and of the more general National Extension Service type, were expected to be implemented through five stages: conception, initiation, operation, consolidation, and finalization.

The first stage, taking approximately the first three months of the three-year project, was to be devoted to an intensive survey of the selected development area. On the basis of this survey blueprints and estimates for the proposed development work were to be prepared during this period.

The second stage, taking about six months, was to be given to the first steps in the implementation of the programme, especially to concrete planning for individual villages and to general psychological stimulation. The necessary staff was to be found and housed, communication within the operational zones was to be established, and steps were to be taken to stock-pile required material for the third stage of operation. Specific activities to be undertaken during this period included establishing the agricultural extension, veterinary and health services (in a limited area); strengthening existing school facilities and opening new schools (in open air or in temporary sheds); reclamation of existing inoperative wells, pools and tanks, etc.

The third stage was to be devoted to rapid extension of programmed amenities to the entire project area. During this period of intensification of development activities all major construction work was expected to be initiated. This 'operation stage' was to last eighteen months, i.e one-half of the life of the project.

The following six months were to be spent in consolidation, and in the process of terminating the development operations. During this period key personnel were to be shifted from the operational zones to other project areas.

In the final stage, covering the last three months of the life of the project, the development agency was to get ready to move, handing over charge of the operation area to normal administrative machinery.

The major fields of project activities have been indicated. At this point it will perhaps be useful to summarize the various areas to be covered by the intensive Community Development Projects:

A. Agriculture and related matters:

1. Reclamation of available virgin and waste land.
2. Provision of water for agriculture through irrigation canals, tube wells, surface wells, tanks and lift irrigation from rivers, lakes and pools.
3. Development of rural electrification.
4. Provision of commercial fertilizers.
5. Provision of quality seeds.
6. Promotion and utilization of improved agricultural techniques.
7. Provision of veterinary aid.
8. Provision of technical information, materials and bulletins, on agriculture.
9. Provision of dissemination of information through slides, films, radio broadcasts, and lectures.
10. Provision of improved agricultural implements.
11. Promotion of marketing and credit facilities.
12. Provision of breeding centres for animal husbandry.
13. Development of inland fisheries.
14. Promotion of home economics.

15. Development of fruit and vegetable cultivation.
16. Provision of soil surveys and information.
17. Encouragement of the use of natural and compost manures.
18. Provision for arboriculture and reafforestation.

B. Communications:

1. Provision of roads.
2. Encouragement of mechanical road transport.
3. Development of animal transport.

C. Education:

1. Provision of compulsory and free education, preferably of the basic type, at the elementary stage.
2. Provision of high and middle schools.
3. Provision of adult education and library services.

D. Health:

1. Provision of sanitation (including drainage and disposal of wastes) and public health measures.
2. Provision for control of malaria and other diseases.
3. Provision of improved drinking water supplies.
4. Provision of medical aid for the sick.
5. Pre-natal and post-natal care of expectant mothers and mid-wife services.
6. Provision of generalized public health service and education.

E. Training:

1. Refresher courses for improving the standard of work of existing artisans.
2. Training of agriculturists.
3. Training of extension assistants.
4. Training of artisans.
5. Training of supervisors, managerial personnel, health workers, and executive officers for projects.

F. Social Welfare:

1. Organization of community entertainment.
2. Provision of audio-visual aid for instruction and recreation.
3. Organization of sports activities.
4. Organization of *melas* (village fairs).
5. Organization of co-operative and self-help movements.

G. Supplementary Employment:

1. Encouragement of cottage industries and crafts as main or subsidiary occupations.
2. Encouragement of medium and small-scale industries to employ surplus labour for local needs and to provide products for outside project areas.

3. Encouragement of employment through trade, auxiliary and welfare services.
4. Construction of brick kilns and saw mills to provide building materials for local needs.

H. Housing:

1. Demonstration and training in improved techniques and designs for rural housing.
2. Encouragement of improved rural housing on a self-help basis.

To implement a programme of this magnitude it was necessary to have an adequate administrative machine equipped with the technical knowledge and effective methods of mass contact. Efforts of the Government of India to evolve such an administrative agency, and to establish special training and orientation programmes have been mentioned earlier. Besides providing properly trained and extension-oriented personnel, these steps were designed to provide unified and co-ordinated direction and control, direct and speedy channels of communication, and a smooth and steady flow of necessary supplies. Thought was given to the problems of evolving effective techniques of approach also.

Ideally the project officials—high and low—were to constitute a team, and in their functioning the projects were expected to evolve a high degree of internal democratization. To formulate the local plans the method of discussion was to be employed; in their implementation the principle of inter-dependence between generalists and specialists was expected to operate. For example, the past achievements and future plans were to be discussed in periodic (generally fortnightly) meetings of the entire Project staff consisting of the Executive Officer, Assistant Project Officers, and the Village Level Workers. The Assistant Project Officers, who were subject-matter specialists, were to help the generalist multi-purpose Village Level Workers by suggesting to them ways and means of solving technical problems in their local setting. In the field itself all types of approaches—individual, home, group, and community—were to be tried. Personal contacts and discussion with individuals, organized visits to demonstrations and model farms, group discussions and meetings (especially during festivals and fairs), 'method' and 'result' demonstrations to acquaint the village people with the technique and benefits of new practices, and effective use of other means of communication such as books and posters, plays, radio, exhibition, competition, discussion, motion pictures, etc., were some of the methods suggested in approaching the village people.

The major principles laid down for the guidance of the Village

Level Workers will perhaps indicate the methods of work better. In general, they follow this spirit and pattern:

(*a*) To get down to the level of a villager, set an example by one's own way of living, get acquainted with him and be accepted as a friend;

(*b*) to use tact and imagination to win the confidence and respect of the villagers and develop an 'intimate partnership' with them;

(*c*) to guide the villagers to see and recognize their needs and problems, inspire them to think and assert themselves, develop in them an urge for change and a desire for better life, and encourage them to release and use their own forces for the improvement of their living conditions;

(*d*) to help the villagers to make their own plans and do things for themselves. They should be made to feel that they are important;

(*e*) to avoid quick action and too many activities. The problems taken up first should be of the kind that a great many people understand and participate in and one where results can be seen in a comparatively short period of time;

(*f*) to be realistic and thorough in building up village development programmes which differ according to felt needs and available resources. The villagers should be helped to keep up their interests in the programmes once they are started. The Village Level Worker should ensure that he is able to do what is recommended regarding the supplies and services required;

(*g*) to discover and train local leaders. They are the people who can 'mould', change, guide and influence the villagers' thinking and action for the common good. They speak their language and can better interpret their needs and problems. The village development programme can and will become a self-help programme only as village leaders are developed;

(*h*) To develop village co-operation. The success of village development programmes depends upon the way village people learn to trust each other and to co-operate with each other. Co-operative and group efforts should start with concrete and simple activities which will give the village people a feeling of group achievement. More difficult co-operative enterprises should be taken up later;

(*i*) to enlist the support and co-operation of governmental and voluntary agencies. Indigenous organizations should be improved and utilized. Group organizations such as women's associations and youth and children's clubs should be organized and encouraged to participate in village development programmes.

6. The Future

The first Five Year Plan provided for a sum of Rs101 crores ($214,437,367) for expenses connected with community development work until 1956. The work was expected to be carried out in partnership by the central and state governments on the one hand, and by village people and the governments on the other. State governments were expected to pay about one-fourth of the total non-recurring expenditure, and share equally with the Centre in recurring costs. The people's contribution to the programme was to be both in money and in voluntary labour. It was to be the government's policy to sanction grants-in-aid for specific projects, the people were either to raise the rest of the money themselves or to put in voluntary labour covering approximately their share in the cost of the projects. While the community development projects had the financial support of the U.S. Government (largely in equipment), the National Extension Service has been financed wholly by the Government of India.

It was expected that by 1961, i.e. during the second Five Year Plan, the entire country would be covered by either Community Development Projects or the National Extension Service. Areas first taken up for less intensive development under the National Extension Service, were to be taken up for more intensive community development later. The ideal is to have the whole of rural India under intensive Community Development Projects by 1966 under the third Five Year Plan.

II

A RURAL DEVELOPMENT PROJECT IN ACTION

1. The People

AS A PART OF THE NATIONAL COMMUNITY DEVELOPMENT PROGRAMME the government of Uttar Pradesh selected, among others, a group of villages in one of the western districts of the state for intensive development. The Project to be launched in this area was not to be a *standard* type of Community Development Project, comprising three Blocks each consisting of nearly 100 villages, nor was it to be a *rural-cum-urban* Project: the selected villages were to be constituted into a Community Development Block. At first only 120 villages were selected for inclusion in the Block, but later, on grounds of public demand and administrative convenience, thirty-three more villages were added to the list. Around the middle of 1953 preparatory work was started, and the Project itself was inaugurated by the Chief Minister of Uttar Pradesh on 2 October 1953.

The area covered by this Project is wholly rural. In fact with the exception of the town in which the headquarters of the Project is located there are no other urban settlements in the area, and the headquarters town itself is excluded from project operations. Judged by average Indian standards the 153 villages in the Development Block are quite advanced agriculturally and economically. An important railway line passes through the area, connecting it both with the seat of the national government and with the district administration centre. There are three railroad stations in the Block—one at the Project headquarters and two in villages of the Development Block. An equally important highway also passes through the area, linking it with some important urban centres of north India. Several regional and local bus services operate on this road.

Besides its tie with the headquarters of the Project—an old, semi-rural settlement and centre of grain trade—this area has immediate connexions with two other cities. One of these is the seat of the district of which the Development Block is a part, and the other is the the seat of an adjoining district. While the people have administrative connexion only with the district headquarters, many villages which are geographically nearer the other district town naturally look to it for its marketing, medical, and educational facilities. No major industries except two sugar mills have developed in this area. The sugar mills, during the three decades of their existence, have contributed considerably to the economic prosperity of the agriculturists in the surrounding villages.

Educational developments within the area itself have been modest and not particularly significant, but in the two prominent district towns as well as in some other distant towns, which nevertheless can easily be reached by train and bus, a number of schools and colleges have grown up and have attracted students from this area. There is a small government dispensary at the Project headquarters, and larger and comparatively better equipped hospitals, as well as several highly qualified private medical practitioners, in the two district towns. There are small branch post offices in nearly all the larger villages of the Development Block, but only the town which serves as headquarters of the Project has a telegraph office.

Notwithstanding these urban contacts, which are important and vital, the villages in the area are self-sufficient to a remarkable degree in several spheres of life.

Two important types of village settlements are found in the area—some are 'single settlement' villages, others are 'nucleated' villages. In the latter, around the nucleus of a central settlement there are one or more satellite hamlets. While some of the smaller villages have a population of 200 persons or less, the larger villages are inhabited by more than 5,000 people. The society is caste-structured, and the economy is mainly agricultural. The Rajputs, Tyagis, Jats, and Gujars are the important landowning, agriculturist castes of this region. These castes are found among both Hindus and Muslims. The relative position and strength of these castes often determine the character and organization of a village. For example, a multi-caste village dominated by the Rajputs is invariably described as a 'Rajput village', and one dominated by the Tyagis is referred to as a 'Tyagi village'. Similarly we often hear of a 'Jat village' and a 'Gujar village', and also occasionally of a 'Harijan village'. However, in referring to some castes as the 'landowning castes', it is not implied that other castes do not or cannot own land. Land is greatly prized by all the sections of the village population, and from the priestly Brahmins at the top of the caste hierarchy to the untouchable Bhangis (sweepers) at its bottom, all castes can cultivate any land they own or can get on lease. Around the agriculturist castes there are a large number of occupational, artisan, and other castes with varying ritual and socio-economic status. In a random sample of ten villages in the Development Block over seventy different castes were counted.

Some of the more important characteristics of the social organization of these village communities can be outlined here in a very general way.

The social organization of these village communities is determined by the interplay of several different kinds of solidarities. Kinship, caste, and territorial affinities are the major determinants that shape their structure and organization. An individual belongs to a family—nuclear or joint, and the family belongs to a lineage, as well as to a large group of relatives having kin or affinal ties with it. These units belong to an endogamous sub-caste or caste; in some instances a number of endogamous sub-castes are grouped as a caste. Most of the Hindu castes are fitted into one of the four major divisions of Hindu society, called *varna.* Solidarities provided by kin and caste tend to merge, but those of territorial affinity belong to a different level. An individual and his family belong also to a village, which is often multi-caste in its composition. The village itself is a part of the network of neighbouring villages, the region, and the nation.

Caste is perhaps the most important single organizing principle in these communities, and it governs to a very considerable degree the organization of kinship and territorial units. In this system of social division, the different segments are kept apart by complex observances related to the concept of ritual pollution. The caste divisions are regarded as divinely ordained and are hierarchically graded. The difference between various segments is defined by tradition and is regarded as permanent. In intergroup relations the caste structure works according to a set pattern of principles: hierarchy and social distance manifest and express themselves in rules and regulations that are calculated to avoid ritual pollution and maintain purity. Marriage, commensality, and physical contacts particularly are governed by strict rules. Castes are endogamous; matrimonial alliances outside of caste are viewed with disapproval and are forbidden by tradition. Complex rules of commensality specify the castes from which a particular caste may accept different kinds of food. Foods are classified into several categories, depending on the degree to which they are susceptible to pollution. Certain types of food get polluted by the touch of a caste lower than or a caste different from one's own, and when so polluted they must be avoided. Some kinds of food, however, are pollution resistant, and are not defiled by the touch of even very low caste persons. Between the easily pollutable and the unpollutable foods there are several intermediate types: foods which are not defiled by the touch of castes having varying degrees of social distance from one's caste, but which become polluted if touched by castes having more than the permitted degree of social distance.

Everyday interaction between the different castes is also governed by caste rules: persons from some castes should never be touched by one, while physical contact with some others should be avoided under special conditions, such as when one is in a state of ritual purity. Caste largely determines occupational choice. With the exception of a few open occupations, such as agriculture, which may be pursued by anyone irrespective of caste, a large number of crafts and occupations are caste monopolies and can ideally be practised only by specific castes. In its functioning an individual caste generally pursues a distinctive way of life, for different castes have different sets of prescribed norms of conduct and expectations regarding standards of behaviour. These norms and expected standards of behaviour cover such aspects of life as observance of rules of purity (especially those of bathing and washing at appropriate hours), public conduct, and even dress and speech. Within a village the caste system manifests itself as a vertical structure in which individual castes are hierarchically graded and kept permanently apart, and at the same time are linked and kept together by some well-defined expectations and obligations which integrate them into the village social system. The horizontal ties of a caste, too, are important, for a caste group living in one village has strong links with its counterparts in other villages, and in several spheres of life members of the same caste living in different villages tend to act together. Although no permanent local or regional councils of individual castes are in existence now in the Project area, elders and influential men in the caste from a number of neighbouring villages still react on an *ad hoc* basis to consider caste matters.

In recent decades a number of forces and factors have influenced the caste system, and have brought about significant modifications in its form and functioning. Development of modern means of communication (especially railways), urban contacts, modern education, and movements of social reform, such as the Arya Samaj and Gandhi's campaigns against untouchability, are important among the factors affecting the caste system. It is now common to hear sharp criticism of the caste system in the villages of this area. Representatives of the urban *élite* working in the rural areas, and even some village leaders, make a point of voicing the opinion that caste as a social institution is man made rather than divinely ordained. The system is still characterized by vertical gradation of castes, and by recognizable social distance between the different castes, but the modes through which this hierarchy and distance are expressed have undergone a definite change.

Notwithstanding considerable propaganda in favour of breaking down the barriers of caste, it still retains its endogamous character. However, rules governing commensality and interpersonal relations between different castes have been greatly modified. In regard to these a dual standard of behaviour is gradually coming to be recognized. Adherence to traditional forms is considered desirable and necessary in the village, but persons going from the village to urban areas take moderately to city ways. Of course when they return to the village they generally have to conform to the local traditions once again. In the villages it is not uncommon to hear about two distinct groups—'the traditionally minded' and 'the progressives', although even the most progressive cannot go beyond a certain point in rejecting the local traditions, and in their actual behaviour tend to conform to its substance. Another fact that deserves to be noted in this context is that women have so far had little hand in this movement for breaking away from the local tradition, and the home is still run on the conservative pattern.

Alongside of 'open occupations' and 'caste monopolies', a number of new occupations, such as government service, have grown up during recent decades and these have been accessible to all irrespective of their caste. Even aside from this some of the caste monopolies are breaking down: untouchable castes have started working as masons, and some higher castes have taken to tailoring as a means of gaining a livelihood. Reference has already been made to the practical non-existence of any established regional organizations of individual castes to act with authority for their members, but conventions and conferences of individual castes to discuss social, economic, and political questions are held periodically, and are indeed very fashionable. Some of these caste organizations publish their own journals.

It is apparent that some of the rigid caste rules have been relaxed and that caste structure is showing signs of weakening in certain other spheres, but this should not lead us to the conclusion that caste has ceased to be a force in Indian village life. On the contrary caste has shown its vigour in a number of spheres. In this region there is considerable inter-caste rivalry. The first elections to local bodies like the Gaon Sabha[1] and Adalati Panchayat[2] were fought not on the basis of programmes and policies, but on the basis of caste. Even in the election to the state legislature this factor was not altogether absent. In the last election, a Tyagi offered himself as a candidate, taking advantage of the tussle between two rival candidates of the predominant Rajput caste. He hoped to win the election on the cal-

[1]Elected village council. [2]Elected village court.

culation that Rajput votes would be divided between the Rajput candidates and that a solid block of Tyagi votes would give him the required majority. He did not win, but it is significant that despite the fact that he had absolutely no record of public service and was running against popular leaders with long records of service and sacrifice he obtained considerable support.

Among kin groups three types of organized units deserve to be noted: the family, the local group of relatives, and the wider group of relatives. In this region it is common to find a house shared by a number of people having close lineal ties, but many of them do not live as one large family; they live as distinct nuclear families organized as separate *chulhas* (literally 'hearths', kin who share the same hearth). The fact that several brothers with their wives and children live in the same house does not prove that they constitute one joint family; because of their separate hearths, each unit is distinctly marked out from the others. The land is often recorded in the name of one person in official records, but in practice each brother cultivates his own share separately. While these individual families are 'nuclear families' in the technical sense, the fact that they share the same house with other kin and are governed by structured patterns of behaviour within the kin group gives them a special character, and they appear to be an intermediate type between the standard nuclear and joint families.

Joint families are not uncommon, but large joint families comprising *all* lineally related males of two or three generations and their wives and children are rare. Where joint families occur they result from the fusion of two or three nuclear families. In the local group of near kin, two units are recognized: the *Kunba* and the *khandan*. Families lineally related to one another up to three generations generally constitute the *kunba*. All families having recognizable lineal relationship with one another constitute the *khandan*. Solidarity existing between such clusters of lineally related families expresses itself on ceremonial occasions and in times of stress and calamity. In the hour of need they are expected to support one another, and mutual consultations among them in regard to all major decisions are regarded as desirable. Informally they function as an effective agency of social control. The outlook of the people is distinctly kin oriented. Notwithstanding a trend towards change from a kin oriented outlook to an interest oriented outlook, in a crisis people still almost inevitably look to their kin for sympathy and support.

A word may here be added about the type of 'regional exogamy' that is practised in this region. In brief the practice follows this pattern: the people of one area (a more or less well-defined group of villages), will marry their girls in another area, and bring wives for their boys from still another area. Thus persons in region A, will give their daughters in marriage to residents of region B, and will seek brides for their sons from region C. The boundaries of these exogamous regions have been defined by long tradition.

Caste and kin-groups, although they have important local units in the village, have a wider regional spread. In a village itself we meet a different type of structural entity; one that cuts across the boundaries of kin and caste and unites a number of unrelated families within an integrated multi-caste community. It generally has a stable population, with a common past and a number of shared values. A village recognizes and emphasizes its individual identity, and in certain situations acts as one unit. Its economy is built largely around agriculture; economically and socially the agricultural castes are extremely important, while the non-agricultural occupations are mostly subsidiary to agriculture. Land is greatly prized and valued, and the community as a whole shares some common problems and acculturative influences.

Because it is largely caste-structured, the community finds itself integrated in terms of traditional patterns that define the interaction between the different segments of the community in the fields of economy, socio-religious life, and village administration. Operating under traditional 'patron-client' arrangement—known in ethnographic literature pertaining to Uttar Pradesh as the *jajman* system, and locally as *kisan-lagdar* or 'agriculturist-affiliated caste' relations—artisans and other occupational castes render to the agriculturist services in their respective fields of specialization; in return the agriculturist gives them a stipulated share of the crops when they are harvested. In special cases cash payment is made by arrangement. Socio-religious life, especially ceremonials and rituals connected with birth, puberty, marriage, and death, are so organized that they require participation by a number of castes at various stages. Among the occupational castes themselves there is often a barter of their traditional services. Because of their common past and a number of shared values the people of a village often have certain common standards of behaviour and characteristic attitudes. It is through these that many villages earn certain types of reputation, such as, ' "A" is a sober village—its people are considerate and co-operative'. 'Internally "B" is divided; the people quarrel a lot among themselves, but they face other villages with complete unity', ' "C" is a village of scoundrels (*badmash*); its people take liberties with law with impunity'.

Power equations in these communities have changed considerably in recent years. It may generally be stated that the local scene was dominated by the important land holders and leaders of village factions. Recent state legislation, particularly the Zamindari Abolition Act[1] and the Panchayat Raj Act,[2] has brought about some significant changes in the pattern of the exercise of authority. With the abolition of *zamindari* and emergence of a class of small proprietary tenants the virtual domination of the village scene by the landlord or landlords has been weakened. In several villages this has meant the end of the domination of one particular caste over all others. Democratic elections to bodies like the Gaon Sabha (village councils) and the Adalati Panchayat (village courts) created under the Panchayat Raj Act provided an opportunity for the different groups in the villages to come out into the open and press their right to positions of power and authority. The contest in most cases was between castes that have exercised power for a long time and the under-privileged, mostly untouchable, groups. In several important villages the latter were able to capture important positions in the elected bodies, in others there were major shifts in alignments of groups, and the dominant group was able formally to maintain its power only by admitting other groups to membership. Because these newly created bodies have sufficient authority to direct village affairs and control village funds, they have attracted considerable attention and interest. Under their impact the nature of village leadership, factionalism, and group dynamics is undergoing changes that may have far-reaching consequences.

2. Agriculture, Education and Health

With these preliminary observations on the social organization of the village communities in this area, we can proceed to sketch the conditions in the fields of agriculture, education, public health, and public works immediately before the setting up of the Community Development Project Block.

At the time of the inauguration of the Community Development Project the total population of the area was 78,337 (42,795 males and 35,542 females), living in 19,899 families. Most of these were engaged in agriculture or subsidiary occupations. Among artisan groups mention may be made of 267 families of blacksmiths, 261 of carpenters, and 116 of masons. The total number of industrial workers temporarily working in the cities was 1,024. Out of 29,340 adult males, 8,058 were literate and 21,282 were illiterate. The proportion of illiteracy was much higher among women: out of 24,699 adult

[1]Under this Act, passed in 1950, hereditary estates were abolished and proprietary rights were given to the tenants.

[2]Passed in 1948 (and amended in 1955) this Act introduced a new pattern of village government by establishing elected village councils and courts.

women only 3,960 were literate, 20,739 were illiterate. Only 3,646 children were enrolled in the schools of the Project area. Educational facilities were not available to a large proportion of children of school-going age.

As has been pointed out earlier, this area is predominantly agricultural. According to the survey that preceded the creation of the Project, 10,458 acres in the Development Block were uncultivated, and 72,465 acres were cultivated. Out of the area under cultivation 38,538 acres were unirrigated, 33,927 acres were irrigated. Under *rabi* (winter) crops there were 16,632 acres of irrigated and 22,754 acres of unirrigated land, and 16,875 and 25,584 acres respectively of irrigated and unirrigated land were under *kharif* (rainy season) crops. Sugarcane was grown on 12,281 acres of irrigated land and 1,833 acres of unirrigated land. A total of 13,493 acres was double-cropped. The following table will give an idea of the main crops in the Project area:

	Name of the Crop	Acres under the Crop		
		Irrigated	Unirrigated	Total
1	Wheat	12,033	11,107	23,140
2	Sugarcane	12,281	1,833	14,114
3	Gram	297	7,638	7,228
4	*Jawar* (millet)	624	6,604	7,228
5	Rice	3,225	2,081	5,306
6	*Bajra* (millet)	21	3,408	3,429
7	Pea	2,155	824	2,979
8	Wheat and gram mixed	560	1,326	1,886
9	Fodder	1,033	253	1,286
10	Barley	197	390	587
11	Maize	16	346	362
12	Wheat and barley mixed	30	97	127
13	Potato	88	1	89

The principal means of irrigation in this area were: canals, wells, tanks, ponds, and tube wells. A branch of the Ganga canal passing through this region irrigated 18,339 acres. Irrigation wells provided water to 11,775 acres. Tanks, ponds, and tube wells irrigated another 3,833 acres. Out of a total of 865 irrigation wells, 308 were bored masonry wells and 355 were unbored masonry wells. The chief means of irrigation through these wells was the 'Persian Wheel'. At the time of the inauguration of the Project there were 481 of these in the area. The number of tube wells was 33. Two of these were state tube wells, 12 were operated by Co-operative Societies, and 19 belonged to private owners.

Agriculture was largely unmechanized and depended on draft

cattle. Before the Project started in this area there were 11,256 bullocks of the local breed, and 8,023 of improved breeds. At the same time there were 3,846 cows of the local breed and 992 of improved breeds. The number of buffaloes in the area was 11,836; 11,405 of the local variety and 431 of a better breed. Out of 62 breeding bulls only 28 were pedigreed. The number of buffalo bulls was 69; 47 of the local variety, 22 of an improved breed. There were also 3,978 goats of local variety, 28 of an improved breed; 2,250 sheep of local breed, 500 of an improved breed; 1,569 pigs of local breed, and 118 of improved breed. A poultry census of the area recorded 3,705 hens (14 being of good breed) and 719 cocks (all of the local breed).

Alongside of traditional agricultural implements certain new types of implements had become popular in this area. Important among them were: chaff-cutters (4,113), soil turning ploughs (386), harrows (22), tractors (6), and carts with inflated rubber tyres, known locally as 'Dunlop Carts' (15). Out of 170 cane crushers only 5 were of the improved type.

The district in which this Project is located is well known for its fruit and orchards, but in the development area itself horticulture was not particularly developed. The total area under orchards was 2,690 acres. Out of this there were 208 acres of old orchards that needed rejuvenation. Most of the orchards had mango trees of a degenerate local variety. The well-known larger varieties of mango popular in the other parts of the district had been introduced, but as yet they were grown on a very limited scale. Papaya was more popular, and there were 6,097 papaya trees in the area. Vegetables were being grown on only 97 acres.

The total number of Co-operative Societies, before the Project came into existence, was 43. They had a membership of 1,394, and a share capital of Rs43,350. They had transacted business amounting to Rs160,848. There were 2 larger Co-operative Unions whose membership included 25 societies and 166 individuals. They had a share capital of Rs11,615 and had transacted business amounting to Rs105,865. Through these societies and other government agencies improved seeds, chemical fertilizers, and new agricultural implements were being popularized. Their work in this sphere in the year preceding the inauguration of the Project (1952–3) included the following:

1. *Sale of fertilizers:*
   - i Ammonium sulphate—288 tons.
   - ii Super-phosphate—62 tons.
   - iii Ground-nut cake—1,836 maunds.[1]
   - iv Mixture—60 tons.

[1]A maund is equal to 82 pounds.

2. *Sale of improved implements:*
   i Akola hoes[1]—10.
   ii Levelling *karhas*[2]—27.
   iii Gurjar ploughs[3]—35.
   iv Cultivators—12.

3. *Sale of improved seed:*
   i Wheat—7,557 maunds.
   ii Barley—20 maunds.
   iii Gram—96 maunds.
   iv Rice—68 maunds.
   v *Jawar* (millet)—37 maunds.
   vi *Sanai*[4] (for green manuring)—65 maunds.
   vii *Dhencha*[5] (for green manuring)—17 maunds.
   viii *Moong*[6]—50 maunds.

There were very few cottage industries in the area. Woodwork, basket making, and hand-loom weaving were important among these, and employed 1,634 people when the Project was established.

In the 153 villages selected for development there were 39 primary schools with an enrolment of 2,098 students. These schools had 73 teachers. There were 5 Junior High Schools, with 912 students and 31 teachers, 1 Higher Secondary School, with 125 students and 8 teachers, and 1 Intermediate College, with 260 students and 9 instructors. In addition, there were 4 Sanskrit Pathshalas[7] and 1 Arabi Madarsa[8] with 175 and 75 students respectively. The former employed 6 teachers; the latter only 3.

A survey of community works and organizations at this time showed that the area had 5 Panchayat houses[9] and 14 Gandhi Platforms.[10] One more Panchayat house was in construction. There were 10 organized units giving periodic dramatic performances or organizing community singing of devotional songs, 33 village gymnasiums, and 31 sports clubs. The gymnasiums had a membership of 422 and the number of persons participating in the activities of the sports clubs was 496. There were 35 wireless receiving sets; all but 7 of these

[1]An improved type of iron hoe.

[2]An improved implement used for levelling the earth.

[3]A light soil-turning plough made of iron.

[4]San hemp or fibrous hemp, *Crotalaria juncea.*

[5]A local crop used for green manuring.

[6]A legume, *Phaseatur radiatus.*

[7]Traditional school where Sanskrit is taught. Other subjects are taught along classical lines in these schools.

[8]Schools run on traditional Islamic lines. Arabic language and Muslim theology are the principal subjects taught.

[9]Office of the village council.

[10]Village platforms for public functions, named after Gandhi.

were communal. There were 442 drinking water wells; 295 of them in need of sanitary repairs. These wells were being ignored because of the increasing popularity of hand pumps, which numbered 3,235. About 135 miles of unmetalled[1] roads needed repairs, and the construction of 195 culverts was required.

3. The Project Administration

The decision to establish a Community Development Project Block in this area was announced in March 1953. The District Planning Committee provisionally selected 120 villages for inclusion in this Block. The Deputy Project Executive Officer, who was to be the officer-in-charge of the Project, was appointed in July 1953, and was asked to conduct a general survey of the area. The purpose of this survey was to gather information regarding conditions obtaining in the selected villages, with a view to finding out their needs and formulating a three-year development plan for the area. The Dy PEO,[2] a young man with training in Economics and Commerce, was an officer of the state co-operative service, and before selection for this job had worked for some years in the Co-operative Department. He had undergone a brief orientation course in principles and methods of extension work. For a month he was without any assistants, and had to conduct a part of the survey with the help of the secretaries of village councils and the supervisors of the Co-operative Department. In August seven Village Level Workers were posted to this Project. With their assistance he completed the survey, and prepared a tentative development plan. The Project was formally inaugurated on 2 October 1953.

When the Project started functioning the necessary staff had not been appointed. Two Assistant Project Officers—one for agriculture, another for co-operatives and village participation—were appointed in October 1953. Two more—one for statistics and information and another for social education—were appointed in December of the same year. An Assistant Project Officer for women's welfare and education was added to the staff in August 1954. Even at the end of the first year of Project activities, there were no technical subject-matter specialists to assist the Deputy Project Executive Officer in the fields of roads and drainage construction, and animal husbandry. No appointments had been made to the posts of Health Visitor and Sanitary Inspector. Out of four sanctioned posts of midwives only one had been filled, although shortly afterwards the three remaining vacancies were also filled. By the end of the first year the sanctioned

[1] Mud roads.
[2] Abbreviation for Deputy Project Executive Officer.

strength of Village Level Workers had been reduced from 25 to 20, but only 17 appointments had been made. Within this period two out of four Field Teachers (social education organizers) had been appointed, and one more was appointed shortly afterwards.

The administrative organization of the Community Development Project Block in the early part of the second year of the Project can be presented in the following diagram:

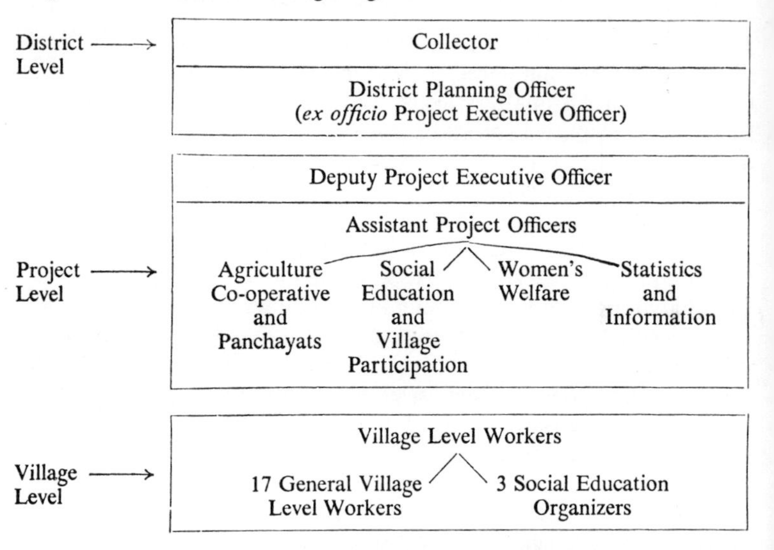

The all-India pattern of administrative organization of the Community Development Projects has been sketched earlier. Like all other development Projects in the State of Uttar Pradesh this Block was controlled by the Development Commissioner, the link between the Project and the state headquarters was the Deputy Development Commissioner for western U.P. Through the Development Commissioner it was connected with the national Community Project Administration.

It is necessary to point out that this new structure marked a departure from the traditional pattern of administrative organization. Under the old system the collector was recognized as the head of district administration, but was principally in charge of land revenue administration. In his capacity of District Magistrate he was also in charge of maintenance of law and order in the district. His position was recognizably superior to that of other district level officers of various departments, but the latter were *technically* and *administratively* under their respective officers on the state level and their intermediaries who were in charge of inter-district units. On the whole the administration was departmentalized, each department having a hierarchy operating on the state, district, sub-division (*tahsil*), and village levels. On the district and its subordinate levels the collector informally co-ordinated government activities in some measure, but except in emergencies he rarely intervened in the work of departments not directly under him. Because of his status he was respected and feared by the other district level officers who generally carried out his wishes and suggestions. When intervention was necessary the collector approached the official superiors of the district officers rather than give them orders directly.

In actual practice the different departments had a large measure of independence; their policies and plans were determined at state headquarters, and transmitted to the district officers. The district officers transmitted them to their subordinates on the sub-divisional level, who were responsible for putting them into action through their subordinates operating on the village level. Under the British régime, when emphasis was more on law and order than on development, this system worked, but with the intensification of development activities certain modifications and adjustments in the system became inevitable.

The old system had three main defects. First, because of the lack of inter-departmental co-ordination and co-operation there was no unity in the welfare measures carried out by the different agencies of the same government. With an administrative organization of this type an integrated approach to the development problems of the rural areas was difficult. Often the Agriculture Department did not know what the Department of Livestock and Animal Husbandry was doing. Worse than this was the situation created by the fact that certain departments working in closely related areas, such as agriculture, co-operatives, and sugar-cane development, pursued independent and conflicting policies which created confusion in the villagers' minds. There was much avoidable duplication of work.

Secondly, under the old system each department had its separate village level staff, which, because of the seasonal nature of work, found itself overloaded in the busy season and practically idle in the slack season. For financial reasons each department could only have a limited field staff which had to look after a large number of villages. In the busy season, or whenever there was an emergency, this proved to be inadequate.

Thirdly, under this system the technically better qualified people on the district and sub-division level were for most of the time administering their small offices and overseeing the work of their subordinate officials. As a result, while the village people got inefficient service from inadequately trained people, those with better technical qualifications spent a good part of their time in routine administrative activities.

Under the reorganized administrative pattern of the Community Projects, an effort was made to overcome some of these defects. By placing the district level officers of the development departments under the administrative control of the Collector and the District Planning Officer, conditions were created for better inter-departmental co-ordination. This relieved the officers of a part of their routine administrative duties, enabling them to devote more time to the subject of their technical specialization. The same results were achieved by placing the sub-divisional officers of these departments under the Deputy Project Executive Officer on the Project level. Through the multi-purpose Village Level Worker an effort was made to evolve a government functionary who combined the duties and responsibility of the field agents of several departments. In the VLW[1] the village people could easily recognize the state appointed extension and welfare agent. Thus the confusion caused by the multiplicity of a large number of departmental agents was avoided. Being in charge of a smaller unit, a population ranging between 3,000 to 5,000, the VLW could maintain more effective contact with people in his area, and, as peak periods of activity in different spheres of extension and welfare work do not coincide, the VLW could be kept usefully occupied all the year round, without being unduly burdened in any one season.

Since he was essentially an extension agent and social worker, the Village Level Worker could not replace *all* village officials. Indeed no attempt was made to achieve this. In view of the administrative nature of his work the *Lekhpal* (village accountant), a land records and revenue official on the village level, was retained; his duties were not assigned to the VLW. As village councils and village courts had recently been created, it was felt desirable that they should have the services of a full-time Secretary. In the first year of the life of the Project the offices of the VLW and the Panchayat Secretary were kept separate. In the second year, as an experimental measure, the VLW was asked, in addition to his normal work, to act as the Panchayat Secretary for the village in which he was living and the Panchayat Secretary was asked to function as a multi-purpose Village Level Worker for one or two villages of his Adalati Panchayat area. In the third year the experiment was abandoned and the Project reverted to the pattern of the first year. Officials of the Co-operative Department were retained only to man the Seed Stores in the area; other of its personnel operating among the people in the villages were withdrawn. The Village Level Worker combined in his duties the functions of the

[1]Abbreviation for Village Level Worker.

field agents of agriculture, co-operatives, veterinary, public health, and rural welfare departments.

In drawing up the three-year schedule of Project activities, the model provided by the central and state headquarters was largely followed. In the territorial break-up of the targets, attempts were made to take into account the specific needs of the individual villages. Immediate as well as long-term targets were modified periodically in the light of directives received from state headquarters. The Village Level Workers were assigned to groups of villages covering the entire development block. They lived in the villages and reported fortnightly at Project headquarters to attend staff meetings. At these meetings they presented brief reports of their work during the fortnight and under the direction of the officers prepared a schedule of activities for the coming fortnight. They could also report their problems and difficulties at these meetings.

The Deputy Project Executive Officer and the Assistant Project Officers were stationed at the Project headquarters, but were expected to spend approximately three weeks each month in the field. The principal responsibility of the former was to supervise the efficient implementation of the development programme in the Block. The APOs[1] had partly to supervise the work of the VLWs in their respective fields, but their main job was to give technical guidance to the latter in the execution of projects within the areas of their technical specialization.

A number of important persons who were residents or representatives of the area were associated with the activities of the Project through the District Planning Committee, the Project Advisory Committee and the Development Block Committees. These committees consisted of both officials and non-officials. The Project Advisory Committee and the Development Block Committee were more immediately concerned with the work of the Project. The non-officials in the Project Advisory Committee were: all members of the District Planning Committee living in the Project area, all Sarpanches[2] of co-operative societies in the area, all members of the State Legislative Assembly and Council living in or representing the area, the President of the District Board and members of the Board living in the area, five members nominated by the government, and one representative of each of the sub-blocks of the Project. Officials having seats in this committee were: the Collector or his nominee (as president), the Deputy Project Executive Officer (as secretary), and all sub-divisional officers of development departments stationed in the area. The Community Development Project Block area was divided into

[1]Abbreviation for Assistant Project Officer.
[2]Elected members of the executive committee.

a number of sub-blocks, and an advisory committee was constituted for each of these sub-blocks. These were called Development Block Committees. These committees consisted of all Pradhans[1] of Gram Sabhas in the sub-block, members of the Board of Directors of all Co-operative Unions within the area, the headmasters of Junior High Schools in the area, members of the state legislature and the district board living in or representing the area, five interested residents of the area to be appointed by the Collector on the advice of the District Planning Committee, all Assistant Project Officers, and all Village Level Workers of the area. The committee was to elect its own chairman, and one of the Assistant Project Officers was to be nominated as its secretary by the Collector on the advice of the District Planning Committee. These committees were to review the progress of work in their respective areas, and sanction grants in aid for specific projects.

The Project reported its activities and achievements to the Community Project's Administration, through the district and state headquarters, every month. It was periodically visited by higher officials from district, state, and national levels, who inspected the work in progress and made suggestions for improvement.

4. The Development Programme

On the basis of a survey of the existing conditions and of local felt needs, a three-year programme setting up targets in different fields of development activities was drawn up. The following tables summarize the targets and their breakdown over the three-year period:

1. *Targets in the Field of Agricultural Extension and Animal Husbandry*

A. IRRIGATION

	Particulars of the Programme	Target 1953–4	1954–5	1955–6	1956–7
1	(*a*) Number of state tube wells to be constructed	2	—	—	—
	(*b*) Area in acres to be irrigated by these wells	1,000	—	—	—
2	(*a*) Number of co-operative tube wells to be constructed	25	5	5	—
	(*b*) Area in acres to be irrigated by these wells	7,500	1,500	1,500	—
3	(*a*) Number of private tube wells to be constructed	3	2	2	2
	(*b*) Area in acres to be irrigated by these wells	300	100	100	100

[1]Elected head of the village council.

4 (*a*) Number of masonry wells to be constructed	10	25	25	10
(*b*) Area in acres to be irrigated by the wells	100	250	250	100
5 (*a*) Rejuvenation of derelict wells	—	50	50	—
(*b*) Increased area in acres to be brought under irrigation	—	250	250	—
6 (*a*) Boring of masonry wells	12	30	50	10
(*b*) Increased area in acres to be brought under irrigation	120	300	500	100
7 (*a*) Number of Persian wheels to be installed	10	25	25	10
(*b*) Increased area in acres to be brought under irrigation	100	250	250	100
8 (*a*) Small pumping sets to be installed on wells	2	4	4	2
(*b*) Increased area in acres to be brought under irrigation	60	120	120	150

B. PURCHASE OF IMPROVED SEED

Name of the seed	Quantity to be purchased, in maunds Targets for			
	1953–4	1954–5	1955–6	1956–7
1 Rice (early variety)	—	200	400	—
2 Rice (late variety)	—	50	100	—
3 *Sanai*	—	1,000	2,000	1,500
4 Maize	—	100	250	—
5 Cane	10,000	15,000	15,000	—
6 *Moong*	—	50	100	—
7 Wheat	25,000	25,000	30,000	—
8 Gram	1,000	1,000	5,000	500
9 Peas	500	500	2,500	300
10 *Berseem* or lucerne	10	10	15	15

C. DISTRIBUTION OF IMPROVED SEED

Name of the seed	Quantity to be distributed, in maunds Targets for			
	1953–4	1954–5	1955–6	1956–7
1 Rice (early variety)	—	150	200	—
2 Rice (late variety)	—	50	75	—
3 *Sanai*	—	500	1,000	—
4 *Dhencha*	—	100	200	—
5 *Moong*	—	50	75	—
6 *Lobia*[1]	—	10	20	—
7 Wheat	8,800	11,000	13,000	—
8 Gram	400	800	1,200	—
9 Peas	100	200	500	—
10 *Berseem* or Lucerne	8	10	15	—

[1]A legume used as a vegetable, fodder, and green manure, *Vigna catiang*.

D. AREA TO BE SOWN WITH IMPROVED SEED

	Name of the seed	Area in acres		
			Targets for	
		1953–4	1954–5	1955–6
1	Wheat	17,000	20,000	22,000
2	Barley	300	500	700
3	Gram	500	1,000	1,500
4	*Berseem* or lucerne	700	1,000	1,500
5	*Jawar*	—	1,500	2,000
6	Rice (early variety)	—	500	700
7	Rice (late variety)	—	3,000	5,000

E. DEMONSTRATIONS TO BE GIVEN

Type of demonstration		Number of demonstrations to be given in		
		1953–4	1954–5	1955–6
1 *Varietal*	i Wheat	25	100	100
	ii Gram	100	200	200
	iii Peas	100	200	200
	iv Rice	50	100	100
	v Maize	50	100	100
	vi Sugarcane	50	100	100
	vii Cotton	20	40	40
2 *Manurial*	i *Sanai*, ii *Dhencha*, iii *Moong*	—	100	100
	iv Ammonium sulphate	200	500	700
	v Oil cake	200	500	700
3 *Cultural*	i Cane	70	100	120
	ii Wheat	50	100	100
	iii Cotton	50	75	100
	iv Rice	25	50	70
	v Maize	10	20	25

F. SALE OF IMPROVED IMPLEMENTS

	Type of implement	Number to be sold in			
		1953–4	1954–5	1955–6	1956–7
1, 2, 3	Shabash plough, Meston plough, Gurjar plough[1]	30	25	30	50
4	Cultivators	50	100	100	50
5	Hand hoe	70	200	200	—
6	Chaff-cutter	10	15	15	50
7	Single hand hoe	50	200	300	50
8	Tractor	1	2	2	1
9	Improved sickle	50	200	200	—
10	Paddy weeder	50	180	200	—
11	Levelling *Karha*	4	10	10	—

[1]Improved types of light soil-turning ploughs made of iron.

G. MANURE AND FERTILIZER TO BE DISTRIBUTED

	Type of manure or fertilizer	Quantity to be distributed in 1953–4	1954–5	1955–6	1956–7
1	Ammonium sulphate	2,000	3,000	3,000	2,000
2	Superphosphate	200	200	200	100
3	*Sanai*	—	500	1,000	1,500
4	*Dhencha*	—	100	250	300
5	*Moong* (type 1)	—	100	150	200
6	*Lobia*	—	10	20	30
7	Castor cake, Groundnut cake and *neem* cake } oil seed cakes	1,000	2,000	2,000	1,000

H. PREPARATION OF FARM-YARD MANURE

	Programme	Number to be constructed in 1953–4	1954–5	1955–6	1956–7
1	Digging of manure pits	500	2,000	2,000	1,000
2	Covering of manure heaps	500	2,000	2,000	1,000
3	Construction of cattle urine preservation beds	20	200	100	50

I. HORTICULTURE

	Particulars of the Programme	Targets for 1953–4	1954–5	1955–6	1956–7
1	Area in acres to be brought under orchards	50	100	200	150
2	Number of orchards and groves to be rejuvenated	5 (50 acres)	15 (150 acres)	15 (150 acres)	—
3	Number of fruit trees to be planted:				
	i Mango	—	1,000	2,000	5,000
	ii Papaya	—	5,000	5,000	2,500
	iii Lemon	—	2,000	2,000	1,000
	iv Guava	—	4,000	4,000	4,000
	v *Ber* (*Zizyphus jujuba*)	—	1,000	1,000	500
4	Number of fuel trees to be planted:				
	i *Sheesham* (*Dalbergia sisso*)	—	5,000	7,000	10,000
	ii *Babul* (*Acacia arabica*)	—	5,000	7,000	10,000
	iii *Neem* (*Azadirachta indica*)	—	5,000	7,000	10,000
5	Nurseries to be started:				
	i Central	1	—	—	—
	ii Smaller	2	10	10	—
6	Vegetable seeds to be distributed:	190 lb	100 lb	100 lb	100 lb
7	Number of seedlings to be distributed	5,000	15,000	25,000	30,000
8	Potato seed to be distributed	100	200	300	300

J. ANIMAL HUSBANDRY

	Particulars of the Programme	Targets for			
		1953–4	1954–5	1955–6	1956–7
1	Supply of pedigree animals:				
	i cows	16	10	10	10
	ii bulls	10	10	10	10
	iii buffaloes	10	10	10	20
	iv buffalo bulls	2	5	5	5
	v hens	200	400	400	200
	vi cocks	20	40	40	40
2	Improved eggs to be distributed	500	1,000	1,500	1,500
3	Castrations to be performed	500	1,500	2,000	3,000
4	Inoculation of cattle against:				
	i Maemurligic septicaemia	—	30,000	30,000	30,000
	ii Rinderpest	14,000	30,000	30,000	30,000
5	Opening of veterinary hospital	1	—	—	—
6	Number of cows to be artificially inseminated	100	500	1,000	1,500
7	Opening of poultry development block	1	—	—	—
8	Opening of poultry development 'key centres'	1	—	—	—
9	Construction of footbaths	2	4	4	2
10	Model cattle sheds	2	4	4	2
11	Vaccination of poultry against Ranikhet disease	500	1,000	1,000	500
12	Fisheries development:				
	i Number of fingerlings to be distributed	—	200	300	100
	ii Area of tanks to be used for fisheries development	—	1 acre	2 acres	1 acre
13	Number of cattle to be treated at the veterinary dispensary	5,000	8,000	10,000	5,000
14	Cattle fairs to be organized	6	8	10	8
15	Cattle exhibitions to be organized	1	2	2	1

K. CO-OPERATIVES

	Particulars of the Programme	Targets for 1953–4	1954–5	1955–6	1956–7
1	Number of new primary societies to be formed	5	30	10	—
2	Number of new unions to be formed	1	—	—	—
3	Number of newly formed seed stores to be opened	1	—	—	—
4	Number of new consumers' stores to be opened	1	1	1	—
5	Number of co-operative farming societies to be established	1	1	2	—
6	Number of industrial co-operatives to be established	—	2	5	—
7	Number of new members to be enrolled in				
	(*a*) societies	250	1,000	1,000	—
	(*b*) unions	25	50	50	—
8	Increase in share capital				
	(*a*) societies	Rs2,000	Rs5,000	Rs5,000	—
	(*b*) unions	Rs1,000	Rs1,000	Rs1,000	—
9	Total money value of business to be done in Rs.				
	(*a*) primary societies	Rs200,000	Rs250,000	Rs300,000	Rs325,000
	(*b*) co-operative unions	Rs125,000	Rs150,000	Rs200,000	Rs500,000

2. *Targets in the Field of Public Health and Rural Sanitation*

	Particulars of the Programme	Targets for 1953–4	1954–5	1955–6	1956–7
1	Number of wells for drinking water to be dug	5	10	10	5
2	Number of hand pumps to be installed	10	30	30	20
3	Number of bathing platforms to be built	5	20	20	10
4	Number of wells to be disinfected	400	500	500	500
5	Pucca drains to be constructed (in yards)	250	1,000	1,000	500
6	Lanes to be paved (in yards)	250	1,000	2,000	500
7	Number of soak pits to be constructed	10	50	50	30
8	Number of village cleaning drives to be undertaken	2	2	2	2
	(*a*) Number of villages	15	50	50	30
	(*b*) Number of houses	500	1,000	1,000	1,000
	(*c*) Number of times the drive is launched in the year	2	2	2	2

Targets in the Field of Public Health and Rural Sanitation—continued

9	Number of villages to be provided with kerosene street lamps	20	100	100	50
10	(*a*) Number of primary smallpox vaccinations to be performed	10,000	12,000	15,000	—
	(*b*) Number of secondary smallpox vaccinations to be performed	20,000	20,000	30,000	—
11	D.D.T. spraying				
	(*a*) Number of villages to be covered	1	5	5	—
	(*b*) Number of houses to be covered	600	1,500	1,500	—
12	Number of maternity centres to be started	1	1	1	—
13	Number of medicine chests to be provided	56	—	—	—

3. *Targets in the Field of Social Education and Youth Welfare*

	Particulars of the Programme	Targets for			
		1953–4	1954–5	1955–6	1956–7
1	Number of community centres to be opened	5	10	10	5
2	Number of community radios to be installed	5	10	10	5
3	Number of libraries to be established	5	10	10	5
4	Number of books to be bought	150	1,500	1,500	1,500
5	Number of reading rooms to be established	5	10	10	10
6	Number of information centres to be opened	1	1	1	1
7	Number of new schools to be started				
	(*a*) Primary schools	2	4	4	2
	(*b*) Junior high schools for boys	—	1	1	—
	(*c*) Adult Literacy classes	40	40	40	20
8	Number of sight seeing programmes in project to be undertaken	4	10	10	10
9	Number of cinema shows to be held	5	100	100	50
10	Number of camps for field staff to be held	—	1	1	—
11	Number of workers to be trained	—	30	30	—

12	Number of camps to be held for village leaders	1	1	1	—
13	Number of youth leaders to be trained	50	50	50	—
14	Number of *akharas*[1] to be established	15	30	30	15
15	Number of *bhajan mandalis*[2] to be organized	1	5	5	1
16	Number of *kisan melas*[3] to be organized	2	2	2	1

4. *Targets in the Field of Communications and Public Works*

	Particulars of the Programme	Targets for			
		1953–4	1954–5	1955–6	1956–7
1	Number of primary schools for boys to be opened	5	5	10	10
2	Number of primary schools for girls to be opened	2	2	2	2
3	Number of Junior High Schools for boys or boys and girls to be opened	1	1	1	—
4	Number of higher secondary schools to be opened	—	1	1	—
5	Number of seed stores to be opened	1	—	—	—
6	Number of Panchayat-Ghars to be opened	5	7	10	5
7	Number of Gandhi Chabutaras to be built	5	7	10	5
8	Number of hospitals to be established	1	—	—	—
9	Number of maternity centres to be started	1	3	—	—
10	New pucca roads[4] to be built (in miles)	½	3	3	½
11	New kachcha roads[5] to be built (in miles)	20	100	100	50
12	Pucca roads to be repaired (in miles)	3	10	10	5
13	Kachcha roads to be repaired (in miles)	100	200	200	100
14	Number of bridges to be constructed (Total span in feet)	3 (18)	7 (42)	10 (60)	3 (15)

[1]Wrestling pits.

[2]Units for singing religious and devotional songs.

[3]Conventions of agriculturists combining recreation with deliberations of matters connected with agriculture, much like the country fair in rural United States.

[4]All-weather roads covered with stone, tar or cement.

[5]Mud roads difficult to use in the rainy season.

5. *Targets in other Fields: Harijan*[1] *Welfare and Cottage Industries*

Particulars of the Programme	Targets for 1953–4	1954–5	1955–6	1956–7
A *Harijan Welfare:*				
1 Number of wells for drinking water to be constructed	2	5	5	4
2 Number of wells to be repaired	10	20	20	10
3 Number of Harijan conferences to be held	2	5	5	2
4 Number of recreation centres to be opened	1	2	2	1
B *Cottage Industries:*				
1 Number of improved *gur bhattis*[2] to be established	—	20	20	10
2 Number of improved *kolhus*[3] to be established	—	10	10	7
3 Number of *charkhas*[4] to be distributed	—	50	50	30
4 Number of bee-keeping outfits to be distributed	—	20	20	10
5 Number of tuitional classes to be opened	—	2	2	—
(*a*) Hide and carcass utilization centres	—	1	1	—
(*b*) Classes in carpentry and blacksmithy	—	1	1	—
6 Number of brick kilns to be started	5	6	6	—

5. Achievements

Having outlined the organization and targets of the Community Development Project, we can proceed to describe its main accomplishments during the first eighteen months, i.e. the first half of its life.

A. *Agricultural Extension, Animal Husbandry, Co-operatives and Irrigation*

Irrigation: After the establishment of the Project, twenty-two co-operative tube wells were constructed under the supervision of the State Agricultural Engineering Department. This increased the number of such tube wells in the area to thirty-four. Experience with these wells pointed to three main difficulties: some engines failed; some proved uneconomic, and on the whole their range of utility was

[1]Literally 'children of God'; the term refers to untouchable castes.
[2]Furnace for processing jaggery or unrefined sugar.
[3]Oil press.
[4]Spinning wheel.

1. VLW working in the plant nursery.

2. Demonstration of the Japanese method of rice cultivation.

3. New varieties of sugar cane introduced by the project.

4. Demonstration of new methods of sowing sugar cane.

greatly limited because of the absence of masonry channels. To overcome the first two of these difficulties efforts were made to devise ways and means of operating the engines efficiently and economically. To remedy the third defect steps were taken to construct masonry channels in order to enlarge the area under the command of the tube wells. The District Planning Committee offered subsidies of Rs1,500 per well for construction of two miles of channels and drains around each well. This work was taken up first in four villages, where 1,826 yards of masonry and 9,248 yards of ordinary drains were constructed. Plans were in hand to extend this to four more wells. Construction of four more tube wells was about to be taken up.

In addition to these co-operative wells people were encouraged to have private tube wells. During the first half of the Project's life, three new private tube wells were bored. During this period the government decided to increase the number of state operated tube wells from 2 to 10. Work on three out of eight of these wells sanctioned by the government was begun during the period of observation.

It has been pointed out earlier that out of 865 irrigation wells in the area, only 308 were scientifically bored when the Project started functioning. During the first eighteen months of its existence thirty-nine more wells were scientifically bored, and twenty-five new Persian Wheels were fixed.

As provision for more and better irrigation was one of the most pressing needs of the agriculturists, it received priority in the development programme. The government spent on its own Rs40,000 on this item. Village people were granted loans amounting to Rs49,600 to enable them to undertake construction of irrigation wells and tube wells. This effort was subsidized by grants amounting to Rs11,000. People contributed their voluntary labour substantially to this work. According to a Project report the value of such labour was estimated to be Rs305,593. As a result of all these concentrated efforts about 62·4 per cent of the total agricultural land in the Development Block was brought under irrigation.

Propagation of improved seeds: Efforts were concentrated on the propagation of improved seed of wheat and sugarcane. In the first year of the Project 900 maunds of an improved wheat seed—Panjab 591—were distributed through the Seed Stores. This seed was to have been returned in kind, with 25 per cent interest, after the harvest, but unfortunately a substantial part of the crop was damaged by rust. In the second year, 6,150 maunds of this seed were distributed, bringing about 70 per cent of the wheat area under improved seed. Practically all the sugarcane area was under some variety or other of improved sugarcane, but efforts were being made to popularize cane 321 and cane 345[1] in place of cane 312 which hitherto had dominated the scene. The first two varieties are believed to be better than the last one, and are more suited to the soil and climate of the area. An improved variety of rice—paddy type 1—was also popularized, and rice seed weighing 119 maunds was sold. As the local variety of rice, known as Lalmati, is very similar to the improved variety and is well adapted to the area, no effort was made to saturate the area with the improved variety. An effort was made to replace the old variety of pea with a new one; 380 maunds of improved pea seed were sold. It was estimated that about 70 per cent of the agricultural land was under improved seed after the first year and a half of the Project's life.

Manures and fertilizers: Because of the insufficiency of wood fuel in this area a large quantity of dung is used as fuel rather than being turned into fertilizer. As a long-term measure, trees to be used as fuel have been planted on 204 acres of land. To overcome the immediate shortage of manure efforts were made to popularize green manuring and the use of oil cakes and chemical fertilizers. During the first year of its activities the Project sold 630 maunds of *sanai* seed, bringing about 33 per cent of the area under some type of green manure. In the second year the target was 1,000 maunds, and it was hoped that this would provide green manure to about 50 per cent of the agricultural land. An attempt was made to educate the village people in the use of oil cake, an invaluable source of nitrogen, for fertilizer. These efforts were partly successful and in the first year oil cakes weighing 1,388 maunds were sold. Chemical fertilizers were more popular. In the first year alone the Project sold 8,938 maunds of different types of such fertilizers.

Improved agricultural implements: During this period 181 improved implements costing Rs8,195 were sold to the agriculturists of the Development Block.

Horticulture and vegetable growing: With a view to popularizing horticulture and vegetable growing one central nursery and seven small nurseries were started by the Project. Seedlings and plants were supplied to the area through these nurseries.

It was realized that people were reluctant to plant orchards because the trees remained unproductive for the first few years. People were more inclined to invest in projects that brought them quick returns. In conjunction with the Department of Horticulture the Project prepared and promoted a scheme which allowed certain types of intermediate crops to be grown in the orchard area in the earlier, unproductive years. This was enthusiastically received by some

[1]Improved varieties of sugarcane.

people, but at about this time its plans for consolidation of land holdings were announced by the government. Fearing that their land might go to someone else after the planting of an orchard, agriculturists decided to postpone such ventures until the completion of consolidation. Even the assurance that ownership of the orchards would not be disturbed by consolidation could not revive their earlier enthusiasm. Notwithstanding this setback orchards were planted in an area of 130 acres.

Co-operation of the local schools was sought to promote the programme of kitchen gardens and vegetable growing. As a result of this drive 613 kitchen gardens were planted in this area, and vegetable seed weighing 49 pounds and 5,000 seedlings were sold. Special efforts were made to popularize the growing of potatoes. In the first year improved potato seed weighing seven maunds was sold. In the second year the quantity of this seed sold to the agriculturists of the Block was a little more than forty maunds.

Other agricultural activities: The Project organized extensive anti-locust operations, as locusts had laid eggs in several hundred acres of the Development Block. People gradually came to realize the value of D.D.T. in meeting the locust menace and in crop protection in general.

In the first year the Village Level Workers gave 2,445 varietal and manurial demonstrations to present concrete proof of the superiority and value of improved seed and new fertilizers.

To promote a healthy spirit of competition among the agriculturists a number of crop competitions were organized by the Project. In the first year there were five district level and 520 village level competitions. In the first half of the second year there were two district level and 212 village level competitions. One of the agriculturists from the Project area got the third prize of Rs1,000 for wheat in the district competition: his yield was more than twenty-six maunds per acre.

Animal husbandry: In the first year eight pedigree bulls and three breeding buffaloes were given to the villages of the Development Block. People were granted loans to buy fourteen Hariyana cows[1] and ten Murra buffaloes.[2] Three goats, two pigs, and two sheep of good breed were also given to the agriculturists.

The Village Level Workers were supplied with modern instruments for castration and with medicine chests for treatment of cattle. They performed 1,760 castrations and treated 8,477 cattle. During this period they inoculated 30,826 cattle against H.S. and 35,310 against rinderpest. The construction of a building to house a Veterinary Dispensary had almost been completed and an artificial insemination

[1]An improved breed of cows. [2]An improved breed of buffaloes.

centre had started functioning. Only forty-five cows had been impregnated at the centre, and efforts were being made to make its existence and services known in the Development Block.

Growing of fodder crops was encouraged. Besides traditional fodder crops such as *jawar*, *methi*,[1] and peas, the Project introduced *berseem* in the area. As a result of its efforts, *berseem* was grown in an area of eighty acres.

With a view to encouraging poultry farming the Project sold twenty-four fowls and six roosters of good breed. A group of five villages was selected for intensive poultry development. The Project obtained an incubator and a 'foster mother' machine, and in the first half of the second year covered by this survey, 450 eggs were being hatched for the distribution of chicks in the Block.

Co-operatives: A new Co-operative Seed Store was started, increasing the number of such stores to six in the development area. Efforts were intensified to enlist new members in the existing societies and to start new primary societies. When the Project was established there were only forty-three primary societies. As a result of the drive to start new societies, fifty-four more were started, increasing their membership by 1,803 and capital by Rs34,202.

B. *Public Health and Sanitation*

Village Sanitation: To promote consciousness of sanitation needs and practices among the villagers 'clean your village' drives were organized in twenty-five Project villages. These improved the general sanitation of the villages very considerably. It was, however, realized that such periodic drives could not solve the problem of rural sanitation. The villages on the whole were insanitary; in larger villages especially the problem was very acute. The installation of a large number of hand pumps in recent years has aggravated the problem further. It has resulted in the general neglect of the village wells, many of which are still needed and are in use but are in a most unhygienic condition. Secondly, in the absence of proper drains and soakage pits water invariably runs into the village lanes and keeps them muddy and dirty all the year round. Steps were taken to repair and clean the wells, and also to improve the sanitation of village lanes. Nine new wells were dug and 'model sanitary repairs' were made to twenty-seven wells. Encouraged by the initial response, a plan was drawn up to have at least one model well in each of the 153 villages under the Community Development Project, and this work was in progress in the first half of the second year of the Project. To improve the condition of village lanes it was decided to pave them with bricks. In the first year of the Project 3,080 yards of village lanes were paved; in

[1]Fenugreek.

the second it was hoped to pave 2,745 yards more. This programme had appreciable success in four villages, and three villages—two of them large villages—had plans to get all their lanes paved by the end of the second year.

Epidemic and malaria control: The Village Level Workers performed 16,294 vaccinations against smallpox. As a malaria control measure twenty-nine villages were sprayed with D.D.T., and paludrine tablets were given to a large number of people.

General medical treatment: The Project helped the Government Dispensary at its headquarters with medicines and instruments worth Rs2,500. The Village Level Workers and midwives were supplied with medicine chests for first aid and simple treatment of common ailments. In all 5,401 people received medicines through the staff members of the Project.

C. *Social Education and Youth Welfare*

Social Education: In the first year twenty-nine adult education classes were started for men and four for women. The general response to the former was not very enthusiastic, and most of them had to be closed down by the end of the year. The classes for women were also not too well received, but it was decided to continue them. Through these classes 544 adults were made literate, and were given general information about the aims and objectives of rural community development.

Libraries: Twenty-nine mobile libraries were established by the Project. Each 'library' consisted of a box containing thirty to fifty books. These were made available to adult literacy classes and community centres.

Schools: Subsidies amounting to Rs9,500 were granted for construction of new school buildings in five villages. A number of existing schools in the Development Blocks were helped with materials and equipment.

Youth welfare: Seven *Yuwak Dal* or Youth Club organizations were set up in Project villages along the lines of 4-H Clubs. Under the auspices of the Project, twenty-eight gymnasiums and *akharas* were started.

Other activities: A mobile propaganda unit of three persons was organized to popularize the development programme in the Block. This unit addressed village audiences almost all over the Project area.

Two development exhibitions were organized by the Project at its headquarters. Stalls bearing on different aspects of community development, such as agriculture, animal husbandry, public health and cane growing, were prepared. Cottage industries and rural handicrafts were also given an important place in these exhibitions. There were many competitions and entertainment programmes in which the village people were invited to participate.

D. *Communication and Public Works*

The Project gave special attention to the building, repair, and maintenance of village roads in the area. Roads measuring forty-five miles were repaired, forty-six new culverts were built, and twenty-nine old culverts were repaired by the Project. During the first half of the life of the Project a cement road half a mile long was constructed and work was in progress on a road five miles long. It was realized that because of limited financial resources this work could not be undertaken on a large scale, and for this reason special care had to be taken to keep the country tracks in good repair, and build new mud roads where they were needed. Earth work was done on 231 miles of country roads to keep them in good shape, and new roads measuring fifty-one miles were built. Much of this work was done by *shramdan* or people's voluntary labour.

Panchayat houses were constructed in three villages, and work was in progress in four more villages. New school buildings were constructed in six villages. In addition to these one more building was constructed to house a seed store.

E. *Women's Welfare*

Under the auspices of the Community Development Project four adult classes were started for women. Besides reading and writing the curriculum included sewing, knitting, embroidery, and home economics. With a view to extending this work to other villages, a training camp for women teachers was organized in which eleven candidate teachers received training. Upon returning to their respective villages after training, these teachers were expected to organize women's welfare centres and adult education classes there.

Maternity centres were started in four villages under trained midwives. In the first year the midwives rendered service at 305 childbirths and gave pre-natal and post-natal advice to a much larger number of women. The centres distributed powdered milk to undernourished children. An important part of the centre's activities was to train the village *dais*[1] in modern methods of conducting childbirths and infant care. Twenty-two *dais* were receiving training during the second year of the Project. The midwives were also supplied with medicine chests, and treated a large number of women for common ailments.

[1]Untrained village midwives; generally middle-aged women who assist at childbirths.

6. Comment

This survey covers only eighteen months, i.e. the first half of the life of the Project. The implementation of the development programme during this period shows that in action the Project had to deviate considerably from some of the targets that it had set for itself in preparing its initial plan for this region. The full or partial acceptance of some of its innovations and the rejection of others were governed by a series of human factors inevitably linked to the process of externally induced change. Some of the major problems in this area will be examined in the chapters that follow.

III

RESPONSE TO CHANGE

1. The Village Level

IN ORDER TO APPRAISE the impact of the community development programme on the different segments of the rural population on the village level, in this chapter attention will be focused on the response of the people in two villages of the western U.P. Community Development Project Block described earlier. These two villages, called 'Rajput Village' and 'Tyagi Village' on the basis of the most important castes inhabiting them, are fairly representative of the villages of this region. Rajput Village has a population of 5,142, and is among the largest and most prosperous villages of the Development Block. Tyagi Village represents the more numerous smaller settlements, and has a population of 757 people. Being centres of considerable development activity, these villages provide an excellent base for the study of human response to directed change.

Rajput Village is a large and complex settlement; its population being divided into two important religious groups and twenty-eight castes and caste-like groups. The Hindu group, further sub-divided into twenty-one different castes, is approximately fourteen times larger than the Muslim group which is sub-divided into seven caste-like groups. The Rajputs, belonging to the Kshatriya or warrior group of Hindu society, are the dominant caste in the village. With a population of 2,164, they are not only the most numerous group, but as substantial landowners they also dominate the economic and political scene in the village. The Brahmins (traditionally priests) are a small but significant minority. They number only 281 persons, but because of their higher ritual status and education they are regarded as an important segment of the village population. The Vaishya caste (traditionally traders) has a population of 154 people. These three are regarded as the 'upper castes' in the village. On the next lower level there are fifteen artisan and occupational castes with 'clean' status, each having a more or less well-defined traditional occupation. The total population of these castes is 1,225. On the lowest level are three untouchable or Harijan castes: *Chamar* (agricultural labourers), *Jatiya* (leather-workers), and *Bhangi* (scavengers). Together they number 931 people. The small Muslim group consists of 387 persons. Although Islam does not recognize caste distinctions, this group is divided into seven caste-like segments. Traditional rules govern inter-marriage and commensality between these groups, and they still tend to follow their hereditary occupations. However, beliefs and observances regarding ritual purity and pollution that largely govern intercaste relations in Hindu society, are not found in the Muslim group. The Muslim Rajputs, like their Hindu counterparts, are an agricultural 'caste'; the rest of the Muslim 'castes' are occupational.

Tyagi Village also has two major religious groups; Muslims constitute 55·8 per cent and Hindus 46·2 per cent of its population. Tyagis,[1] both Hindu and Muslim, are the most important group in the village. They are the leading landowners in the village. Because of their more substantial land-holdings the Hindu Tyagis dominate the village scene. There are ten Hindu castes in the village, and the Muslims are divided into six caste-like groups.

The population of these villages can be classified into three distinct groups according to their socio-economic status:

A The upper group of agriculturists, and upper-status and higher income segments of the population, consisting mainly of the dominant agricultural caste as well as the upper castes and a few people with better economic status drawn from the other castes.

B The middle group of less well-to-do agriculturists, and artisans and occupational castes.

C The lower group of low-status and lower income castes (consisting mainly of untouchables, and other poor agricultural labourers).

There is a small but significant section which may be called the rural *élite*. It includes mostly people from the higher income and higher status groups, who have some education and urban contacts, and have active interest and influence in village and inter-village politics. Politically conscious, vocal, and assertive members of the lower groups, especially those rising to positions of village leadership through elections to the recently instituted units of village self-government, can also acquire membership in this select group, although there is considerable initial resistance to their admission from the rural gentry and the established village leadership.

[1]The Tyagis are an important agricultural caste of this region. They claim to be non-priestly Brahmins. Literally the word Tyagi means 'those who have renounced'. They trace the origin of their caste name to their having renounced three Brahmanical functions, viz. the study of Vedas, functioning as priests, and acceptance of alms. Muslim Tyagis are converts to Islam from the Hindu Tyagi caste.

Leadership in these communities is diffused. Persons occupying positions of prestige and power in kin groups and castes, as well as in informal groups and factions, may not be formally recognized as 'village leaders', but their role as decision-makers in day to day life is really vital and effective. Persons with recognized abilities in certain fields, such as 'good agriculturists', individuals with 'experience in law courts', and those with knowledge of 'herbs and drugs' also function as opinion leaders, and their influence often extends much beyond their speciality. Many recognized 'village leaders' are village politicians, with some education and considerable outside contact, and function as a link between the world of the villagers and the outside world of cities and the administration. Many of them devote a substantial part of their time to these activities. Outsiders having effective contact with the villagers also enjoy enormous prestige and influence in the village. Persons like the Principal of the Intermediate College in Rajput Village—an outsider now living in the village because of his position in the college, can wield considerable influence. Many vital decisions affecting Rajput Village can be attributed to this individual. The Deputy Minister for Planning in the U.P. Government, who also represents this region in the state legislature, is a greatly respected figure in the two villages. So are some other politicians prominent in regional politics.

Both these villages have been exposed to urban influences. Rajput Village is three miles from an all-weather road, and a little more than five miles from the *tahsil* headquarters. Tyagi Village is about three miles from the *tahsil* headquarters; and a mile of the road connecting the two is improved. Rajput Village has separate primary schools for boys and girls, and has attained the distinction of setting up an Intermediate College largely through the co-operative endeavour of the people. Tyagi Village had no school at the time when the Community Development Project Block was established. An earlier effort to start a school had proved abortive. Muslim boys, however, had some facilities for religious instruction in their village mosque. For modern medical treatment people from both the villages have to go to the government dispensaries or private practitioners in nearby towns. The villagers did not have a trained midwife before the establishment of the Project.

Community development activities were organized in Rajput Village by a resident multi-purpose Village Level Worker. The Project also appointed a trained midwife in this village. For about a year the teacher in charge of the adult education classes for men was paid an honorarium by the Project. The teacher conducting the social education class for women was also given an allowance from development funds. Tyagi Village was at first served by a Village Level

Worker who lived in a nearby village. Later on, development activities for this village were assigned to the secretary of the village council who was stationed there. The adult education classes for men were subsidized for a year by the Project. There was no midwife or women's social education class in the village. Both villages were regularly visited by other Project officials. Important visitors to the Project were invariably taken to these villages, for they were regarded as good examples of successful development activity organized by the Project.

In the sections that follow an attempt will be made to examine the response of the village people to state sponsored activities in the fields of agricultural extension, public health and youth welfare. A separate section will be devoted, to its efforts to mobilize people's voluntary labour in village development work.

2. Agricultural Extension

The agricultural extension programme of the Community Development Project included activities in the fields of agriculture, animal husbandry, and village co-operatives. These activities were not new to this region, and people in both Rajput Village and Tyagi Village were generally familiar with some of the innovations that were being promoted in these spheres by the field agents of the government. With the inauguration of the Community Development Project, however, a more concentrated and integrated effort was made to get the programmes in these fields accepted, and consequently the impact of this drive was felt by a much larger section of the village people.

Agricultural extension activities of the Project covered the following fields:

i Introduction and propagation of improved seed.
ii Introduction and propagation of chemical fertilizers and new manures.
iii Introduction of improved agricultural implements.
iv Introduction of new agricultural techniques.
v Promotion of kitchen gardens and planting of orchards.
vi Provision of adequate irrigation facilities.
vii Organization of agricultural co-operatives.
viii Provision for cattle care and better cattle-breeding facilities.
ix Other activities such as crop protection measures, crop competitions to stimulate interest, etc.

In respect to the propagation of improved seeds the Community Development Project sought to work through three well-marked stages: introduction, propagation, and saturation. However, in respect to the two major crops of this area, namely wheat and sugarcane, the Project was not required to build from the beginning, as people were generally familiar with several improved varieties of seed on account of the previous efforts of the Agriculture Department and the Cane Development Union in the area.

In Rajput Village, during the first half of the life of the Community Development Project, approximately 1,418 maunds of improved seed were bought by the people from the Co-operative Seed Store in the village—741 maunds in the first year, and 677 maunds in the second year. While only 887 acres were under improved seed in the first year, through the efforts of the Project this acreage was increased to 1,504 acres in the second year. The Project promoted two improved varieties of sugarcane—sugarcane 313 and 421. In the first year of project activities 45 per cent of the land under sugarcane was sown with improved seed. In the second year there was a rise of 10 per cent, and 55 per cent of the land under sugarcane was sown with improved seed.

Similar progress was also reported from Tyagi Village. In the first half of the life of the Project, people of this village bought approximately 440 maunds of improved seed from the Agriculture Department and the Co-operative Seed Store located in a nearby village. In the second year of project activities 95 per cent of the area under wheat was sown with improved seed as against only 70 per cent in the first year. The area under sugarcane was 250 acres in the first year, and 300 acres in the second year. With the exception of about 40 acres in the first year and 25 acres in the second year, all this land was under improved varieties of sugarcane.

The record of the Project in this sphere appears to be quite impressive, but it should be remembered that one improved variety of wheat, namely Panjab 591, and several varieties of sugarcane sponsored by the Project had become fairly popular in this region long before the establishment of the Community Development Project. As a part of its agricultural extension programme the Project introduced several other improved varieties of seed, such as wheat P.710 and 720, barley C.251 and K.12, gram I.P.25, *moong* type-1, maize type-41, pea type-163, and cotton 35/1 and F.216. Of the total area under improved seed in the two villages at the end of the period under study a little less than 3 per cent only was under the new seeds introduced for the first time by the Community Development Project.

Some of the chemical fertilizers and manures recommended by the Project were already in use in this area. In Rajput Village agriculturists bought 185 bags[1] of ammonium sulphate from the Co-opera-

[1]A bag of ammonium sulphate weighs 2 maunds and 18 seers.

tive Seed Store and 150 bags from the Cane Development Union offices during the first half of the Project's life. Compared to the sale of this fertilizer in the year preceding the setting up of the Project, the increase in the first year was 21 per cent and 25 per cent in the second. During this period the agriculturists of Tyagi Village bought 141 bags of ammonium sulphate; the increase in sale during the first year was 18 per cent and in the second 24 per cent more than that of the year preceding the inauguration of the Community Development Project. The use of groundnut oil cake as a fertilizer was also promoted by the Project. In Rajput Village 76 bags[1] of groundnut cake were sold. The use of this fertilizer was more popular in Tyagi Village. In the first year 146 maunds of groundnut cake were sold. In the second year there was a slight decrease; the quantity sold being only 124 maunds. Special effort was made to popularize green manuring. In Rajput Village 47 acres were sown with 35 maunds of *sanai* seed bought from the Co-operative Seed Store. In the first year *moong* type-1 was introduced as a green manure crop, but its growth was poor, and results as a fertilizer were disappointing. Consequently in the second year it was practically abandoned by the agriculturists. Approximately three maunds of *sanai* and *moong* seeds were bought by the agriculturists of Tyagi Village in the first half of the Project's life. In this village also *sanai* was successful and *moong* was a failure.

Efforts to popularize improved agricultural implements, initiated earlier by the State Department of Agriculture and the Cane Development Union, were pushed forward by the Community Development Project. Within the period of this survey, 22 iron cultivators, 11 improved hand hoes, 15 Meston ploughs, 16 inflated tyre carts, and 1 tractor were bought by the villagers in Rajput Village. Agriculturists could borrow dibblers and the seeder from the Seed Store free of charge. In Tyagi Village agriculturists bought 6 cultivators and 4 improved ploughs. The Village Level Worker demonstrated at least 14 types of agricultural implements to the people.

A series of improved agricultural techniques, including the methods of line sowing, trench sowing of sugarcane, Japanese method of rice cultivation, and dibbling for seed multiplication were popularized by the Project. To this end 82 demonstrations were given by the Village Level Worker in Rajput Village. Approximately 38 per cent of the agriculturists had taken to the method of line sowing in sugarcane cultivation. The trench method was new, and a beginning was made with about 15 acres in the first year. The Japanese method of rice cultivation and dibbling were not received very enthusiastically by the people.

[1]A bag of groundnut cake weighs 1 maund and 30 seers, approximately 140 pounds.

In the period covered by this survey 32 demonstrations were given by the Village Level Worker in Tyagi Village.

The Project made a special effort to promote planting of orchards and kitchen gardens. In Rajput Village orchards were planted in an area of seven acres, with 635 mango saplings and grafts. With the co-operation of the local schools and youth clubs 228 kitchen gardens were planted. In the first year vegetable seeds and seedlings were supplied free of cost; in the second year they were given at subsidized rates. Two thousand five hundred trees, to be used as fuel, were planted in an area of 7 acres.

In Tyagi Village four kitchen gardens were planted as a result of the efforts made by the Village Level Worker.

After the inauguration of the Project two tube wells were bored in Rajput Village. One of these was operated by the Irrigation Department of the U.P. Government. It was electrically operated, and irrigated approximately 800 acres. The other tube well belonged to the local Intermediate College, and was constructed with a subsidy of Rs5,000 from the State Co-operative Department. Run with a diesel engine, this well could irrigate 400 acres; although in the absence of proper channels it irrigated only about 50 acres. The Project did not have any direct hand in the boring of these wells. However, through its efforts 2½ miles of masonry channels and 1½ miles of ordinary channels were constructed, which considerably increased the area under the command of these wells. Interest-free loans were granted to two agriculturists to dig two irrigation wells and fit them with Persian Wheels. These wells were expected to irrigate about 20 acres of land. No irrigation projects were undertaken in Tyagi Village.

Through the efforts of the Village Level Worker and other officials of the Project the multi-purpose Co-operative Society of Rajput Village was strengthened. When the Project was established this Society had only 88 members. In the first half of the second year of the Project's life this had been increased to 222. Each member had to buy at least one share for Rs20; to be paid in five equal yearly instalments. In the first year only Rs440 were collected as share money. At the end of the second year Rs2,452 had been paid by the members. Loans amounting to Rs12,660 were given to 149 members for improvements in agriculture. The Co-operative Seed Store run by the Society supplied improved seeds, implements, and fertilizers to the members. The membership of the Co-operative Society in Tyagi Village was increased from 40 to 52. It advanced loans amounting to Rs2,343 for agricultural improvements.

Cattle-breeding and cattle-care received considerable attention from the Village Level Workers in both the villages. Before the Project started there were 12 cows, 16 buffalo cows, and 31 bulls of good breed in Rajput Village. The Project gave one pedigree bull and one breeding buffalo to the village. Through cattle shows and public lectures efforts were made to encourage scientific methods of cattle breeding. The Village Level Worker had been provided with modern instruments for performing castrations. With these he castrated 57 calves. In co-operation with officials of the veterinary department, the Village Level Worker inoculated 2,683 cattle against different epidemic diseases. He gave treatment to 206 cattle brought to him for this purpose. Villagers were encouraged to take advantage of the artificial insemination centre at the Project headquarters. No serious efforts were made to encourage poultry farming. Similar work was done in Tyagi Village also. Purchase of 5 cows and 2 buffaloes of good breed in the village was made possible partly because of money advanced by the Project. The Village Level Worker castrated 3 calves, performed 1,000 inoculations, and treated 70 cattle. A pig of good breed was given to the Bhangis for improving the breed of pigs.

The Project encouraged the cultivation of traditional fodder crops like pea and *rij*, and introduced *berseem*. In the first year of the life of the Project fodder was grown on only 72 acres in Rajput Village. In the second year it was extended to 117 acres. In Tyagi Village 25 acres were under these crops in the first year, and 30 acres in the second.

Among other activities in this field reference may be made to crop competitions and crop protection against pests. Four crop competitions were organized in each of the two villages. From the small fees paid by the entrants three prizes were awarded to those whose crops were adjudged to be the best in the village. In Rajput Village insecticides were sprayed on 150 fruit trees and on infected crops covering about 10 acres.

The Response:

In view of the high priority given to the agricultural extension programme the Project officials largely concentrated their energies on it. The results, at least on the surface, appear to be impressive.

Considerable progress was made in popularizing improved seeds of wheat and sugarcane. People were already familiar with these, but the concentrated efforts of the Project coupled with the facilities it provided, made their extension possible on a much wider scale. In regard both to wheat and sugarcane people still claimed that the *desi* (local) varieties grown by them previously were better in taste and nutritive value. But because of their experience with improved seeds, extending to over a decade, they had slowly learned that they were better in yield, in resisting rain and disease, and in bringing higher prices in the urban markets. As a result, the improved varieties were being accepted by an increasing number of people. Success in regard to sugarcane was more pronounced, as it was grown primarily as a cash crop, and the sugar mills definitely encouraged the improved varieties. Although the people found the new varieties of sugarcane unsatisfactory for domestic use, they practically discarded the local variety because it was not acceptable to the mills on account of its poorer sugar content. The resistance in regard to the adaptation of improved wheat was greater because it formed a staple in their diet. The extreme reluctance with which people greeted the other kinds of improved seeds, which the Project was introducing in the region for the first time, is illustrative of the general attitude of the village people towards innovations of uncertain value. They were not unwilling to adopt a seed of proved worth, but showed great hesitation to experiment with items about the merits of which they were not convinced. Because experimentation of this type on a large scale was likely to disturb the precarious balance of their agricultural economy, their reserve and hesitation can be easily understood. On the whole they tended to trust their own experience and judgement much more than the explanations of government officials who were traditionally held suspect by the village people.

The increased sale of chemical and other fertilizers suggests that the people were learning to appreciate their utility. In regard to chemical fertilizers there were two more or less conflicting trends of thought; while some people expected almost miraculous results from the fertilizers, others feared that 'they would sap the fertility and "strength" of the soil' and 'burn the crops'. In a significant section of the agriculturists there was a strong feeling that the fertilizers adversely affected the nutritive value of the crops. As one agriculturist put it 'they (the chemical fertilizers) are like a strong aphrodisiac—temporarily stimulating, but harmful in the long run'. Various government agencies in the past and the Project more recently tried to popularize these fertilizers, but failed to educate the people in their proper use. The consequences of this neglect in some cases were painful. Acting on the dictum that 'the more fertilizer you use, the better your harvest will be', some persons applied over-doses of chemical fertilizers and ruined their crops. The adoption of new green manuring crops has been slow but steady. Through experience people have come to know its utility, and the results of the use of *sanai* so far have been sufficiently encouraging to persuade more people to extend its cultivation.

Factors of the size of land-holdings, conditions of draught cattle, and financial position of the individual farmer largely determined the adoption and use of improved agricultural implements. As most

5. Road-building by voluntary labour.

6. Volunteer road builders resting from their labours.

7. A Rajput leader. 8. A Tyagi leader.

9. An Influential upper-caste elder.

10 An Influential untouchable elder.

agriculturists have small and scattered holdings, they do not find tractors very useful. Even those who have sufficiently large holdings, have a pronounced distrust of such machinery because of the fear of mechanical breakdowns and uncertainties of repairs. There are two tractors in Rajput Village. One of these, bought during the first year of the Project, is owned by an individual and has given excellent service; the other, owned jointly by a group of lineally related families, has given all kinds of trouble. Not only did it have frequent breakdowns, but its use by many families raised a number of complications. With this example before them others were not encouraged to venture into co-operative buying and joint ownership of tractors. Because of its high cost, few people could dream of buying a tractor by themselves. Other less costly implements, especially cultivators, chaff-cutters, and light iron ploughs were being increasingly adopted.

The village people did not show any great enthusiasm in adopting new agricultural techniques. The most pronounced success in this field was in spreading the method of line-sowing of sugarcane. This has three visible advantages which the agriculturists were quick to perceive: weeding was easier, the plants could be more easily tied together to prevent them from falling down, and it facilitated cutting of the cane when crops were ready. However, two factors hindered the adoption of this method. Most substantial landowners, until recently, did not take enough personal interest in what was being done in their fields. The work was largely left to unskilled labourers, who preferred working along traditional lines. Consequently, in spite of over a decade of propaganda, demonstration, and persuasion only about 38 per cent of the cane growers in Rajput Village adopted this method. Line-sowing of wheat and rice, dibbling for seed multiplication, and the Japanese method of rice cultivation were generally regarded as too time-consuming, and being unaccustomed to the regularities and systematic work involved in these techniques agricultural labour resisted them.

Orchards involve considerable initial outlay, with no prospects of immediate returns. As such their appeal was limited to more substantial agriculturists. However, the Project introduced an ingenious programme under which other crops could be grown in the land in which orchards were newly planted. This, coupled with the prestige of owning orchards and the possibility of gaining profits in cash from them in a few years' time, encouraged some agriculturists to contemplate planting orchards. But little actual progress was made, because plans for consolidating land holdings were in air and people were unwilling to invest time and money in a project on land which might be transferred to someone else in the process of land consolidation. Notwithstanding official assurances that orchard land would not be disturbed, very few people went ahead with this programme. The reported number of kitchen gardens planted in Rajput Village is somewhat deceptive as a large number of these 'gardens' consisted only of a few plants of tomatoes or egg plant. This work was undertaken largely by school children. While most parents were indulgent in this regard, few took these ventures seriously. The efforts to encourage planting of fuel trees were erratic and unsystematic. As such the results were not very substantial. Another factor affecting this programme adversely was the unavailability of land for this purpose. As there is little surplus land people use every inch of it for more productive and profitable purposes.

The Project had little direct control over the major means of irrigation—the state operated tube wells and irrigation canals. In view of the great cost of irrigation projects and its limited resources the Community Development Project could do little about multiplying them, although in both villages there was a pronounced felt need for more irrigation. The state tube well in Rajput Village was generally welcomed. People resented the high cost of irrigation, and the high-handed and corrupt ways of the operator, but the well was nevertheless regarded as a boon by many. Because of the possibilities of land transfer in the proposed consolidation of holdings, people were not willing to invest in individual irrigation projects to meet the requirements of their individual fields. To the credit of the Project it must be added that the construction of irrigation channels under its direction and encouragement effectively increased the area under the command of the tube wells.

Notwithstanding the increase in the number of members and share capital, the co-operatives are still far from becoming a regular and vital part of the village people's life. A considerable section of the agriculturists views them as an official outside organization; as something alien to the village and not quite dependable. Their membership is confined largely to persons of higher status and upper income groups, and positions of responsibility in them are occupied mostly by village politicians. The average agriculturists do not feel encouraged to join them for three main reasons. First, their rules are intricate and are not easy for ordinary villagers to grasp. Second, in having to deal with them the people are required to sign a large number of papers and this they do not like to do for the fear of getting involved later in legal and administrative complications. Third, money and grain obtained from the societies have to be returned on a specified date, and in this respect the societies are much less accommodating than the village money-lenders. In regard to seed obtained through the co-operative seed store there were further complications.

It was to be returned not only by a specified date, but in a 'pure' condition. Officials in charge of the store used their personal judgement in determining the purity and acceptability of the seed, and this often led to extortion and bribery. Because they distrust the minor officials handling the affairs of the co-operatives the village people tended to distrust the societies as such too.

The activities of the Project in the field of cattle care and cattle breeding were widely known. The pedigree bull and breeding buffalo provided by it were appreciated by the villagers, but they did not improve the situation materially as no ways were devised to handle the scrub bulls that were mainly responsible for the poor breed of cattle. For religious reasons these scrub bulls could not be disposed of or even castrated. For lack of adequate training in performing castrations, the Village Level Workers, especially the one in Tyagi Village, were not too enthusiastic about this part of their duties. The fact that they were supplied with a medicine chest, and had received training in treating common diseases of cattle was not sufficiently publicized. Besides, the time of the Village Level Workers was occupied by pressing matters relating to agriculture, and as such they could not give much attention to the treatment of sick animals. The drives to inoculate cattle against epidemics was a success. The village people were impressed by the fact that their villages suffered much less cattle loss due to these epidemics than the other villages where similar efforts were not made.

The general response of the people to the introduction of fodder crops was encouraging. The progress made in Rajput Village was especially impressive.

Crop competitions were organized more for fulfilling formal obligations, than for generating a healthy spirit of competition in regard to the acceptance of improved agricultural techniques. The more well-to-do and prosperous agriculturists thought it below their dignity to enter any such competition; the average agriculturist resented having to pay an entrance fee and signing a form confirming their wish to enter the competition. The fee was regarded as an undesirable taxation. The hesitation in signing a paper reflected the village people's general attitude of distrust towards government officials, and their fear of the possibility of getting involved in unwanted legal complications. Since only a limited number entered the contests, the prize money derived from the fee paid by the entrants was so small that it could not motivate anyone to enter the competition. Thus a vicious circle was created.

Measures of crop protection organized by the Project were on such a small scale that they did not arouse any positive kind of response in the people.

3. Sanitation and Public Health

The public health and sanitation programme sponsored by the Project comprised the following activities:

i Village sanitation drives, including digging of compost and soakage pits.
ii Renovation of old wells and model sanitary repairs to other village wells.
iii Paving of village lanes.
iv Epidemic and malaria control.
v First aid and simple treatment of common diseases.
vi The opening of maternity centres.

In the period covered by this survey three sanitation drives were organized in Rajput Village, and four in Tyagi Village. Village lanes were cleaned with the help of students and others voluntarily contributing their labour to this work. Through the initiative of the Village Level Workers three soakage pits were dug in Rajput Village, and four in Tyagi Village. These were meant to prevent dirty water from running into the lanes and making them muddy. With a view to cleaning up the village, and preserving cow-dung manure better, manure and compost pits were dug outside the village. Sixty-four compost pits were dug outside Rajput Village and twenty-two outside Tyagi Village.

As a result of the introduction of hand pumps, a large number of wells in the villages were being ignored. Families with modest financial means, who could not afford to instal pumps, had to continue using these old, insanitary and increasingly uncared for wells. When there were breakdowns in the pumps, their owners also had to take recourse to the wells. The poor untouchable section of the village population had to depend completely on these wells. In Rajput Village three wells, all in the residential quarters of the untouchables, were renovated and improved according to prescribed sanitary standards. Their parapet walls were raised, and pulleys were fixed to iron rods on them. Washing and bathing platforms were constructed at some distance from the wells. The drainage around the wells was improved to prevent water from collecting near them. This was a cooperative undertaking: the Project contributed half the share of the cost of construction in the shape of required materials, such as cement, iron rods and pulleys, and the people contributed the other half by raising cash contributions or by contributing their labour. In Tyagi Village the well in the quarters of the untouchable Chamars was repaired, and a hand pump was installed in the quarters of the Bhangis (untouchable scavengers). While the Project offered a 50 per cent subsidy to the untouchables for this purpose, it made only a one-third contribution towards the cost of repairs of wells to the higher castes. Efforts were made to persuade them to have similar repairs made to their wells. In Tyagi Village the village council repaired a well used by the higher castes with the aid of a one-third government subsidy.

Lanes in these villages got very muddy in the rainy season and people consequently found it very hard to move about in the village. The problem was further aggravated after the introduction of hand pumps in the village. Persons installing hand pumps did not think it worth their while to invest also in proper drainage and soakage pits. As a result water freely ran into the lanes and kept them muddy and unclean all the year round. The position was particularly bad in Tyagi Village. As there was a pressing need for paving the lanes with bricks, the village council prepared a plan which was implemented with technical guidance and financial aid provided by the Project. The village people contributed approximately two-thirds of the cost from the funds of the village council, out of voluntary deductions from the price of sugarcane supplied by them to the mills, and by doing earth-work on the roads. The Project helped with one-third of the cost, and also provided technical supervision. Within the first half of the life of the Project 1,365 yards of the village lanes were paved, and a project was taken in hand to pave the lanes in the quarters of the untouchables also. For the latter a 50 per cent subsidy was provided by the Project. At the time of this study proposals were afoot to pave the lanes in Rajput Village also. Cane growers had sent an application to the Union authorizing them to make a uniform deduction from the price of cane supplied by them to the mills. People had started contributing their labour by carting earth and bricks. The work of paving, however, had not been taken in hand.

Measures to control epidemics were confined to performing primary and secondary vaccinations. In Rajput Village the Village Level Worker performed 1,388 vaccinations. One hundred and thirteen vaccinations were performed in Tyagi Village.

Active steps were taken to control malaria in both these villages. In the first year the Project sprayed 154 houses with D.D.T. In the second year, with the help of Youth Club members, 352 houses were sprayed. The Village Level Worker distributed 500 tablets of paludrine. In Tyagi Village 20 houses were sprayed, and 200 tablets of paludrine were distributed.

The Village Level Workers were supplied with medicine chests, and were trained to render first aid and simple treatment. In Rajput Village 754 people took advantage of this service. In Tyagi Village 842 persons received medicines from the Village Level Worker.

Because of the lack of availability of trained persons and the considerable financial cost involved, maternity centres run by trained midwives were started in only a few key villages. The midwife stationed at Rajput Village assisted at 235 childbirths. She gave pre-natal and post-natal advice to 432 women. Powdered milk provided by the Project, when available, was given by her to poor children. According to her records 971 children got milk at one time or the other. She trained five *dais* in modern methods of delivery. Tyagi Village was occasionally visited by the midwife from a nearby centre.

The Response:

The programmes in this field touched a very considerable proportion of village people, but they were not pushed forward with the urgency and enthusiasm that were shown in the agricultural extension programme.

The importance of sanitation is generally understood by the people on the upper levels in the village community. The idea that filth causes disease is now fairly common. However, no practical ways have so far been devised to keep the village clean. Village councils have statutory powers to compel people to dig soakage pits so as to prevent water used in their houses from running into the lanes, and also to force them to have their garbage and manure pits outside the village. In both Rajput Village and Tyagi Village several resolutions to this effect were passed, and notices were issued to certain individuals threatening them with fines if they did not conform to the prescribed minimum standards in this regard. However, the resolutions and threats were both ineffective. People reverted in a few weeks. Some of the cultural factors involved in this failure are discussed in Chapter VI.

Sanitation drives have come to be looked upon as the conventional type of 'social service' rendered by political leaders and social reformers. Visiting politicians often showed their interest in village development by taking up the broom and cleaning a small portion of a dirty village lane. 'Clean-up drives' are also a necessary part of the preparations to receive important political and official visitors to the village. In both Rajput Village and Tyagi Village, people participated in these drives more in a spirit of compliance to the wishes of government officials, than with a determination to make and keep the village clean. Another factor that motivated them was their desire to impress the visitor. This was understood and exploited fully by the officials.

The soakage pits, when they were first dug, were greatly appreciated by the people. However, the method of construction recommended by the Project was not particularly suited to the soil and the general living conditions in this region. The soakage pits failed to serve their purpose after two or three weeks. People showed little interest in repairing or in digging them again, and officials often became alive to the problem only when an important visitor was expected. In view of the fact that the first reactions of the people to the soakage pits were favourable, a different method of construction —involving less physical labour and requiring repairs only after longer intervals, would perhaps have proved much more successful.

As the value of manure was well understood in the community, the Village Level Workers did not experience much difficulty in convincing the agriculturists of the utility of compost pits. The project failed not because of lack of understanding on the part of the agriculturist, but because of certain traditional work patterns which have a strong hold on the people. As pointed out later in Chapter VI also, the work of cleaning and taking out garbage and cow dung is traditionally regarded as women's work, but women from the upper castes are not expected to be seen carrying them to the outskirts of the village. As very few families can afford to hire servants for this purpose and even those who can do not trust them; the traditional practice of having the womenfolk deposit refuse and cow dung on a heap near the house, was continued. Because of the large size of the community these difficulties were especially noticeable in Rajput Village. A second factor contributing to the failure of this project here was the caste constitution of the village. Most of the agriculturists in this village belong to the upper castes which are governed by rigid norms which distinguish sharply between separate spheres of men's and women's work. There are strict rules concerning what the women of these groups can and cannot do. For these reasons the compost pits in this village were largely used only by those who happened to live on the outskirts of the village in the vicinity of the pits. They were used by a much larger proportion of the families in Tyagi Village. Because of the comparatively small size of the settlement, women did not have to go a long way to reach the compost pits in this village. Secondly, traditional rules determining what Tyagi women could do were less rigid, and carrying manure to the pits did not involve any loss of prestige for them. However, Muslim women influenced by urban Islamic ideas of the seclusion of women could not follow the example of Hindu women.

The programme of making model sanitary repairs to village wells, and of renovating old wells, was received rather coldly by the upper income groups. Most of the families had either installed hand pumps, or they could share one with a neighbour. As hand pumps have now come to be regarded as a mark of prestige, as well as a much desired convenience, most families on this level preferred to save for investing in a pump rather than spend any money in renovating the wells. The untouchable groups, however, had a real need for them. In their case the Project subsidized the cost of construction by 50 per cent. Many of them found a sense of achievement in having completed these projects. The new look of the well—a well that they could call their own—conferred certain prestige on them as a group. As such they were quite enthusiastic about this aspect of the public health and sanitation programme.

The work of paving the village lanes was successfully completed in Tyagi Village and was enthusiastically taken up in Rajput Village for two main reasons. First, there was a real need for improving the condition of the lanes. Secondly, completion of such a project was a visible evidence of progress adding greatly to the prestige of the village. The officers of the Project recognized and exploited these factors in pushing forward their plans, but there were a number of practical difficulties in the way of implementing the project. First, it was not easy to raise contributions in cash from the people. Most of them simply did not like having to contribute money from their personal funds. Recourse could be taken to one of the two alternatives: the officials could either impose a semi-official levy at a flat rate bearing a certain relation to the total land revenue paid and collect it with the land revenue, or they could persuade the agriculturists to accept a voluntary deduction at an agreed rate from the price of sugarcane supplied by them to the mills. As the former course would have bordered on coercion and administrative pressure, and would have been contrary to the spirit and principles of extension work, the Project authorities rightly chose the second alternative. But that too was not without its peculiar difficulties. There were many agriculturists who supplied a large quantity of sugarcane to the mills, but who had only small sections of lane near their houses to be paved. They felt that their financial contribution to the project would be out of all proportion to the direct gain to themselves. In fact, certain *pattis* (distinct residential areas of the village) which produced most of the sugarcane, had proportionately very little lane surface to be paved. They resented having to pay for the paving of lanes in the non-sugarcane producing parts of the village. Secondly, there were certain families who, because of the type of land they owned, were growing more wheat than sugarcane. As no deductions were to be made from the price of wheat sold by them, the sugarcane growers felt that these families were being let off very lightly. Thirdly, there was the problem of the group of agricultural labour and the poor untouchables who were hardly in a position to contribute in cash, or even to make a proportionate contribution in labour for that would have meant many of them going without wages for a number of days. Finally, most people were not willing to entrust the money to the village council and its head, because of the fear of misuse of funds. These factors delayed the formulation of a plan for Rajput Village. A way out was found by evolving a somewhat complicated plan. Contributions raised in a residential quarter were to be earmarked for expenditure only in that quarter. As the needs of the different quarters were different, the rate of contributions to be raised from each was regulated according to their individual needs. Wheat growers and persons in business were to make proportionate contributions in cash. Both these groups had also to contribute their labour by carting earth and bricks. Those who had a long part of the lane in front of their houses were to contribute proportionately more towards the project. The poorer people were to contribute labour, the worth of which was stipulated to be approximately one-third of what the agriculturists were contributing. The funds were not to be spent by the village council and its Pradhan, but by a committee under the general direction of the college Principal. So as not to offend him, the Pradhan was included in this committee. Through these diverse sources approximately two-thirds of the cost of the project was to be raised from the village; the rest was to be met from the Project budget. The plan covered a substantial part of the village, leaving only the quarters of the untouchables. In their case the Project was willing to provide half the cost of paving, but the untouchables were too poor to find the rest of the money and could ill afford to lose wages by contributing labour as their share.

In Tyagi Village, fortunately, there were no such complications. The more substantial agriculturists had larger houses, and proportionately greater areas of lanes near their houses to be paved. The ratio of sugarcane and wheat grown by them was more or less the same. The non-agriculturists were willing to do their share by contributing labour, and in this the agriculturists did not have unreasonable expectations from them. The village council and its Pradhan were generally trusted by the people. For these reasons the work was planned and completed in record time. There was difficulty only from the untouchables, some of whom did not want to co-operate with the rest of the villagers. In view of the fact that the Project offered subsidies at a higher rate to the untouchables, it was decided to leave their lanes temporarily unpaved. That was taken up as a separate project later.

In the first flush of enthusiasm the people of Tyagi Village completed their major project of paving over 90 per cent of the village lanes. This enhanced the reputation of the village, and the villagers were justifiably proud of their achievement. Their village was often described by the officials as a 'model village'. In about six months, however, they felt that it was not enough to have the lanes paved; it was necessary for them to make arrangements for keeping them clean. The village council found itself without funds to repair the pavements, and it could not afford to hire sweepers to clean them regularly. At the end of the period covered by this study, thought was being given to this problem, but no solution was in sight. At several points ditches had formed in the lanes in which foul water collected. The Project took care to get them clean only when an important visitor was expected. The people were still enthusiastic about their achievements, but a sense of greater responsibility was gradually dawning upon them. They were coming to realize that they had not achieved a complete solution of their problem.

People were familiar with smallpox vaccination, but secondary vaccinations given by the Village Level Workers were new to many, for there was a general feeling that vaccinations were given only once in life and that, too, at an early age. As vaccination was compulsory, and people were used to them, there was no resistance to this programme. On the whole the people were co-operative. But little educative propaganda was carried out to convince them about the utility and significance of secondary vaccinations, and as such there was, generally speaking, considerable scepticism about them.

Propaganda by the Project, coupled with the influence of educated villagers, has succeeded in informing a considerable section of village people that malaria is caused by mosquitoes. But the efforts to eradicate malaria were few and inadequate. While houses were sprayed with D.D.T., no effort was made to do anything with the ponds and waterlogged ditches that bred mosquitoes. D.D.T. spraying was liked because of its novelty. Some people thought that it was meant to 'improve the air'. Its significance in malaria control was not understood by most of the people. Paludrine was introduced as a cure for malaria, but very few people knew that it could also be used as a preventive. Even as a curative drug, it was not given in proper doses and its use was stopped as soon as the temperature of the sufferer dropped.

Very few people knew that the Village Level Workers had medicines and equipment for simple treatment of common ailments and for first aid. When his limited supplies were exhausted, replacements were not forthcoming for long periods. The Village Level Workers were too preoccupied with other matters to be able to give adequate attention to this part of their work. In view of the uncertain hours of their work they could not schedule a set hour for giving medical relief to the people. Finally, many people did not trust the adequacy of their training, and as such relatively few of them took advantage of their services in this field regularly.

The opening of the Maternity Centre and the appointment of a trained midwife was at first received very enthusiastically by the people. However, difficulties arose in the first four months. They could never clearly understand her role and functions. Traditionally they could distinguish between the role of a trained doctor, and of an untrained village *dai* who assisted at childbirths. The role of the midwife, who was something between the two, was new to the village people. Because of her official position, clean clothes, and sophisticated language, village women at first regarded the midwife as a qualified doctor, and expected modern medical treatment and injections from her. Many of them were disillusioned when they discovered that she was neither trained nor officially permitted to do this. They hesitated in calling her to assist at childbirths, because, unlike the village *dais*, she refused to do any cleaning, and would not massage the mother and the baby in the weeks following the birth. For this they had to hire an untrained village *dai*. Although the midwife did not demand any payment for her work, people felt obligated to give her some kind of a present for her services. Calling her thus involved most people in double expenditure: a prescribed payment to the *dai*, and a present or gift of money to the midwife. Because of their suspicion of strangers—especially city people and officials—many of the poorer families could never muster courage to call her. They had a fear, without any foundation, that she would charge exorbitant fees.

Out of seventy women interviewed regarding her work only about 10 per cent were convinced of the utility of the midwife to the community. Modern methods of pre-natal and post-natal care were explained by her to 40 per cent of them. Of these only 5 per cent had grasped the essentials of the ideas she tried to communicate. As some of her ideas conflicted with the traditionally held views of the people, they were generally sceptical about them. A remark heard often enough from village women was, 'What will she teach us? Do we have to learn how to bear children from this woman? Were no children born in the village before the midwife was appointed?'

The programme of distributing powdered milk to village children was not sufficiently publicized. The midwife resented having to do this because it involved considerable record keeping and sending of reports. When the first supplies of powdered milk were received, she did not have clear instructions about its distribution. By the time the instructions were received, the milk had deteriorated. Subsequently, supplies of milk were not regularly received. Because of the frequent absence of the midwife from the village on account of sickness and personal work, this part of her programme never functioned well. Most village women interviewed in this connexion were amused at the idea of giving powered milk as a substitute for or supplement to mother's milk.

An important part of the duty of the midwife was to train local *dais* in modern methods of delivering children. For about six months no efforts were made to do this. Later on, however, frantic memos were sent to her to start training some village *dais*. It was not easy for her to find suitable persons, even though the Project was willing to offer small stipends to the trainees. Traditionally, only middle-aged women of lower castes do this work professionally in the village. Most of them thought that they had much more experience and knowledge than the midwife, who was a comparatively younger person. Younger girls could not be selected for this purpose because common village women would not regard their training an adequate substitute for experience. With much effort five women were persuaded to enter this training. Most of them were attracted by the stipend rather than by a desire to learn. When there were delays in the payment of the promised stipends (and they were not infrequent) some of them lost interest and became irregular in meeting with the midwife and taking instruction from her. Some of them were so set in their ideas that they had considerable psychological resistance towards the new methods suggested by the midwife. At the time of this study these *dais* were still under training and as such it is not possible to evaluate the response of the village women towards them.

4. Social Education and Youth Welfare

The Project's activities in this field covered the following:

- i Organization of adult education classes for men and women.
- ii Organization of clubs for village youth and children along the lines of 4-H Clubs.
- iii Organization of Community Centres and units for community singing of religious and devotional songs.

In the first year of the Project's life adult education classes for men were conducted both in Rajput Village and Tyagi Village. In the former a school teacher was given an honorarium to conduct the classes in the evening. Forty persons were enrolled, but only about twelve attended them regularly. The instruction consisted mainly of teaching the adults to read and write. Occasionally development subjects were also discussed. In Tyagi Village an educated young man from the village conducted these classes. Thirty adults joined them, but only seventeen persisted long enough to get the certificate of adult literacy. The intent and method of instruction in this village were much the same as in Rajput Village. For lack of enthusiastic response from the people the Project decided to abandon these classes in the second year of its activities. The teacher in Rajput Village, with the help of members of the Youth Club, agreed to run them without any honorarium. Some teaching aids, such as books, slates, and blackboards were provided to them by the Project. In Tyagi Village, however, the teacher refused to work without payment, and the classes had to be discontinued.

A social education class for women was run in Rajput Village. During the first year twenty-five women were enrolled, although only five or six were attending the class regularly. Besides reading and writing, they were also taught sewing and knitting. With a view to making such classes more useful a refresher course for the teachers instructing in them was organized. The teacher from Rajput Village participated in it. An educated girl from Tyagi Village was also selected for training. She was later to start a centre in her village.

A youth club was initiated in Rajput Village, with sixty-four members. Most of the members were students of the local Intermediate College, but a special effort was made to persuade non-school-going youth to join the club also. Each member had to take up an individual project such as calf-rearing, vegetable growing, or the raising of a crop on a small patch of land. Groups of these young club members participated in social service activities, particularly in village sanitation drives. With the help of the Project they built up a small library of 122 books. There was considerable enthusiasm among the village youth for the staging of plays, and towards this end they organized a 'dramatic association' to function under the club. They successfully staged two plays. The people of the village responded by contributing liberally to this association. Approximately Rs375 were raised, and utilized for buying curtains, wigs, costumes, and other accessories useful for the future plays to be staged by the club. Members of the club also took considerable interest in Indian games and forms of recreation and such Western games as volley ball. They played a series of matches with youth clubs in other villages. Youth club activities were not begun during this period in Tyagi Village.

In the last two months of the Project's activities covered by this survey a *Balmangal Dal* (or 4-H Club for small boys) was also started in Rajput Village. Equipment for children's games and play, such as swings, slides, etc., costing about Rs400 were provided by the Project.

With a view to developing Village Community Centres, the Project staff made efforts to gather people for community singing of religious and devotional songs. These units were organized in both the villages. The unit in Rajput Village, consisting of about a dozen active members, continued functioning, but the one in Tyagi Village lost interest in about four months. Musical instruments for these units were provided by the Project. Mobile libraries of the Community Development Project were used by some of the members of these units. A regular Community Centre could not be developed in Rajput Village. Tyagi Village, however, distinguished itself by having a fairly active Centre. People gathered there not only for reading the newspapers subscribed to by the Centre, and for discussing village, national, and world affairs, but they also held regular fortnightly 'discussion meetings' and exchanged views on a wide variety of subjects.

The Response:

This aspect of the community development programme touched only a limited number of people. As such, very few villagers had any knowledge about the educational activities of the Project.

The adult education classes initially attracted few people, and even from among them a large section gradually dropped out.

Those who continued attending the classes for men were mainly younger people who had not been able to complete their schooling, or persons who, having completed their school grades, had relapsed into virtual illiteracy. All those who had joined these classes were interviewed in connexion with this study. Nearly all of them were convinced of the utility of education, but only 30 per cent found the adult classes, as they were being run, 'useful' or 'interesting'. Taking the two villages together, out of the seventy who joined the classes only twenty-nine continued attending them. Most people left them because they 'had no time', 'were too tired in the evening', and because they 'were ridiculed by others for attending school like small children'. To many the classes were dull and uninteresting.

The classes for women in Rajput Village could not be run properly during the period covered by this study. The only son of the teacher conducting these classes died in an accident on his way to participate in a *shramdan* project. Because of the shock of her loss she could not concentrate on her work. As the boy had lost his life on a mission sponsored by the Project, the authorities did not think it proper to remove the mother from a Project position, which carried a small stipend. The women who were in the class were not too enthusiastic about it. According to them 'no work was done there', 'the teacher was engrossed in her own worries', and even 'the knitting and sewing lessons were too common; much below the standard of what many women in the village already knew'.

The failure of these classes as a media of communication will be examined in Chapter V, and some of the cultural factors hindering their progress will be discussed in Chapter VI.

An excellent pilot project for organizing Youth Clubs was prepared by the Planning Research and Action Institute of the Uttar Pradesh Government. The unit which was organized in Rajput Village, however, deviated from the principles laid down in the pilot project in many ways. To begin with, the members were not very carefully selected. The Assistant Project Officer for Social Education, who had undergone special training for this work, was too much tied down to his routine duties. For over three months, after coming into existence, the club lacked direction. Indian games and sports were almost its only organized activities. On their own initiative the members did some sanitation work, but their enthusiasm cooled down in a few weeks. Later, they got some guidance from the Project staff in choosing their individual projects of farming, vegetable growing, and calf rearing, but this direction was neither regular nor systematic. As stated by an inspecting official: 'The youth club members were more interested in cultural activities, such as staging plays, and in sports, but had too little interest in agricultural projects.' Sixty out of the sixty-five members of the club regarded the two plays, successfully staged by them, as their major achievement. Forty-four complained about lack of continued guidance from Project officials in their agricultural and animal husbandry projects.

As mentioned earlier, the Project could not develop an effective Community Centre at Rajput Village. This can be attributed to the large size of the village, to the lack of effective interaction between different parts of the village, and to the traditional forms of recreation in the village. Here people spend most of their spare time in informal 'smoking groups' formed mostly along the lines of factions in the village. Actually no serious effort was made to bring people together. The unit performing the singing of religious and devotional songs, was for all practical purposes the only functioning part of the Centre. This unit had about twelve regular members, drawn mostly from the adult class and the youth club. The elders in the village did not quite approve of it, because, being members of the Arya Samaj movement they were against idolatry, and *keertan* is associated with idol worship and unreformed Hinduism. However, there was no overt opposition from the elders.

In Tyagi Village the Centre was a much greater success. Since this was a small village it was easier for people to get together. Although there were factions in the village, the presence of some 'neutral' leaders kept them under control. Members of divergent factions could still meet on a common platform. The reputation of being 'progressive' earned by the village in the last five years was an additional inducement for the people to join the Centre and the discussion group.

The unit for community singing of religious songs met with greater resistance in this village. The sizeable Muslim group could not join it as a matter of religious principle. Because of their pronounced Arya Samaj leanings the more important Hindu leaders of the community were also lukewarm towards it from the very beginning. For lack of enthusiasm and support the unit ceased functioning in a few months.

5. MOBILIZING VOLUNTARY LABOUR

The Community Development Project operated, as far as possible, on the principle of working in partnership with the people. It made outright grants covering the entire cost of a project only in a few exceptional cases. Generally people were expected to contribute money and labour towards the completion of the programmes initiated by the Project. As mentioned earlier they did contribute *shramdan*, or unpaid voluntary labour, as a part of their share in a number of projects. In public works, especially road-building, the importance of this type of contribution was greatly emphasized. Getting a specified piece of work done was only one of the major motives behind the *shramdan* drives; they were aimed also at encouraging the 'cult of dirty hands' and the 'dignity of labour', and were expected to develop a spirit of co-operative teamwork among the people.

As in other villages of the Development Block, in Rajput Village and Tyagi Village the Republic Day celebrations included a '*shramdan* week', in which the village people completed a specified project wholly by their unpaid voluntary labour. This was an annual feature of Project sponsored development work in the villages. For other individual projects also the co-operation of the people was sought. Under the guidance of the Project, the people from Rajput Village built a 1½ mile long hard surface road, and a 2-mile long mud road. They repaired another road which was about three miles long. In addition, they also helped in the construction of the Seed Store, in the renovation of wells, and in the construction of two culverts. In Tyagi Village, *shramdan* was done mostly in connexion with the paving of village lanes, renovation of wells, and construction of the school. Most of the unskilled work connected with these ventures, such as digging of earth, and carrying or carting earth and bricks, was accomplished in this way. A road, 2½ miles long, was repaired by the people.

The Response:
The Government of Uttar Pradesh lays great emphasis on mobilizing people's labour for development work. With this end in view, in its Panchayat Raj legislation it has made a provision authorizing village councils to secure five days of compulsory *shramdan* every year from residents of the village. The village council can impose fines on those who do not co-operate in *shramdan* projects organized by it. Very few village councils have so far taken recourse to this extreme method.

The idea of *shramdan* is not new to these village communities. In Rajput Village, the people had given their enthusiastic support in the building of both the Sanskrit School and the Intermediate College. All segments of the village population had contributed free voluntary labour in this work. In building the village mosque, the Muslims of Tyagi Village had also depended in a large measure on the voluntary labour of their group.

Projects giving direct and immediate benefit to the people, such as renovation of wells and paving of village lanes, secured reasonable co-operation from most of the village people. However, the Project-sponsored '*shramdan* weeks', mostly to build or repair roads, did not receive the same enthusiastic welcome from them. Out of a random sample of 128 participants in a *shramdan* week organized separately in Rajput Village and Tyagi Village, only thirty-one had a clear or partial idea of the basic aims of the movement, the rest viewed it as a form of *begar* (forced, unpaid labour). A majority of these individuals said that they had participated in these drives only in compliance with the directions of the government and the leaders of the village.

From a close observation and analysis of four *shramdan* drives, two in Rajput Village and two in Tyagi Village, certain points emerge that explain differences in reactions to *shramdan*.

The village *élite* as well as the upper income and higher status groups have, on the whole, welcomed the *shramdan* drives, and through them the construction and repairs of roads. They gained from it in two ways. First, the repaired and newly built roads facilitated the transport of their sugarcane and grain. Secondly, in these drives they could assert their position of leadership and prestige in the village. As is explained at some length in Chapter VI, because of their status they assumed supervisory roles in this work, and left the hardest and less desirable part of the job to be done by the people of the lower status and lower income groups. Even their token participation won the praise and acclaim of officials and outside political leaders. The poorer groups, on the other hand, had no practical and visible gain from these projects. Few among them owned bullock carts, and most of them did not have large quantities of sugarcane or wheat to be transported to the urban markets. Their work did not win much praise from outsiders. All that they got often was a formal acknowledgement from the lower officials and some village leaders. They not only had to work hard, but they also lost the wages for the day, which they might otherwise have earned. This explains why many of them viewed the thing as a revival of *begar*, a practice under which influential landowners and government officials compelled the poorer people to work without wages or at nominal wages and which is now prohibited by law.

Regarding the utility of these road-building and road-repairing *shramdan* drives, even some of the village leaders were sceptical. Three out of the four projects observed by us were arbitrarily begun, without any consultation with the village people. The aims of the particular projects were not explained to those who were actually to work on them. Excessive reliance was placed on some established village leaders to bring a specified number of people with them for work. In two cases in which new roads were to be constructed, the officials had not even done the preliminary measuring and marking. Several of the participants were picked up from their homes without any prior notice and more or less pressed into service. Unusual activity was shown by the officials when some important visitor was about to see *shramdan* in action; otherwise they were quite relaxed and slack. For these reasons, many responsible village people regarded the activities as a 'show', something which the officials had to do to justify their existence. To the credit of the officials it should be said that some of them worked as hard as most of the villagers themselves on these projects, and this won for them the appreciation and friendship of the people.

In conclusion, it may be said that projects emerging out of the felt needs of the people got their best support; those that were officially induced had only limited success. To develop *shramdan* into a powerful movement of village self help, more imagination and careful planning than was displayed in these four drives are needed.

6. Comment

Although the ideal of the Community Development Project was to work for the many-sided development of the entire community, from the foregoing account of its work in two villages it is clear that its significant and best organized activities were confined to the field of agricultural extension, and consequently the group of agriculturists benefited the most from them. A closer analysis of the agricultural extension work itself reveals that nearly 70 per cent of its benefits went to the *élite* group and to the more affluent and influential agriculturists. The gains to poorer agriculturists were considerably smaller. Being suspicious of government officials they did not seek help from the Project as often. As this group had little influence in the village and outside, and was in no position to offer any material help in the furtherance of Project objectives, the officials largely ignored it. For the economic development of this group, as well as for that of the artisans and agricultural labourers, no programmes were initiated by the Project. Some programmes for the welfare of women, younger people, and the untouchables were undertaken, but their organization lacked imagination, and consequently they failed to make the desired impact. In the sphere of public health and sanitation some significant steps were taken, but they only touched the surface of the problem. They were far below the needs of the community, and did not in any appreciable measure change the attitude and outlook of the people towards nutrition, hygiene, and health. The social education programme made the least impact. It was treated as a step-child, and was started more as a formal obligation than for its basic aims of awakening the community to its own needs.

An analysis of the motivation of village people in accepting the Project-sponsored programmes shows that they offered their co-operation mainly for the following reasons:

i *Economic advantage and convenience.* Several programmes in the sphere of agricultural extension, such as some new seeds and improved implements, were accepted for their visible economic advantage. Factors of convenience and practical utility governed the acceptance of certain items, such as the hand pumps and chaff-cutters.

ii *Prestige of the individual, family, kin-group, caste, and village.* Co-operation with the Project opened up the possibility for some individuals to acquire a position of leadership in the village; others found it as a means by which they could assert their traditional leadership. Recognition by officials and outside leaders conferred a distinct honour on these individuals and enhanced their influence in the village. Adoption of 'progressive ideas' added to the prestige of the family, kin-group, or caste also. Ownership of a tractor or an orchard added to the prestige of the family and the kin-group. Construction of new wells in their section of the village contributed in some measure to the prestige of the untouchable groups.

The building up of the reputation of the village was another significant motive in the acceptance of certain programmes. A village which built a new school, constructed a public building, or paved all its lanes could earn a reputation in the vicinity for being 'progressive'. Competition between individuals, families, kin-groups, castes, and villages was also at the back of the acceptance of many programmes.

iii *Novelty of innovations.* Several items of the programme, such as new agricultural implements and improved techniques, were tried out of curiosity. While a number of innovations were rejected because of their strangeness and people's lack of familiarity with them, some others were enthusiastically adopted because they were so novel.

iv *Compliance to the wishes of government and 'village leaders'.* A large number of programmes in many spheres were accepted in a spirit of compliance to the wishes of the government and the influential village people. A remark heard often enough in these villages was, 'If the government wants us to do a thing, we should do it.' The tremendous prestige of national leaders like Nehru and Pant, and the influence of local leaders like Thakur Phool Singh who were associated with the programme was also a reason for its acceptance by a considerable section of the village people.

The main obstacles in the way of the greater acceptance of the programme were:

- i The general apathy of a considerable part of the village population.
- ii Suspicion and distrust of officials and outsiders.
- iii Failure on the part of the Project to evolve effective and adequate media of communication.
- iv Tradition and cultural factors.

These factors have vitally affected the implementation of the programme. In view of their critical importance they will be examined at some length in the chapters that follow.

IV

STATE OFFICIALS AS AGENTS OF CHANGE

1. Officials as Agents of Change

THE INDIAN RURAL COMMUNITY development programme, at least in its initial stages, can be viewed essentially as an externally directed programme of technological and social change. Although there was general recognition that it should ideally develop into a movement of village self-help, and should ultimately enable the people to undertake responsibility for their welfare and for progressive improvement in their standard of living, it became evident that under the present conditions the government would have to take an active interest in promoting both the welfare and the educational aspects of the programme for a considerable time. Under these conditions the officials who were called upon to implement the development plans on behalf of the state, had to assume an active role of leadership and have had to function as innovators and agents of change in the communities under their charge. This has marked a significant departure from the traditional view of the officials' role and functions in Indian village administration.

In evaluating the role of development officials as agents of change, it is necessary to consider a series of related questions. Viewing the administrative machine as a whole, it is essential to examine its organizational and operational suitability for the task that it has been called upon to undertake. In this connexion the problems of communication, both inside the administration of a Community Project, and between the Projects on the one hand and the people on the other, also merit attention. Problems connected with the orientation and training of the individuals who constitute this machine demand special scrutiny as the effectiveness of the plans depends in a large measure on the success of the officials in adapting themselves to their new role and functions. The questions of practical programme planning, especially those of timing and balance, can be of crucial significance in determining the ultimate success or failure of the development plans.

2. Organization and Methods of Operation

The planners of the development programme had given considerable thought to the subject of evolving an administrative structure that would be equal to the task of meeting the challenging problems posed by the movement. In this connexion they had to examine critically the existing administrative structure of the country and appraise its suitability for the new action programmes that the government intended to undertake. It was felt that while the existing machine was satisfactory for a normal 'law and order' and 'revenue' administration, it needed substantial modifications to suit the requirements of a welfare state. With the contemplated changes in the structure of administration, it was necessary to develop certain operational principles that would be more in keeping with the needs of the changed situation.

The administrative organization of the Community Projects and the National Extension Service,[1] as well as of the Western U.P. Community Development Project Block considered in this study,[2] have been outlined earlier. In that connexion some of the merits of the new administrative pattern *vis-à-vis* the old one have been noted. Some of the practical results of these administrative innovations can now be examined.

To create the proper 'climate for rural development', and emphasize the urgency and national significance of the programme, the administration of Community Projects was made the main responsibility at different levels of highly placed officials with appropriate powers. The creation on the national level of a central Community Projects Administration, with the Community Projects Administrator as its head; the appointment of Development Commissioners, with wide powers, on the state level; the active and responsible association of the Collector or Deputy Commissioner with rural development on the district level, and the placing of the individual projects under a full-time executive officer, were some significant steps in this connexion. These measures, coupled with the active interest of the political executive, have had considerable effect in changing the administration's general attitude towards the problems of rural reconstruction and welfare.

In the first Community Projects Administrator the country found a man of dynamic personality; one who had a missionary zeal for rural development, and a capacity to communicate his enthusiasm to

[1] Chapter I, pp. 14–18. [2] Chapter II, pp. 35–40.

his co-workers. His nation-wide tours helped to create a certain sense of idealism and dedication among those who were engaged in implementing the development plans.

The effectiveness of the Development Commissioners depended on their personality and attitudes, and on the general tone of their relations with important figures in the political executive. There was a general feeling that the Development Commissioner, with his position, prestige, and wide powers has been able to co-ordinate and speed up development activities on a state-wide basis, much better than would have been the case under the earlier departmentalized system.

On the district level, however, the Collector was not very effectively drawn into development work. In British India, this official enjoyed enormous prestige and authority as a symbol and representative of the imperial power, and was mainly concerned with the administration of law and order and of land revenue in the area under his charge. His functions in these fields had become the mark of his position, and to the common people his place remained largely unchanged. Even among the officials, there was at best an intellectual rather than an emotional and psychological acceptance of the fact that under the re-organized administration the head of the district had become the chief executive of welfare and development activities among the people under his charge. The development duties were regarded as a minor addition to his traditional, and more important, law and order functions; if they did not minimize the importance of his high office, they were certainly not regarded as adding to it. In actual practice, the District Planning Officer functioned as the district level head of the Community Projects and National Extension Services. Because of his numerous other preoccupations the Collector delegated considerable responsibility and authority to the District Planning Officer. Yet, the association of the Collector with some of the development meetings and activities invested them with prestige and his more effective participation could invigorate them still further.

The general reaction to this official change in the role of the Collector was somewhat mixed: while some people welcomed his transition from 'a symbol of authority' to the position of 'the servant of the people'; others deplored the change and read in his 'humble welfare activities' a sign of the general 'weakening of administration'. Individual collectors, too, reacted differently to the change. Depending on their personal equations some of them cast aside their traditional aloofness and threw themselves vigorously into development work; others continued to concentrate on their normal administrative responsibilities, undertaking only the bare formalities of the new duties assigned to them in the sphere of planning and development.

The office of the Project Executive Officer was new in the structure of village administration. As an emerging role it was still being defined. It did not carry with it the prestige or power of a magistrate or a police official, and an 'officer' without powers or authoritarian functions appeared somewhat a paradox to the average villager.

Another important feature of the administrative re-organization in connexion with the development projects was the provision for unified direction and control at all administrative levels. The first reactions to this change were not too enthusiastic. To this point state administration had been largely departmentalized, each department having its hierarchy of state, district, sub-divisional, and village level officials. The Collector, being the head of the district administration, had functioned as a co-ordinator, but normally he did not interfere with the internal administration of the various departments. In actual practice each department had considerable autonomy, and its district level representative managed its affairs subject to the direction and control of his official superiors on the state level. In the administrative reorganization several 'nation-building' or 'development' departments (such as agriculture, animal husbandry, co-operatives, *panchayats*, etc.) were brought under the administrative control and direction of the Collector and the District Planning Officer. The supremacy of the Collector on the district level was no longer a fiction, it had become a hard everyday reality. All the district level officials of such departments had now to apply for leave of absence or for reimbursement for travelling allowances to the District Planning Officer. Their separate offices were pooled together and brought under the control of the District Planning Officer. The officers affected by this change viewed it as a blow to their prestige, and as a curtailment of their administrative powers. They resented the dual control over them, for now they were under the technical control of their departmental superiors, and under the administrative control of the District Planning Officer and the Collector. A frequent criticism made by the technical personnel thus brought under the control of the District Planning Officer was that under this arrangement technical specialists were subordinated to a layman. What perhaps aggravated the situation in the district in which this Project was located, was the fact that the District Planning Officer was a comparatively younger official of the state co-operative service. He belonged to the same class of service as many of the officials brought under his control, and was in fact junior in respect to length of service and salary to some of the people whom he supervised under the new organizational plan. In the status system of the

Indian bureaucracy seniority in service and emoluments are the major determinants of an official's position, and subordination to a junior person belonging to the same class of service was viewed by many as a blow to their own prestige. This problem was solved in some other districts either by appointing to the post of the District Planning Officer a senior person holding a rank equivalent to that of an Additional District Magistrate or a junior officer of the Indian Administrative Service. Subordination to such officers was resented much less by the district level heads of development departments.

Similar problems arose on the project level also, for in the administrative organization of the projects the technicians and 'subject-matter specialists' were placed under the control of an Executive Officer who was not acquainted with fields of technical specialization. But there the discontent and disharmony was not as deep and as apparent as it was on the district level. Two factors mainly account for this. The Executive Officer controlling the technical men, titled Assistant Project Officers, belonged to a superior class of service, and had a considerably higher salary and a decidedly better official status than the technicians. Secondly, as a result of their orientation and training in extension methods, most of the Assistant Project Officers were sensitized to the need for a reorganization which contributed to more effective and co-ordinated teamwork.

One of the most important innovations in administrative reorganization made at the time of the establishment of the development projects was the creation of the office of the multi-purpose Village Level Worker. This was a bold and imaginative step, and has gone a long way to remove the confusing multiplicity of development workers from the village scene. It has also provided opportunities for close and continuous interaction between the village people and the government in regard to questions of rural welfare and development. It has made it possible for planners and development workers to penetrate more effectively into village society. Because of his new and emerging role the Village Level Worker has not been without his problems and difficulties. In view of the critical importance of his role in development planning for rural India, an attempt at a more extended consideration of his position and problems has been made in Appendixes I and II.

Another notable feature of the new administrative structure was the association of the representatives of the local people with the official organization of the Project through various advisory committees. It is not possible to evaluate the role and effectiveness of these committees here, for during the period covered by this study they had not really started to function properly. Most of them had been constituted and had convened once or twice, but their meetings were neither regular nor frequent. Some members were not aware of their exact duties, responsibilities, and powers. In considering and approving matters brought to their attention by the officials in only a few instances did any of the members press their local claims; in the first few meetings official proposals were approved more or less in the form in which they were presented to the committee.

Besides making changes in the administrative structure, the planners of the development programme gave a great deal of thought to the problem of developing suitable working principles which would lead to more efficient and effective implementation of the plans.

The most significant change contemplated in this sphere was a dramatic switch-over from 'authoritarian' methods to 'democratic' methods. This involved 'inner democratization' of the administration, and the substitution of a more positive philosophy of partnership between the people and the government for the traditional paternalistic attitude to problems of rural welfare. In the orientation and extension training programmes, development literature, and conferences and seminars the necessity of such a change was repeatedly emphasized.

For developing a democratic outlook the staff of the Project was to work as a team. The traditional authoritarian 'boss-subordinate' relationships were to yield to the new concept of co-operative and democratic functioning of the development units; the superior officials were not to oversee and 'inspect' the work of their subordinates, they were to work jointly with them to solve the practical problems and difficulties arising in the field. Methods of discussion and consultation were to be increasingly used by the Project staff of different levels for a proper understanding of their respective problems and difficulties. With a view to providing opportunities for such discussion and exchange of ideas and experience, provision was made for fortnightly meetings of the Project staff in which all development officials from Village Level Workers to the Deputy Project Executive Officer were to participate. Occasionally the District Planning Officer and the Collector also were to attend these meetings. Personnel stationed at the Project headquarters from other government departments, such as sugarcane development, public health, and public works were regularly invited to these meetings. In general these staff meetings proved to be useful, but their organization and heavy agenda prevented their development as a forum for free and full discussion of problems and difficulties encountered by the actionmen in the field. A considerable part of the time of these meetings was taken by the presentation of individual progress reports by the Village Level Workers. The officials present commented on these, and assigned work to the VLWs for the next fortnight. New projects to be undertaken were then explained to the staff. Toward the end of the session the Village Level Workers were given a little time to explain their problems and difficulties. Because of the pressure to show results and realize the set targets, the officers were not very receptive to new ideas. They generally tended to brush aside the views that questioned the possibility of meeting the specified targets. As the officers themselves were under pressure they had to push their subordinates hard to use every possible means to achieve the desired results. Many of the officials were aware of the difficulties of their subordinates, but in view of a general lack of appreciation of these difficulties from their own superiors, they felt helpless. They received orders and instructions from the higher authorities to produce results, and in turn communicated them to their subordinates for implementation.

The traditional norms governing 'boss-subordinate' relations also came in the way of the contemplated inner-democratization and team-work. Higher officials viewed their role largely as that of 'inspecting officers', and continued to supervise and appraise the work of their subordinates. While this was a necessary part of their duties, excessive concentration on this aspect alone gave a distinct authoritarian tone to the administration. Because of their higher status in regard to official position and pay, many of them resented any views that departed from or questioned their own policies and methods of work. Theoretically the subordinates could express themselves freely, but in practice they realized that it only antagonized their official superiors. As their promotion and prospects depended greatly on the goodwill of the officers, they found it more practical and profitable to adopt an attitude of uniform compliance to the wishes of higher officials. In some instances individuals coming forward with new ideas and suggestions were snubbed as 'trouble-makers' and 'lazy talkers', and this largely fixed the one-way pattern of communication under which subordinates received orders and instructions for execution from their official superiors. The Village Level Workers complained about this attitude of the Assistant Project Officers and the Deputy Project Executive Officer, and these two felt somewhat the same way about their official superiors on the district and state level.

Similarly, in theory it was understood that the development programme was a giant educational undertaking, and that for lasting benefits it should be built up in partnership with the people. But the urgency of getting things done reduced many projects to high-pressure drives, having little room for understanding co-operation by the people. Time and again officers pointed out that extension principles were good but very slow; 'when problems have to be tackled on a "war-footing" only "executive methods" can get quick results'. The covert acceptance of this view by a considerable section of the officials was largely responsible for the perpetuation of a paternalistic flavour in development administration.

Another important principle adopted for the administration of the development projects was that of basing the local programme planning on 'felt needs' of the people, and of implementing these plans, as far as possible, through existing local agencies. Although there was considerable use of the phrase 'planning according to *felt needs*', none of the officers connected with the western U.P. Project had any idea of the exact methods of ascertaining these needs. They worked on the assumption that the needs of the rural areas were generally recognized and well known, and that the budget-frame provided to the individual Projects by the national Community Projects Administration fairly represented the requirements of the rural areas. While it was true that the major areas in which welfare work was required were well known, priorities in local planning could only be fixed on the basis of specific knowledge of the requirements of individual villages. The model budget circulated by the central headquarters was intended only as a rough indication of the ground to be covered, and had no sanctity attached to it. In planning their development activities most officers, however, tried to play safe, and conformed their activities as closely as possible to those outlined in the model budget. This appears to have been done on such a large scale that the Community Projects Administration felt compelled to remind the Projects that they were under no obligation to follow the model rigidly, but were expected to fix their priorities and to make financial allocations according to their specific regional needs. The outline of the three-year development programme for the western U.P. Project was, however, prepared more or less on the lines laid down in the model budget provided by the centre. In preparing it the Project administration was further handicapped by the fact that it was understaffed, and had had very little time to get acquainted with the people of the region and their requirements. Projects and targets set in the initial three-year programme outline were modified and altered from time to time, but these changes, rather than reflecting the needs and wishes of the people, were a reflection of the views and preferences of visiting dignitaries—political and official.

In this Project, programme planning followed more or less the set pattern adopted in the other parts of the state. The scale of priorities fixed for the Project did not very much indicate the particular needs of this region; conformity to the state-wide pattern was regarded as more desirable than planning for specific local needs. In view of the comparatively improved agricultural practices in this region, proportionately greater attention to public health and medical welfare could very well have been given by the Project but the officials did not think it safe to depart from the general pattern.

From time to time the Project received plans and directives from the state headquarters which it had to implement, notwithstanding the fact that they were not particularly suited to the area. A few examples will suffice. In this region people practise a local variant of the improved method of rice cultivation known as the 'Japanese method'. A comparatively small acreage was under rice in this area, and the method in use was almost as productive as the Japanese method. Yet because the Japanese method was being popularized throughout the state, even in this Project a great deal of time and energy had to be spent on it in compliance with directives from state headquarters. The same amount of effort could have been used much more productively in other areas of development work. Similarly, the Project officials had to spend a great deal of time exploring the possibilities of launching a sericulture project (and even making some initial preparation for it) in the clear knowledge of the fact that this region was unsuited for it. Project officials had to make special efforts to dispose of certain kinds of unrequired seeds sent under the direction of state headquarters, even though there was no local demand for them because of the unsuitability of the soil for the crop. Directives from headquarters appeared to have a kind of special sanctity, and were regarded generally as above criticism by the Project officials.

On the village level the plans lacked balance: the maximum benefit from development activity went to upper-level agriculturists on the one hand, and to a limited extent to the lowest group of untouchables on the other. The sizeable middle group of artisan and occupational castes was practically ignored. While some items of the development programme received disproportionate attention; others, such as social education classes, were lifeless and were run as a matter of routine. On the whole care was taken to time the projects well. Where this was not done, lack of co-operation and participation was evident in the response of the people. Adult education classes started during peak periods of agricultural activity failed to attract an appreciable number of students. Similar classes for women scheduled to suit the convenience of the teacher did not draw many candidates because at that time they were required at home for domestic work. *Shramdan* drives during the busy agricultural season got at best limited and grudging co-operation of the people.

In implementing the programme through or in association with the existing development agencies the Project experienced several difficulties. It was expected to make effective use of the existing co-operatives in the Project area. Where they did not function properly the Project was to revitalize them. A number of new co-operatives were to be started under the Project. The co-operatives were, thus, expected to play a vital part in furthering the development objectives of the Project. But the officers were almost wholly unaware of the factors that had hindered the growth of the co-operative movement and limited its appeal to a very narrow and small section of the village population. Similarly, great reliance was placed on newly established democratic units of village self-government, especially the village councils, to function as the local agents of the welfare programme. The optimism of the planners in this regard was somewhat excessive, because these bodies had been instituted only recently, and a clear picture of their role and problems in effective village administration had yet to emerge. The success of the Project in enlisting the co-operation of the Cane Development Union and the local schools was commendable. The former provided a well-organized association of agriculturists with whom the Project could deal directly. The Cane Union not only made contributions in cash for village development work from its Common Good Fund, but also provided a channel for its members to contribute to other development projects. Agriculturists from a large number of Project villages contributed in cash towards programmes such as road-building, school construction, or paving of village lanes, through the Cane Union. On application from the members of a particular village the Union office made the desired subtraction from the payment for sugarcane owed to these villagers and passed the money to the Project office on behalf of the villagers for the specified purpose. This proved advantageous to the Project in three ways. First, the village people preferred a deduction from the price of sugarcane sold by them to an individual cash payment from their funds. Second, when the majority of union members expressed a wish to make such contribution nearly all the cane-growers from the village agreed to accept the cut with them. Thus, because of the group spirit and action even such people contributed who otherwise probably would not have done so. Third, the Project could collect all the contributions from the Union office instead of undertaking the uncertain and time-consuming task of seeking the money from individual households. The schools, in the same way, provided the Project land on which to start its plant nurseries, and a place as well as the personnel to run their adult education classes. They were also a great help in initiating the 4-H Club programme.

Evaluation and experimentation were expected to occupy an important place in the working of the projects. Through them the planners and administrators were expected to obtain the necessary correctives for the successful implementation and continuation of the programme.

Apart from evaluation by independent official and non-official agencies, *self-evaluation* by the officials themselves was to have an important part in guiding the progress of the Project. The Project administration had no built-in mechanism charged with the responsibility of evaluating and appraising its successes and failures. The Assistant Project Officer for information and statistics was kept busy compiling figures and information for the numerous reports that the Project had to send out to state and national headquarters and present periodically to important visitors. The achievements of individual Village Level Workers were reviewed in the fortnightly meetings, but specific projects as a whole were rarely appraised. The various Monthly Progress Reports and Quarterly Progress Reports laid heavy emphasis on achievements and on targets met, and rarely spoke of any failures. Many of the officers were somewhat sceptical concerning the utility of evaluation itself. The first evaluation report of the Programme Evaluation Organization was regarded by some of the officers as a generally true statement of many of the obvious realities of the situation, but they failed to see in it any insights that could materially improve the situation.

Because of pressure to produce results the Project could not give any time to experimental 'pilot projects' under controlled conditions. Had these been tried, a careful study of their problems, progress and possibilities might have given important leads regarding the wisdom of their extension to a wider region.

The major problems of communication between the Project personnel and the village people will be analysed in the next chapter. It may be pointed out here that within the administration of the Project, there was mostly a one-way channel of communication, from the top down. There was considerable reluctance on the part of those who administered the Project to communicate their problems and grievances to the state or national authorities. They were generally afraid that raising problems and difficulties too often would annoy the higher authorities who might begin to regard them as 'obstructive' or 'trouble-makers' or 'failures'. Because of the alleged sensitivity of their official superiors they thought it best to comply with their ideas and wishes without question. For this reason, even when they were directed from the top to implement certain projects for which there was no locally expressed need and which were obviously doomed to failure, the Project officials were unwilling to present their views openly. They were particularly careful not to criticize any of the 'pet' theories and projects of important persons occupying high political and administrative offices.

3. Orientation and Training

The community development programme called for a new approach to the problems of rural welfare. In order to orient the officials selected for implementing the programme in this approach, and equip them psychologically to fit the new administrative organization, special training programmes were initiated. The training programme for the Village Level Workers included, besides the principles of extension work, theoretical and practical instruction in regard to their diverse areas of work. Officials occupying the ranks of District Planning Officer, Deputy Project Officer, and Assistant Project Officer, had to undergo short orientation courses, mostly of six weeks' duration. These courses were intended primarily to acquaint them with the spirit and methods of extension work. For higher officials, especially at the state and national level, no special programmes were organized, but they were encouraged to participate in seminars, conferences, and discussions where modern approaches to extension work, with special reference to India, were discussed.

The most significant result expected from these orientation and training programmes was a fundamental change in the outlook of the officials towards their work. In the new arrangement and according to the new philosophy they were not to feel and work like mercenaries, but as a vital part of a great national experiment. The dignity of labour was emphasized in these courses, and the desirability of accepting the gospel of 'dirty hands' was dramatically demonstrated by personal participation in activities demanding hard manual labour on the part of important political leaders and high government officials. Individual and group achievements of officials were to be judged not by impressive figures in official records and reports, but by the resulting benefits at the grass-roots level. Implementation of the development programme was not to be regarded as a routine duty, it was to be taken up with a sense of dedication and missionary zeal. Preparing the ground for 'inner democratization' within the administration, and fostering a spirit of co-operative teamwork among the officials, was viewed as an important function of these programmes.

Another basic change expected from these courses was a shift from 'executive' or 'administrative' methods to 'extension' methods in approaching the people and in implementing the programme. A number of earlier government drives, promoted with great official fervour, were shortlived, and had not left any lasting impression on the village people. In the rural development programme the educational aspects of development activities were regarded as the most

11. Demonstrations of a "model" well and soakage pit.

12. A women's social education class.

13. Schoolboys being fed at a celebration at the village Intermediate College.

14. A project officer working with village youth.

vital, for it was the hope of the planners that the village people would, as a consequence of their experience with this government-directed welfare work, learn in time to undertake the responsibility for it themselves.

These efforts had considerable success in creating a psychological atmosphere conducive to rural community development. On the whole the official world was shaken out of its complacency and invested with a sense of urgency in regard to the necessity for making an organized and concerted effort towards solving the problems of rural areas. If the educational programmes were not entirely successful in re-orienting the officials' attitude and approach, they at least suggested to them the availability of an alternative. It is true that participation by the officials in projects involving manual labour was more in the nature of a gesture than a real contribution, but it did leave an impression on the people, and was a definite help towards changing the attitude of subordinate employees engaged in development work. It was impossible to change established norms of the officials' thinking and action in a short time, but an excellent beginning towards that end was made.

The success of the training programmes in creating the psychological atmosphere for 'inner democratization' was more limited. This can, in large part, be attributed to a lack of balance in the programme. While the duration of the training for Village Level Workers was longer and consequently more effective, the courses for higher officials were all too brief, and in most cases not very well organized. The results were confusing. While the Village Level Workers came out of the training centres expecting to find a democratic atmosphere of co-operative teamwork in the field, their immediate superiors were not sufficiently sensitized to the contemplated changes, and were not mentally prepared for a fundamental change. They were ready for a token democratization, perhaps, not for a total modification of their traditional role. The Village Level Workers were generally bewildered and frustrated. They did not find the change in the attitude of their immediate superiors which they had been led to anticipate; and their superiors thought that the Village Level Workers were hoping for the impossible in expecting any far-reaching and radical change in their subordinate status and its attendant role.

The acceptance of the superiority of 'extension' methods over 'administrative' methods was neither complete nor unconditional. In general, the Village Level Workers were oriented to this view much better than were their immediate superiors. Among the latter, many had mental reservations about the utility and efficacy of this approach. To some it was too theoretical and doctrinaire; to many others it was just too slow. According to most officials, the pressures under which they were working did not leave them the option of trying time-consuming methods of discussion and eliciting the leadership of the local people.

In planning the orientation and training programmes the Community Projects Administration could not anticipate the many problems and difficulties that were likely to arise in the field. This was a new venture in Indian public administration, and there was not much time for planning and organizing these programmes. Where the training was of a longer duration and more intensive, it left a lasting impression on the trainees; shorter courses barely touched the surface of the problems. Generally the Village Level Workers left the training centres much better equipped, psychologically and technically, for their jobs and the new programme than those under whom they were to work. Realizing the inadequacy of its officer-level training programme, the Community Projects Administration organized several symposia and seminars for their benefit. Many of these were imaginatively organized, but they nevertheless failed to prove an effective substitute for intensive and sustained training. The feeling of most of the officials was that refresher courses and 'sight-seeing' tours arranged for them were hurriedly planned, and failed to be the positive educational experiences that they could have been had they been arranged with more imagination and thought.

With the experience gained during the administration of the first Community Projects, it should be possible for the Community Projects Administration to devise more realistic and effective training programmes for its officials. In doing so it will be desirable for them to harmonize administrative reforms and modifications with the orientation and training of their field agents.

Closely related to the problems in the general area of orientation and training are the questions of providing suitable working conditions for the officials.

In regard to their work load the officials felt that they had to work much harder in the development jobs, but that their normal duties were not excessive. However, from time to time, they were assigned certain other tasks, such as taking censuses and making surveys, making spot checks, and writing reports for the government on matters having no direct bearing on their development work. It was the feeling of many that these unexpected assignments upset their normal schedules, were time-consuming, and reduced their efficiency as far as their usual and normal tasks were concerned.

Another problem that worried many officials was that of providing proper incentives for more and better work. In the reorganized pattern of administration many felt that their chances for promotion were considerably reduced. Positions carrying superior status and better pay in their parent departments went to those who were actually working in those departments. Opportunities for promotion in the Department of Planning and Development were very few and higher administrative jobs carrying responsibility and larger emoluments often went to officials who were drawn from the revenue department. In the course of our research we were told time and again that the Community Projects Administration had failed to evolve any system of recognizing especially meritorious work by suitable awards and promotions.

A third problem about which concern was expressed by Project officials was that of getting timely support and supplies from state and national headquarters. There were episodes when required seeds and fertilizers were received long after they could be of any use to the people. Similarly, publicity materials urgently needed by the projects came in very slowly and in too meagre quantities. The Project officials had good reasons to worry on this account because for the successful completion of many of the projects programmed by them they had to depend on state headquarters for the required supplies. When they were unable to keep their promises they lost the confidence of the people. Often this involved the failure not only of the project in hand but also of a number of others that were to follow. The village people would then openly express scepticism about the government's promises at a crucial time when their support was most needed and, knowing the past record, the officials could not give them assurances in respect to matters which they themselves could not directly control.

4. Conclusions and Comments

A great deal of thought and planning have gone into the modification of the traditional administrative structure to adapt it to the requirements of the rural community development programme. By setting up orientation and training programmes, and by making a conscious effort to evolve a set of operational principles to guide the officials engaged in development activity, the planners have shown both foresight and a genuine interest in equipping the officials to function as agents of change. Through periodical publications, and seminars and conferences, the government has tried to evaluate the success of its plans, and has provided a forum for exchange and communication of ideas. By and large, it has selected men of patriotism and strong motivation to implement the projects. The attitude of the national administration has not been one of complacency. It has shown considerable adaptability, and has been receptive to new ideas. To the credit of the planners it must be said that they have not hesitated to deviate boldly from established practices, where the need or wisdom of such departure, was indicated.

The lessons learned in implementing the Community Projects under the first Plan can provide valuable correctives for the future of the rural community development movement in the country. Problems in the entire area of administrative reorganization, as well as orientation and training need to be reviewed critically. Human factors involved in the change-over from the old pattern of organization and methods of work can now be appraised empirically. This experience should enable the planners and the administrators of the development programme to devise more effective training programmes, and alter the administrative machinery suitably. Questions connected with the working conditions of the officials —especially those of work load, effective area of operation, incentives to more and better work, and delegation of responsibility, still require a careful examination.

Planning so far appears to be from the top down. It would be naïve to suggest that the process can be suddenly reversed. Notwithstanding the theoretical acceptance of the principle of grass-roots planning, it would be unrealistic to assume that the village people are able to undertake complete responsibility for it at present. Yet while the state will have to retain a position of leadership, and take considerable initiative in regard to questions of rural welfare, it is necessary to examine the implications and results of the present trends in planning. Because of undue curbs on Project autonomy its officials hesitated to demonstrate much initiative. What was worse, they tended on the official level to accept orders from above, i.e. from the state headquarters, without question or comment, and this often despite pronounced private reservations. As an outcome of this trend the officials were oriented less towards the village people, and more towards the pleasing of their official superiors.

A related problem merits serious attention in this connexion. In changing over from a 'bureaucratic' to an active 'social service' role, government officials as a body must preserve their identity. In India, social service so far has been closely associated with political work, and political leaders have often been identified as leaders of social reform. Because of lack of perspective and improper understanding of their new role, some officials have come perilously close to viewing their functions as political functions. A young democracy must guard carefully against the development of such a trend. The permanent executive will always have to work under the direction and control of the political executive, but it should never identify itself too closely with the latter. Party politicians often tend to use government agencies for immediate party ends. Safeguards must be devised to minimize the use of state-sponsored programmes and official machinery towards such objectives. Better understanding and appreciation of the spirit and methods of modern extension work by the politicians is necessary for prevention of the use of the movement for short-sighted political ends.

The desirability of rigorous and penetrating evaluation cannot be too strongly emphasized. A large number of Project-sponsored activities are directed along the lines of traditional government 'drives' rather than according to the proved principles of extension work. Visible accomplishments under such pressure and stimulation and completion of physical targets are greatly valued, and too little attention is given to the question of finding out if the movement is really acquiring roots in the village society. Impressive progress reports of Project achievements can mean little in terms of the basic objectives of the Plan if these achievements do not arouse an understanding interest and creative response among the people. Sympathetic but honest evaluation could wean the official away from the kind of self-deception that a quest after impressive records as such sometimes entails. It could help towards a better definition of ends as well as towards the development of suitable means for attaining them. Only through insights provided by such work can we hope to transform 'bureaucrats' into 'agents of change'.

V

PROBLEMS OF COMMUNICATION

1. Communication in Social Change

THE RURAL COMMUNITY DEVELOPMENT PROGRAMME IN INDIA as conceived and partly implemented by the state under the first Five Year Plan is essentially a democratic movement of village self-help. The basic objective of the movement, as viewed and expressed by the planners, is to create in the Indian masses a burning desire for change, which, through progressive adaptation of modern techniques, will lead to their achieving higher standards of life. For this reason the programme emphasizes *education* more than *service*. It is realized that the problem is not simply one of village people adopting modern ideas and techniques offered to them by the extension agencies of the government; it is also a problem of adapting these ideas and techniques to suit the culture and values of the people and of developing acceptable and effective channels of communication. In recognition of this need the Plan has laid considerable emphasis on offering the programme to the people in their own language and symbols. Viewed in terms of its ultimate aims, the movement is a gigantic educational experiment aimed at creating a more positive and forward looking view of life in village India, and thereby at achieving a socio-economic transformation of the village scene. The successful implementation of the programme in all its varied aspects consequently involves a series of problems in the area of communication.

In this chapter an attempt will be made to examine some of these problems in their cultural context, with particular reference to the Community Development Project Block in western Uttar Pradesh.

2. The Approach

In the blueprints outlining the Community Development Projects and the National Extension Service some thought has been given to the questions of developing effective techniques of mass contact and of evolving suitable media for communicating the development programme—its ideology and methods—to the village people. In the extension training of the multi-purpose Village Level Workers and in the orientation courses of higher development officials, special attention was given to these problems. An effort was made to change the traditional, the bureaucratic and impersonal, outlook and psychology of the officials by training them to approach the people with sympathy and understanding. In order that the educational goals of the programme may not be defeated, the service programme was to be implemented through carefully considered steps that were calculated to secure understanding acceptance of the proffered items.

The methods of communicating the programme to the villager, recommended in the development literature and emphasized in the training of the officials, can be classified under three main categories:

1. Contact.
2. Demonstration.
3. People's participation.

The extension agents of the Projects were to contact individual persons and families, as well as recognizable groups in the village and all the people of the village collectively. For certain items of the development programme, such as the acceptance of a new agricultural practice or the joining of an agricultural co-operative, approaching an individual and his family was regarded as the best method. For some other items on the Project schedule that needed group action, such as making sanitary repairs to a well or the formation of a co-operative society of weavers, it was necessary to approach a group. In the case of the repairs to a well all the people living in the territorial sub-division of the village where this well is located had to be approached, and for the formation of a handloom weaver's co-operative it was essential to contact the caste of weavers in the village. A number of projects called for collective approach to the entire village. Efforts to build roads by *shramdan* or people's voluntary unpaid labour, or raising contributions to get the village lanes paved are two of the many items that called for such a collective approach.

The method of demonstration was to be used mainly in agricultural extension. The main idea behind these demonstrations is to give a convincing proof to the people that practices recommended by the Project are practical and easy in operation and profitable in results.

The people's participation in all phases of development activities was regarded as the most important part of the education process implied in the programme. Gratuitous service to an unconvinced population was to be avoided as far as possible.

As demonstrations and participation by the people depend ultimately on the success with which villagers have been approached, it might be useful to sketch the methods of contact tried in the western U.P. Project.

3. Communicating the Programme

The decision to launch a rural Community Development Project Block in this area was announced in March 1953. The selection of villages to be included in the Block was made by the District representatives of the rural *élite* from this area. Principally through word of mouth, information was passed along to people that the government was shortly to start a many-sided programme of rural development. Among literate villagers, especially those who had regular urban contacts and affiliations with political parties, there was some awareness of the national programmes of this type. Information regarding the Community Development Projects was being broadcast by the All India Radio, but it is doubtful if this contributed much to the information about the existence of such plans of the few owners of wireless receiving sets in this area. The cinemas at the district headquarters and the Project headquarters regularly showed documentary films and newsreels about community development programmes in action, and these in a very general way contributed to the information of a small section of village people. Through them this information circulated to some more people in the villages. The national press had given very considerable publicity to the first Five Year Plan and its constituent parts, but it could not affect the village people much as very few copies of such publications are subscribed to by village people. Weekly newspapers published at the district headquarters and the publications of the Panchayat Raj Department contributed a little more to knowledge regarding the proposed Project and its aims.

One of the most important sources of information in the pre-inauguration period was the political meetings attended by village leaders, in which leaders from the district and the State outlined the proposed undertaking. When the Deputy Project Executive Officer of the Project started a survey of the area with a view to formulating a three-year development plan some more information about the Project was spread. The secretaries of village councils, village accountants, and Co-operative Supervisors assisting him in this work were instrumental in this. The impact of all the sources of information sketched above, however, was not very great. In a survey conducted at the end of the first year of Project activities in two villages of the area, it was found that only 8 per cent of these who knew about the existence of the Project had come to know about it before its formal inauguration in October 1953, through one or more sources described above.

The inauguration of the Project by the Chief Minister of Uttar Pradesh was preceded by a concentrated drive to attract as many people as possible to the function at which it was to be launched formally. The inauguration ceremony itself was accompanied by great fanfare. The Village Level Workers, Panchayat Secretaries, Lekhpals, in fact all village level officials of the government, had gone from house to house in the villages of the Development Block, asking people to attend the function and give a rousing reception to the visiting dignitary. The village where the ceremony was held was especially cleaned for the occasion. Development slogans, such as *Jag uthe gram, khil utha desh* (villages are awake, the nation is blossoming); *panch raj parmeshwar raj* (rule by village representatives is like rule by God); *swachchha gharon men Lakshmi was karti hai* (clean houses are the abode of Lakshmi, the goddess of wealth), and *machchhar jiwan ka nash karte hain, ham machchharon ka nash karenge* (mosquitoes destroy life, we shall destroy the mosquitoes), were written in bold letters on the walls of the houses all over the village. The site of the function was impressively decorated. The function attracted the rural *élite* as well as a large number of others from the villages of the Development Block. A number of speeches, climaxed by one from the Chief Minister inaugurating the Project, were made on the occasion. The central theme of all these speeches was the subject of village development, and the speakers, after describing what the government was doing for the villages exhorted the people to take up the challenge and assume responsibility for their self-development.

In the period that followed several methods were used to communicate the programme to the people. Important among them were:

1 *Slogans.* Reference has already been made to the slogans that were written on the walls of the houses in preparation for the visit of the State Chief Minister. These slogans were written by school teachers and students under the direction of the Village Level Workers and other Project officials. This activity was later extended to many other villages of the Project area. Development slogans were also used in connexion with national celebrations such as the Indian Independence Day (August 15), the Republic Day (January 26), and the birth anniversary of Mahatma Gandhi (October 2). On these days processions of school children and villagers were organized which went around the villages shouting these slogans.

2 *Pictures and posters.* Shortly after the beginning of the Project

some posters and pictures were distributed in a number of villages in the Development Block. Because of the limited supply sent from the national and state headquarters their distribution was restricted to headquarters of public bodies, such as Panchayat offices, schools, and co-operative seed stores. At these places they were prominently displayed. These posters and pictures related mostly to the importance of co-operation, the value of education, the necessity for sanitation, and the role of village councils as instruments of rural welfare and development. After the first set distributed at the time of the inauguration of the Project no more were received from the headquarters and consequently their use as a medium of communication remained extremely limited.

3 *Pamphlets and publications.* These may be considered under three categories: publications of the central and state governments, publications of the Project, and announcements regarding specific programmes. No publications were received from the central and state headquarters for distribution or sale to the public, and very few were received for circulation among the field staff of the Project. A few copies of two booklets issued by the Planning Research and Action Institute of the U.P. Government in connexion with the 4-H Club movement, one on the cultivation of tomatoes and another on the cultivation of the egg plant, were made available for sale at the seed stores.

During the first half of its life the Project issued three publications. The first of these explained and illustrated a plan under which certain crops could be grown profitably for a few years in areas where orchards had been newly planted. The main idea of this leaflet was to dispel the feeling common among agriculturists that planting of orchards involved an investment which had no prospects of any immediate returns, and that for profits it was necessary to wait until the plants became trees and started bearing fruit. This publication sought to illustrate how with a little planning and care earlier returns can be secured. It also gave estimates of costs involved in planting different types and sizes of orchards, and offered practical hints regarding modern methods of planting different types of fruit-bearing trees. The second publication of the Project was a small collection of development songs called *Badalti Duniya* or 'The Changing World'. These songs were improvised by the man in charge of development publicity in the Project, and had been popularized by him through the numerous meetings he had addressed in the villages of the Block. They had direct bearing on one aspect or another of development work undertaken by the Project. Their tunes were catchy, and were based mostly on popular film or well-known devotional songs. The third publication was a booklet outlining the achievements of the

Project during the first fourteen months of its existence. From time to time leaflets and announcements pertaining to specific project activities, shows, and exhibitions were also issued.

4 *Movies*. The Project owned a portable projector and generator, and financial provision had been made for the appointment of a full-time person to operate them. These were to be used for showing films produced by the Films Division of the Government of India. This organization has produced two types of films—documentary films, showing the progress that is being made in the country under the First Five Year Plan, and instructional films, illustrating the techniques that are being promoted by the development projects. The Planning Research and Action Institute of the State Government had a good selection of these and other movies on development subjects. However, the Project was unlucky in the instruments and their operator. For a time there was no operator. When he arrived there were frequent mechanical breakdowns which could not be attended to very quickly. When the machines were repaired, the personal problems of the operator came in the way of efficient and effective utilization of this medium of communication.

5 *Tournaments and competitions*. Four types of competitions were organized by the Community Development Project. Sports tournaments were mostly for the members of the 4-H Clubs, but on special occasions, such as the annual Development Exhibition and Fair they were open to all residents of the Development Block. The Project also sponsored crop competitions on the village, *adalati panchayat*, and Development Block levels. People were encouraged to enter their cattle in these shows, and committees of judges awarded prizes to the best cattle in the different classes. Finally, a large number of village and Project Level baby shows were held under the auspices of the Project, and prizes were awarded to the healthiest and cleanest babies.

6 *Exhibitions and conferences*. The Project organized two annual Development Fairs, one in 1954 and another in 1955. Development Exhibitions formed an important part of these fairs. Stalls showing the work of the Project in the fields of agricultural extension, horticulture, cane development, co-operatives, rural health and sanitation, and women's welfare were erected in these exhibitions. Within the exhibition area improved agricultural practices were demonstrated in especially prepared plots. There was a display of improved agricultural implements. Small models of sanitary wells, soakage pits, and several types of hygienic latrines were also constructed. In conjunction with the exhibition a series of conferences of agriculturists, cane growers, members of the co-operatives, and members of village *panchayats* were also held. In these fairs a separate day was

set aside for women. The programme for this day included women's sports, a baby show, and a women's conference. Cattle shows, wrestling competitions, sports tournaments, and poultry shows were also organized in these fairs. The programme for each day concluded either with a film show or a propaganda meeting. Movies both of the popular and the educational type were shown. The propaganda meetings included in their programme popular discourses on development subjects as well as the singing of songs having to do with rural development.

Annually a similar exhibition and conference was also held at the district headquarters. As the Development Block is a part of the district, some of its residents attended these exhibitions and conferences also.

7 *Propaganda meetings.* The Project employed a former *Arya Samaj*[1] propagandist as the head of the song publicity unit. This unit went from village to village in the Project area addressing audiences on development themes. The propaganda and discourses of this unit followed the conventional Arya Samaj pattern. While the leader of the unit preached the other two members accompanied him; either by playing musical instruments or by repeating his lines at appropriate pauses. This technique was familiar to the people and was very popular in this area. To reiterate, emphasize or illustrate the points the unit drew upon Indian mythology and history, popular folk-tales, proverbs and common anecdotes. Its songs became especially popular.

8 *Fraternization.* One of the aims of the orientation courses organized for officials working in the development projects was to create in them a feeling that in the new India they could not live in an *official world* of their own, separate from the world of the Indian villagers. They were expected to make special efforts to come close to the village people and gain their confidence. This brought about some change in the officials' attitudes and behaviour. Officials learned to greet the village people cordially, and started occasionally joining their functions and ceremonies. While the general desirability of fraternization was recognized, no definite steps had either been devised or recommended in this regard. The initiative was largely left with the officials. In 1955 the Deputy Project Executive Officer of the Block tried a somewhat unorthodox experiment. It was so enthusiastically received by the village people that it deserves special mention. On the day of the Holi festival (the spring festival of the Hindus), the entire Project staff at headquarters set out on a mass

[1]A movement for socio-religious reforms in Hindu society. One of the aims of this movement was to bring back to the Hindu fold persons who had embraced Islam or Christianity.

fraternization expedition. A large trailer was attached to the Project tractor. The group equipped itself with two large barrels of coloured water and an adequate supply of colour. They took with them some D.D.T. spraying machines for sprinkling this coloured water on the village people. The propaganda unit of the Community Development Project accompanied the group with its musical instruments, and a microphone and loud-speaker.

The group visited about six villages, singing Holi songs and spraying coloured water on the people they met on their way. In the villages they left the tractor, and went around to the different quarters meeting people and throwing coloured water and powder on them. The propaganda unit sang Holi and development songs on street corners. It was the view of many people especially interviewed on this subject that within their memory nothing like this had happened in their village: government officials had never mixed with them as equals before.

9 *Visits by dignitaries, meetings, and speeches.* Speeches were regarded, in practice if not in theory, as the most effective media of communicating a new programme to the people. Many of the methods of approach sketched above involved considerable speech-making. Meetings were held for visiting dignitaries—high ranking officials as well as important political leaders. If the visitor happened to be a 'very important person' his visit was often preceded by a period of hectic activity in which incomplete projects were completed, some new projects were begun and there was a good deal of last minute mopping and dusting.

Thematic analysis of a dozen speeches of leaders and higher officials reveal a number of recurrent themes. The most common of these contrasted India's present plight with its high position in the past: from a land 'flowing with milk and curds', India had now become a land of poverty and starvation. This was followed by the inevitable appeal that through hard work the country could be restored to its ancient glory. Another rather frequent theme was that India had lost her freedom to the British because of her 'weakness'; unless her people now worked hard to build up the strength of the country there was very great fear that some foreign power may again conquer the land. To avoid foreign domination it was necessary for the village people to take up the challenge and make the country strong. A third theme was that it was Mahatmaji's (Gandhi's) wish to see Indian villages happy and prosperous; he did not live to see the day of realization, but his heir, Jawaharlal Nehru, is determined that his countrymen do so without losing time. The world has recognized the greatness of the Mahatma, and Nehru's views command great respect in international affairs today. If so many other countries have chosen to follow their lead, Indian village people owe it to themselves to rally behind their leaders and make a success of the development programme. Then there was the appeal to do things by citing similar and encouraging examples: if the United States, Russia, and China could build up their national prosperity from humble beginnings, why could India not do the same? Another important theme was that of *the changing times*: with the advent of independence a new epoch had been ushered in, and people have to change their ways to suit its climate. There were frequent references to the importance of villages in Indian national life. A point that was often emphasized in this context was that India's plans for industrialization and her many power projects could never succeed if the village people did not improve their agriculture and produce enough food for people working in the other fields.

These themes were echoed in the speeches and propaganda of lesser political leaders and field workers of the Project, but many of these spokesmen were more 'down to earth' in their appeals and used symbols and anecdotes that could be more readily comprehended by the people. In putting across their ideas to the villagers, and especially in trying to secure their co-operation in action programmes, they also appealed to the people's pride in their caste and village. For example in his speech in a Rajput village a development officer said, 'Look to the Jats. What progress are they making? They do not have half the land you Rajputs have; but they work hard. While a Jat spends his time in the fields, you sit on the platform of your house and smoke hubble bubble (water pipe). When the Jat thinks seriously about required improvements in his land, you only think about petty village squabbles.' Another official said, 'Yours is a large village, perhaps the largest in the Project area. But what are your achievements? What have you done to improve your village? And look at village X. With one tenth of your population they have done ten times more work.'

By using impersonal ridicule certain points were communicated in a very telling manner. In the distribution of prizes following a Cattle Show the District Livestock Officer began his speech by saying, 'An American came to India. In his country he had heard that Indians as a people were very devoted to the cow, and worshipped her as a mother. Naturally he expected that he will find cattle of good breed—healthy and well looked after. And what did he see? Emaciated cows, giving less milk than American goats! We are proud that milk and curds used to flow in our country and say so times without number. But what is our present condition? Some of our cows give just enough milk to make a cup of tea!' On another occasion the same officer said, 'We all regard the bull as sacred. We are right; for an agricultural people a bull is really sacred. When a child is seriously ill, some parents say, "O God! Let our child recover. We shall leave a bull in Shiva's name when the child recovers." And when the child recovers you leave the weakest calf to grow into a bull. Is this a good way of acknowledging your gratitude? You want to deceive God by giving him a counterfeit coin! God does not have to punish you. You punish yourself and your community. Your bull can only have weak offspring. You may not realize it, but your cultivation suffers. Why cheat God? Buy a bull of some really good breed. That will please God and benefit your community.'

The Assistant Project Officer (Social Education) addressed a meeting of women in a village. He began, 'I came to this village to address a gathering of mothers and sisters. For two hours before the meeting I was wondering if there were any mothers or sisters in this village. Do you know why? Can you even guess? I will tell you why. I looked at the children—one, two, ten, twenty, in fact as many children as I could see. Their bodies were unclean and their clothes dirty. Some had sore eyes, all had running noses. Seeing this I thought that this must be a village without any mothers and sisters. Mothers and sisters would not leave their sons and brothers, daughters and little sisters in this shape.' To give one more example: the propaganda unit of the Development Project arrived in a village at 9.30 to address a gathering on the subject of health and sanitation. The leader of the unit began by saying, 'Sorry, we are late. It is dark and we lost our way. Your village is hidden in thick groves, and we could not see even the twinkling of a little earthen lamp. But when we were about half a mile away from your village, we knew that we are near it. Ask me how we knew it? It is simple. You do not yet have compost pits. Uncovered manure heaps in your village emit such a foul smell that from half a mile one could know that your village was near.' Continuing, the leader asked, 'Is there anyone in the village who does not know that cow dung is a valuable manure?' Some people said, 'Everyone knows that.' At this he asked, 'And is there anyone in the village who can honestly say that he does not burn a lot of this potential manure in his *hukka*?'

It is perhaps needless to add that specific items recommended by the Project, such as improved seed, fertilizer, modern agricultural implements, were supported by rational appeals concerning their utility, efficiency, economy, durability, and productivity.

10 *Social education classes and community centres.* As a part of the development programme social education classes and community centres were started in a number of key villages. The former aimed at imparting education for a better life. Although adult literacy formed an important part of their activities they were

expected to prepare the people, in the long run, for co-operative and democratic action in the field of village welfare and development. These classes were organized separately for men and women. The community centres aimed at providing healthy and creative recreation to the people. It was hoped that because of their association with these centres the people will come to have a better understanding of the aims and methods of community development.

11 *Group discussions and individual contacts.* Through group discussion of common problems people were expected to recognize their needs and devise plans to meet them. The field agents of the Project were expected to prepare the ground for such discussions, and take a leading share in informing the people *how* they could do *what* they wanted to do. As several aspects of the development programme involve choice-making by individuals and their families they were also contacted, and efforts were made to convince them of the utility and desirability of innovations recommended by the Project.

12 *Camps and sight-seeing tours.* The Project organized camps for village leaders, youth leaders, and women. The purpose of these camps was twofold: to educate the leaders and key individuals, participating in the camp programmes, in the aims and methods of rural community development, and to prepare them to assume an active role of leadership in village development activities. Similarly, with a view to creating development consciousness among the village people, especially among their leaders, parties of villagers were taken out once a year on sight-seeing tours to other Community Development Projects. The parties of adults included enthusiastic agriculturists and village leaders. Some groups of younger people, consisting mostly of leaders and workers of the 4-H Clubs, were also taken out on such conducted tours.

13 *Work with local Agents of Communication.* Accepting the development of the *community* as its idea, the Project tried, in theory at least, to reach all sections and classes, and attempted to educate and benefit them by its activities. In this field it had a few general guiding principles. An attempt was to be made to use all existing village institutions and organizations for the furtherance of development objectives. As far as possible co-operation of the traditional leaders of the village was to be enlisted for the implementation of the programme. A special effort was to be made to find 'key' individuals, whose example in accepting the new items offered by the Community Development Project was likely to be followed by the rest of the community. In giving *method* and *result* demonstrations connected with the agricultural extension programme, the Village Level Worker had to select people who could later communicate the method or successful results of the demonstration to others in the

15. Drill training of Youth Club members.

16. VLW speaking to an agriculturist.

17. Song publicity-unit of the project.

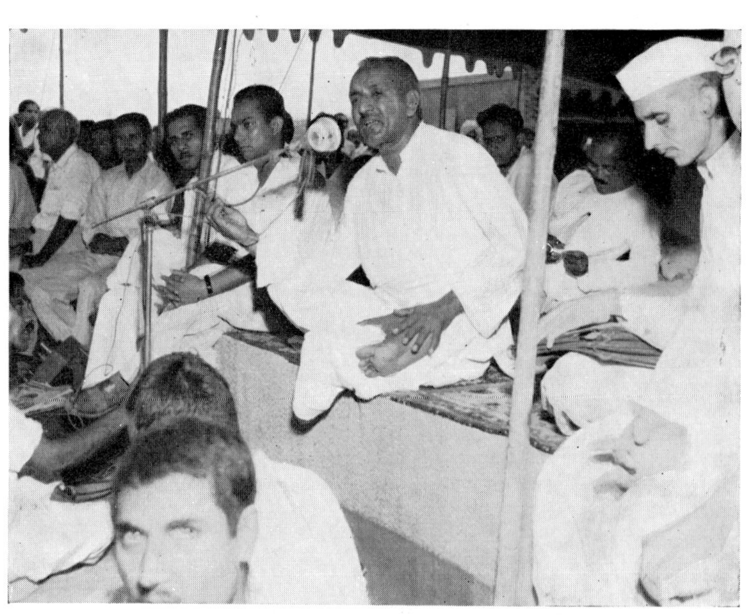

18. An important leader speaking to village people.

community. Care had to be taken in selecting the geographical location of these demonstrations. Ideally they were to be given at places where they could be seen by as many people as possible. Finally, people had to be educated to undertake as many group and community undertakings as possible. Understanding rather than coercion was to be the basis of such group and community activities.

The Community Development Project sought the co-operation of existing village institutions such as the village *panchayat* and the *adalati panchayat* schools, and co-operative societies. Persons holding offices in these bodies or otherwise prominent in their activities were regarded as 'village leaders', and the development officials made a special effort to work closely with them. Some others, who had contacts with politicians and officials, were also included in this category, and were consulted in matters connected with the development project. The response of this group was enthusiastic and encouraging. They had a certain hold on village people, and were invariably helpful in raising contributions and collecting a fair number of people to work for any group or community undertaking sponsored by the Project. For several practical reasons the Village Level Workers chose them to be the recipients of benefits from Project activities such as demonstration and trials. One reason was that these people were eager to attract a good part of the benefit from Project activities to themselves. Another reason was that the officials, being under pressure to show results and to complete the set targets, were only too glad to work with anyone who was co-operative and needed a minimum of persuasion. Thus a group of village people having contacts with the world of officials and politicians largely came to be viewed as the local agents of change. It was hoped that they would quickly adopt practices recommended by the Project, and through them the practices would percolate to the rest of the community.

4. The Response

What was the response of the village people to these direct and indirect efforts of communicating the development programme to them?

Before analysing their response to specific techniques employed for this purpose it might be useful to examine the extent to which knowledge regarding the Project and its activities had penetrated two fairly representative villages of the Development Block at the end of the first year of development activities in the area. For convenience these villages have been called 'Rajput Village' and 'Tyagi Village'. As pointed out earlier,[1] in the former a 10 per cent stratified

[1]Chapter III.

random sample of the male population was interviewed; in the latter, because its smaller size permitted, 50 per cent of the male residents were interviewed.

In Rajput Village, out of a sample of 114 persons, 56 had heard about the Project, 58 had not. Sixty-four perons had attended meetings and functions organized by the Project, although some of them were not aware of the existence and aims of the sponsoring organization. Forty-five persons had knowledge—most partial—about development activities in the village; only 23 knew about Project sponsored activities in other villages. The Village Level Worker had met 59 of these people, but some of them did not know that he represented the Community Development Project. He had sought active co-operation of only 48 of the persons interviewed. The activities for which such co-operation was sought were: agricultural extension (24), village sanitation (32), irrigation (8), other works (10). Only 45 persons could mention some of the innovations recommended by the Village Level Worker. These related to three main fields: 13 people knew about suggested improvements in agricultural practices, 21 were aware of programmes in the field of public health and sanitation, and 11 could list programmes in other fields.

In Tyagi Village, out of a sample of 117 persons, 74 had heard about the Project, 43 had not. Only 21 persons had attended meetings or functions organized by the Project. Almost all the persons who knew about the Project had at least a partial knowledge about its activities in the village; 51 people had some knowledge about its activities in other villages also. Ninety-three people had met the Village Level Worker, but many of them did not know of his connexion with the development project. He had sought the active co-operation of only 24 people. Area-wise co-operation was sought in the following fields: sanitation (13), agricultural improvements (1), irrigation (5), and *shramdan* (voluntary labour) and other activities (25). Forty-nine persons in this sample could not recall any innovations recommended by the Project; 37 people knew about the village sanitation programme, and 33 had some information regarding Project activities in the field of animal husbandry and cattle care. Eighty-six people knew about Project-sponsored improved agricultural practices; although some of them had no knowledge of the existence of the Project itself.

It has been mentioned earlier that only 8 per cent of those who knew about the plans for the local Project prior to its inauguration had some idea about the general national plans for rural community development. They had picked up this information from newspapers, radio, movies, and political meetings. It is not possible to attribute knowledge in individual cases specifically to any of the above sources because most of the informants could not pin-point the exact source from which they derived it. In order of their importance the sources of information could roughly be graded as: political meetings, press, radio, and movies.

The number of radio-owners in the villages is very small, and the community listening sets that a few villagers possess are often out of order for long periods. Thus very few people have access to wireless sets. The few who do have them rarely listen to the village programmes broadcast from the Delhi or Lucknow stations of All India Radio. Their favourite programmes are movie songs, religious discourses, and, in some cases, news. Ownership of a radio set is a mark of urbanization: the owner identifies himself, consciously or unconsciously, with the world of the city and therefore interests himself in items that have a distinct urban appeal. When some of the radio owners were asked to explain why they did not listen to the special rural broadcasts they said, 'We listen to the radio for a change. In the rural programmes we have village songs, and skits and dialogues in a local dialect. Do we not have too much of these things around us already? These programmes do not interest us. If city people were to listen to them they would probably learn something about village life.' When it was pointed out to them that these stations were also broadcasting some useful talks for the agriculturists there was no response from them. Apparently little was known about these programmes. One villager, however, said, 'Are they useful? Are their weather forecasts ever correct?' The same is true of the movies. Very few people from the countryside go to the movies regularly; to most people it is a very special and rare treat. Along with regular films some newsreels or short educational films are regularly shown, but these are regarded as being closer to the advertisement slides than to the main feature. The language of the commentary in these films is often so bookish that village people find great difficulty in understanding it. The number of newspaper subscribers in the rural areas is very small, but the few papers coming into the village do get read, and through gossip and discussion the news gets disseminated in the village to some extent. Information derived from newspapers as well as from political meetings first comes to the village *élite* (specifically, persons who have contacts with urban people, officials, and political workers), and is conveyed by them to their immediate associates in the village. Finally it reaches a section of the others through these intermediaries.

A brief analysis of the general pattern of response towards the different media of communication adopted by the Project can now be attempted.

The use of slogans, although not indigenous to the culture of village communities, has become fairly popular since the days of the resistance movement against British domination in India. In a short and easily remembered sentence the slogans convey a message. It is true that because of the cultural predisposition of the people the slogan is sometimes interpreted by the villagers in a sense different from the one which it is intended to communicate, but it must be said that it is remembered for a long time by a large number of the people. In our investigations it was found that many people learned for the first time through slogans written on the walls that the mosquito was the source of malaria. Many of those who show enthusiasm for village sanitation programmes say that they became aware of its necessity by reading the slogans. In any event, it is one of the most inexpensive ways of offering an idea: the written words catch the eyes of people again and again, and slogans shouted in meetings and processions ring in the ears of some for a good many days afterwards.

Pictures and posters are eagerly sought and carefully displayed by the villagers, but it is not possible to evaluate their utility as a medium of communication because their use in this Project was so limited. Most of these pictures and posters displayed in *panchayat* houses, schools and co-operative seed stores were not particularly imaginative or attractive, did not display much understanding of the village people's interests, and were generally banal and cheerless.

Nor were pamphlets and publications used as a means of propaganda on any extensive scale. Of the three Project publications mentioned earlier, one was an administrative report of Project activities in standard Hindi, and was of little practical utility to the village people. The appeal of the brochure on orchards was limited to men of substantial means who could spare the land and afford the investment involved in the planting of orchards. Copies of this brochure were preserved by many literate agriculturists. It was simply written and easy to understand, and had useful and practical hints on methods of planting different types of fruit-bearing trees. As village people still tend to regard most printed matter as authoritative and correct, it would perhaps have been useful to issue more publications of this type. The third pamphlet issued by the Project was a collection of development songs. It has been pointed out earlier that it was received very enthusiastically, and within a month 970 copies of the booklet were sold. Some of these songs became popular in the Project area in a short time. The reasons for their success are fairly obvious. The songs were written in simple language that stayed close to the village idiom. They used the appeal of Indian history and of mythological and national heroes. They rarely mentioned things that were outside the experience of village people. Being based on familiar and catchy tunes the songs could be remembered easily.

The Project could not use movies for propaganda purposes as much as planned, because of difficulties in getting a suitable operator and in getting the projector and the generator repaired in time after the frequent mechanical breakdowns. In conjunction with propaganda meetings, camps, and exhibitions some films were shown in the villages and at the Project headquarters. They attracted good audiences, but generally failed to hold their interest. Most people were drawn to these shows in the hope of seeing regular films with glamorous stars, spicy dialogue, and lilting love songs. Instead they found that they were being treated to old newsreels and uninteresting short educational films. Documentary records of development activities which are being carried out in other parts of the land and films showing major industrial undertakings are not without significance, but unless they are presented to the villager in an easily understood form they do not mean much to him. As people are predisposed to look for entertainment in the films, it will probably be necessary to balance more of this element with the instructional part. The films shown in this area were rather disappointing: in theme, treatment, and language they were wholly alien to the people, and therefore failed to interest them.

Sports tournaments were largely the affair of school-going children. In these there was sufficient inter-village competition. Officials tried to encourage similar healthy rivalry in respect of the work of 4-H Clubs also. Many of the cattle shows were not properly publicized and a few of them were ill-timed, but on the whole a fairly large number of people entered their cattle in them. The quite substantial and useful prizes offered to the winners were an inducement to many people to enter their cattle. Judging in almost all cases observed by us was impartial, and it was the effort of officials to give prizes to the very best cattle in the show. But this left many people disappointed. Some felt that all villages entering cattle in the show should have been rewarded in some way or the other for their co-operation: a village would not lose face if even one of its residents got a prize. In one case it was found that the leaders of the village which had secured a large number of prizes were half-apologetic, for their very success was viewed by others as a mark of selfishness.

This attitude came out more clearly in the crop competitions. To begin with, competition was not very keen. Their success in one competition did not particularly inspire the winners to make better efforts in subsequent competitions. In the second year's competition one of the winners of the first year said, 'I do not want to be selfish. Others should get the prize this year.' There is little evidence that anyone adopted new practices or took extra care of his crops in order to win a prize in these competitions. Often they were announced when the crops were half ready, and when extra attention could not have made any appreciable change in either the condition or the yield of the crop. In fact only a small fraction of the agriculturists in most villages ever knew about these competitions. Besides, entering a competition involved the payment of a small fee and allowing one's name to be entered in government papers. The average agriculturist resented this. The fee was regarded as an unnecessary taxation, and the reluctance to get their names entered in official records was due largely to the average villager's fear of getting involved in unwanted complications with the government. It is true that on the district and state level competitions very substantial prizes were offered, but relatively few people were aware of the existence of these competitions. Of the few who knew about them not even a fraction had the zest to enter them. The prize money for the village competitions was collected from the villagers themselves in the form of an entrance fee. With a view to enabling a large number of agriculturists to enter the competition, this fee had necessarily to be very small. Even then relatively few people entered the competitions and this resulted in some cases in the first prizes being as ridiculously low as Rs2/8/- (about 50 cents). Such prizes could hardly be an inducement to the competitors. Some of the more well-to-do agriculturists considered it below their dignity to accept such prizes! The Project-sponsored Baby Shows attracted a fairly large number of competitors. As practically all babies entered in these shows were given small presents the parents were quite satisfied. They furthered the development objectives of the Project by increasing the general awareness among the women of the existence of the Community Development Project and by bringing them in closer touch with the midwives and the Assistant Project Officer (Women's Welfare).

Conferences and exhibitions attracted a small but important section of the village people. To the former were invited all the 'village leaders' with whom the Project worked closely. The invitees appreciated this honour. Invitations to attend government sponsored conferences generally added to their prestige in the village community. The proceedings of the conference added generally to their understanding of Project achievements and future plans. Some of these participants expressed the problems and grievances of the village people and this in a way aided the Project officials in understanding local needs and reactions. The exhibitions drew a comparatively larger number of people, but the meetings held in conjunction with these exhibitions were dominated by the 'leaders'. Of course, the Project aimed at getting a much wider audience, and with this end in view made special efforts to get people to attend the exhibitions.

The Development Fairs were announced by colourful leaflets, and people were brought to the exhibitions by Project jeep and tractor. It is doubtful if these exhibitions were educationally a success in the sense that they taught any specific techniques, or even in that they attracted all sections of village people. But their success in attracting a politically conscious and vocal section of the people was certainly worthy of note.

The creation of a separate publicity unit, and the village meetings addressed by them have been mentioned earlier. This was indeed a commendable step. By using propaganda forms already familiar to the people it was able to attract eager and sympathetic audiences. People could grasp the message of development conveyed in songs and discourses punctuated by humorous anecdotes, village proverbs and folk tales more easily than they could from high-sounding speeches with unfamiliar themes, symbols and language. It is not suggested that the ideas communicated by this unit were *accepted*; the important thing to remember is that they were *understood.*

The efforts of the Community Development Project to fraternize with the people have been emphasized perhaps somewhat disproportionately, but with good reason. Past administrative traditions have created a wide gulf between the world of the village folk and the world of the officials. The official is a representative of the urban world, and is marked out by the fact that he is a limb of the all-powerful and paternal mechanism of the state. Under the British regime the villagers generally looked with some awe on the officials, and carried out their orders in fear of the government. In the post-independence period there has been some change in this attitude; in the upper stratum of village society there is a feeling that the government need not be feared to the same degree now as it was feared in the past. But the villagers still feel suspicion and distrust of the officials, and even some well-intentioned approaches of the latter are misunderstood by them. For the successful implementation of the rural development programmes it was felt that the walls of distrust and apprehension separating the village people from the officials must be demolished. It was with this aim in view that an effort was made to orient the officials in new techniques of mass contact and extension work. It was generally realized that century-old traditions could not be undone in a few days, but a beginning in the right direction was made.

In regard to the desirability of fraternization both sides had certain mental reservations. Many officials were not wholly convinced that the new approach would work better. Some of them frankly thought that 'strong-arm' administrative methods were more effective than the 'weaker' approach which treated people as equals. In fact among the village people also there were many who had misgivings about the gradual softening of government attitude. Some people thought that fraternization would impair the impersonal nature of administration and make an impartial and non-partisan approach to internal village and inter-village affairs difficult, if not impossible. In fraternization they saw a danger of officials getting mixed up in local factionalism and village politics. Some of these doubts were not wholly unjustified. Fraternization involved establishing friendly relations, and friendships, according to village norms, involve a series of mutual and reciprocal obligations. Hospitality must be returned in one form or the other, and one must support one's friend. Friendship with a person also means identification with his group or faction, and by implication hostility to rival groups and factions. Naturally the officials have to be very careful in their fraternization moves, for if they identify too closely with one faction their plans can only have partial success. The members of the friendly group will then support the officials not because they are convinced about the utility or efficiency of the programmes sponsored by them, but simply as their part in the obligations of friendship. On the other hand the members of the hostile group will feel it their duty to reject anything offered by officials identified with their rivals, even if they see merit in the programme.

However, the gulf between the world of the village people and of the officials is still so wide that the ideas and programmes of the latter are rarely accepted at their face value. The official gets promises of support publicly, but once he withdraws from the scene the village people dissect and analyse his statements from several angles and try to see all kinds of hidden motives in them. Their final response to a programme sponsored by an official is heavily coloured by the prevailing stereotypes regarding officials. Yet, though a feeling of distrust against the 'official world' is general, the people do distinguish between different types of officials and between individual officials, and there is a certain type which they tend to trust more. It is here that friendly moves and fraternization can succeed. The efforts of community development officials in this direction were, on the whole, very warmly received and were definitely welcome to many. Of course there were some sceptics who did not see in these efforts any evidence of real change, and a few critics who mourned the weakening of the government's authoritarian role and status.

Visits of political dignitaries and important officials, if not too frequent, were generally welcome. The hectic activity on the part of the subordinate officials that precedes such visits stimulates at least temporary interest among the people. Hospitality occupies a very high place in village culture, and visits by important people are viewed as an honour to the village. The village *élite*, especially the leaders, are enthusiastic about such visits because they enable them to establish or strengthen contacts with important figures and celebrities and to demonstrate their importance to their fellow villagers. In the atmosphere of general enthusiasm created by such visits the field agents of the Project find an opportunity to complete many projects which either did not receive any support at all or got only partial support of the village people. The official is not only interested in getting a thing done, his main interest is in getting it done in time to be able to show something concrete to the visitor. In lending support to such programmes the motivation of the village people is different. They are not always convinced about the utility or even the desirability of the programme that they now support with enthusiasm. Traditional norms of hospitality require that something important must be done to please a guest; and for an especially important guest something very special must be done. Then there is the consideration of the prestige of the village. This factor is considerably exploited by the officials. In order to uphold the dignity of the village, the residents do everything possible to impress the visitor. Within a short time compost pits are dug outside the village, soakage pits are constructed at strategic points in the village, and model sanitary repairs are made to some of the village wells. The visiting dignitary is shown these achievements with due ceremony, and in return commends the enthusiasm and efforts of the village people. When the visit is over the compost pits often remain unused, soakage pits are not kept in condition, and the hygienic significance of the repairs to the wells is little appreciated. The field officials have the consolation of having met some of the physical targets, the village people are satisfied that they have done their best to impress the visitor. To be fair to the visiting officials and leaders it should be added that most of them do not naïvely accept as the reality what they see at the surface, but often they do not have a constructive alternative to offer. Many of them probably understand the true motivation behind these 'show projects', but, in the belief that 'every little bit helps' they hope that once having done a thing people will ultimately see its utility and will learn to use it for constructive purposes.

Meetings addressed by well-known figures have become an important but somewhat obscure ritual. The meaning of this ritual is often not quite clear to a majority of the people. Some of the dominant themes and types of appeal contained in these speeches have been analysed earlier. The more abstract and literary speeches mean little to the average man. Their primary utility probably lies in linking village thinking with trends of national thought through the rural *élite*. This in itself is of great significance. However, the effectiveness of this technique in conveying the development ideology and programme to the general populace has serious limitations. The language, symbols, and appeal of these speeches are not easily grasped by the village.

Another factor influencing the effectiveness of this medium of communication is the considerably altered villagers' view of the role of 'leaders'. In the days of the national struggle for independence the leader was stereotyped as a self-sacrificing patriot who gave up personal comfort and security to court imprisonment and physical suffering in the cause of the nation. In the days of the mass struggles, the leaders were more closely associated with the people. Their transition from British jails to high offices and positions of power has brought about a fundamental change in the situation. People have not lost faith in the leaders, but they are beginning to feel that they are now different and more distant. Those who expected independence to bring about an almost magical transformation in the country are somewhat frustrated, and they no longer take the promises of the leaders at their face value.

Officials engaged in development propaganda in the field have shown better understanding of the motivations of villagers in accepting items of the government sponsored programme of change. It is true that their speeches are often the echoes of the lectures of leaders and high officials, but when they descend to the level of the village people and make the kinds of appeal that are a part of the village cultural pattern they attain their first successes in communicating ideas and programmes to the people.

The social education classes and community centres did not play as significant a part in communicating the development ideology and programme to the people as was expected by the planners. The former concentrated largely on adult literacy, and not on education for better life. They failed in achieving even this limited objective for a variety of reasons. To begin with they were not properly timed. On one occasion the start of the classes for men coincided with the start of the sowing season, and another time with the start of the harvesting season. Because of their preoccupation with agricultural activities very few people were attracted to these classes. The second cause of their failure could be attributed to the attitudes and values of the people. Although literacy and education are highly valued by them, only children are supposed to attend the classes in schools. An adult exposes himself to general amusement and mild social ridicule when he starts going to school with a slate and pencil. As a consequence of this attitude adults who registered for these classes slowly dropped out of them, and in the end only a few boys who had failed to complete the school grades were attending them. The classes for women also met with similar difficulties. Teachers in local girls' schools were generally employed to run them. Of necessity they could hold them only in their spare time, i.e. after their regular school hours. However, most women found it difficult to attend them because domestic duties required their presence at home during these hours. Cultural factors limited the utility of these classes still further. The younger daughters-in-law could not join them because the cultural norms of the community did not approve of their 'wandering about' like older women; women with two or three children, on the other hand, were not prevented by such norms from joining the classes, but they had little inclination to do so. Most of them thought that they were too old to go to school. Besides, they could neither take their children with them to the classes nor could they leave them at home.

If such classes are to succeed as a media of communication they will probably have to be organized differently. Their striking resemblance to the elementary school classes predisposes a number of people to avoid them. In respect to their organization and methods of teaching they largely follow the orthodox pattern of elementary schools, and fail to hold the interest of the adults. Recognizing the general failure of this part of their development programme the officials of the Project decided to discontinue the classes for men at the end of the first year of Project activities. The classes for women were, however, reorganized and continued.

The community centres were treated as an adjunct to the adult classes, and their activities were confined mostly to community singing of religious and devotional songs. In most cases only small groups of younger people were interested in them and no efforts were made to organize them with a wider base.

The methods of group discussion and individual contact were used by the extension agents of the Project on a limited scale. As they were confined largely to special groups, such as the village leaders and some key individuals, they will be discussed at greater length in connexion with the local agents of change.

A word may here be added about camps and conducted sight-seeing tours. Two camps were organized by the Project during the first half of its existence. The camp for 'village leaders' was organized in a great hurry. The participants were not chosen with sufficient care, nor was sufficient thought given to the planning of its activities. On the whole this camp left an impression of aimlessness. The Youth Camp was much better organized, and was attended by over 100 young people. Its activities created some stir in the village where the camp was held and also in the neighbouring villages. It left a general feeling that something was being done. The participants themselves were favourably impressed by the results of the camp and felt that personally they had gained by joining it. However, only nine participants of the first camp showed continued interest in the work by joining the follow-up camp held a few months afterwards.

The sight-seeing tours organized by the Community Development Project could not be described as successful. Adequate care was not taken in the selection of villagers to go on these trips. The trips were hurriedly planned and not too organized. In late February and March, when the financial year was about to close, there was generally a great rush to send out such parties to insure that the money budgeted for this purpose did not lapse. Naturally in such haste it was not possible to select the best people to join these groups. In the selection of the Projects to be visited there was considerable lack of foresight and planning. In one case village people from this Project area (which is agriculturally more advanced than many other parts of Uttar Pradesh) were taken out to observe agricultural extension work in another Project where the general level of agricultural development was rather low and where the Project had done very little to improve it. It is only natural that the reactions were unenthusiastic. It is very doubtful if many of those who were taken on these conducted tours returned very impressed or enthusiastic, and there is little evidence as a result of these ventures, that they communicated either enthusiasm or information to other villagers.

Besides the appeals addressed directly to people at large, the Project hoped to be able to work intimately with a smaller group of individuals who were expected to function as local agents of change. For this purpose persons occupying existing positions of leadership in the village as well as traditional leaders were to be used. The underlying assumption in this approach was that if leaders could first be converted to the ideology of change, the task of converting the rest of the community would be greatly facilitated. Implied in this assumption was the belief that people normally looked to this group for guidance and would automatically start emulating their example once they adopted the new practices. It was also hoped that by making them a link between the officials and the people some of the difficulties in communication would be appreciably reduced. Persons elected to local offices by popular vote were regarded as village leaders.

Other important and respected individuals were also included in this category. Group discussions and individual contacts were largely confined to this group. The response of this select group was on the whole enthusiastic, and in the first instance the development officials were greatly encouraged by this welcome. However, these assumptions did not take into account certain vital factors governing the villagers' ways of thinking and acting.

The first mistake was in assuming that these people were *the leaders*. In point of fact, they were leaders, but not the only leaders. They stood midway between the average, more traditional village folk, and the urban world. The village looked to them for guidance in its general relationship with the urban areas and the officials, and their help was sought in legal matters, in contacting and influencing officials, and generally in facing problems that arise out of contact between the village and the outside world. They were not necessarily looked upon as leaders in agriculture, nor were they in any sense decision makers in many vital matters concerning the individual and his family. Because of their association with the officials and the urban ways of life these leaders as a group had come to possess a special status within the community, but the average villager did not trust them without reservations. Some of the common stereotypes regarding government officials applied in a modified form to these village officials who were recognized as having a semi-government status. This group, on its part, sought to maintain its separate and special identity by differentiating itself from the average people and by closer identification with the officials. Among others included in the category of 'traditional leaders' were the important and influential people in the village. Naturally most of them were from the dominant land-owning group. In identifying power and status with leadership, an important and emerging aspect of group dynamics was ignored. While some recent state legislation has created possibilities for the emergence of new leadership, the undue emphasis in working with 'traditional leaders' was construed by some villagers as an effort on the part of the government to maintain a *status quo* in the internal power relations within village communities and indirectly as a step to support the domination of the landowning groups. Thus the policy of the government on the subject of leadership seemed contradictory and confusing.

A closer study of groups dynamics in village communities reveals several different levels of leadership, each with somewhat specialized functions. Many persons commonly described as 'leaders', as suggested earlier, gained this position because of their contact and influence with the officials and regional politicians. Some of them have adopted this role semi-professionally. Their role and functions in village life are fairly well defined and specialized. However, their influence in other spheres is almost negligible. An excellent village politician is rarely a model farmer; the latter is generally an obscure and apolitical person 'who minds his own business'. In adopting agricultural practices people are more likely to follow his example, rather than that of the local politicians.

The same can be said in reference to important and influential people. Their importance often stems from their economic position. In the class system of the village they are invariably so different from a majority of the people, that persons from the lower levels look on them with distrust. Most of them are more feared than respected, and it is not difficult to notice signs of covert antagonism against them among the lower classes. In certain situations close identification with this class becomes a hindrance to the furtherance of development objectives for the whole community. However, these groups can be useful in certain ways. In initiating action through existing agencies of local self-government their help is indispensable. They can raise subscriptions from the village for development work. They can also be depended upon to collect enough people for *shramdan.* For completion of physical targets within prescribed time limit such help appears too attractive to most development officials to be resisted, yet in many cases it defeats the long-term democratic and educational aims of the programme. A target met is an achievement, but if it leaves a feeling among the people that the government is resorting to extortion and forced labour, the loss may outweigh the gain.

Because of the internal complexity of village organization resulting from caste and class divisions and from the existence of factions, it is always somewhat unsafe to work with any one set of leaders. In a given situation it is necessary to understand the levels of leadership and the sources of decision-making. For more effective communication and more understanding acceptance of the programme it is necessary to reach the many diffused sources of decision-making. In addition to the good will of the important and influential persons and the local leader-politicians it is desirable to secure the support of various informal friendly groups and factions, as well as of persons holding key positions in caste groups and large kin groups. Co-operation of local leaders in specialities (such as agriculture and medicine) is often more helpful than the support of leader-politicians only.

It has been pointed out earlier that reliance was not to be placed exclusively on propaganda addressed to the village people either directly or indirectly through some of their established leaders; demonstration and public participation were also to be used as important media of communication. It was feared that mere oral propaganda in support of the proffered items would meet with general scepticism on the part of the people who might dismiss it simply as so much utopian talk. Demonstrations could radically and dramatically alter the situation. If people could *see* that the recommended practices were practical and profitable they were likely to adopt them more readily. Public participation was also viewed as an effective educational instrument. Through it the planners hoped to invest in the people a sense of intimate partnership and to demonstrate to them with concrete results what human muscle was capable of accomplishing.

The experience of this project suggests that both these instruments have to be handled with great care. The general consensus of opinion in the two villages where intensive investigations were carried out in connexion with this study is that demonstrations generally failed to communicate new methods of doing things and were not very successful in creating enthusiasm among the people about their results either. Indeed demonstrations by minor government officials are not new to this area. Agriculture and cane development officials had given routine demonstrations in the villages of this region for over two decades, without much conspicuous success. Some of the methods and techniques suggested by them had been adopted, often with local modifications. Intensification of agricultural extension work and a larger number of demonstrations given under the auspices of the Project have failed to improve the situation. The basic purpose of the demonstrations was not understood by a great many people. The general reaction of the people to these demonstrations can be summarized thus:

i They represent a passing fancy of the government. Like many other moves on the part of the government in the past these demonstrations will be pressed for a few days, and will gradually be abandoned.

ii The officials are paid for their work, and so they have to show something accomplished. These demonstrations are one part of their work. By agreeing to have a demonstration on one's land one obliges a government official; one does not necessarily have to learn anything or do this same thing afterwards.

The motivation of most people in agreeing to have demonstrations in their fields can be classed in three categories:

i If the government desires a thing, it is best to co-operate.

ii If one can oblige an official by agreeing to have a demonstration one should not withhold co-operation.

iii In some of the demonstrations one can get free fertilizer, an opportunity which should not be missed.

In their hurry to complete the targets the officials were only too glad to oblige important people by giving them the benefits of such demonstrations. Very few other people were approached, and when they were contacted their motivations in agreeing to have the demonstrations were rarely examined. In fact there was little hard thought about the choice of people in this respect; completing the prescribed number of demonstrations was more important than imparting techniques to people. In a great many cases the agriculturists sent their servants or children with Village Level Worker when he was giving the demonstrations, and there is little evidence to suggest that the results were either seen or discussed by the people on any appreciable scale.

Public participation in Project activities has mostly been in the form of participation in *shramdan*. These drives, often lasting a week, were organized under the direction of leader-politicians of the village. They could manage to collect a reasonable number of people for this work, but a great majority of participants had very little understanding of its purpose. There was not much overt resistance to it, but a very considerable proportion of the participants viewed it as a form of coercion and submitted to it in a spirit of obedience to government directives.

As the Project operated on a rigid schedule, and the higher authorities laid great emphasis on completion of physical targets, the officials were interested in getting things done somehow rather than in securing *understanding co-operation* of the people. It is true that the people could perceive some of the benefits of what they did under such mild or indirect government pressure, but it is difficult to see how this approach could generate in them a habit of democratic co-operative action.

Communication is a two-way process: it involves *giving* as well as *receiving* information and direction. While this fact has been recognized in defining the role of the Community Development Projects as agents of communication and change, in actual practice the Projects have tended to assume the role of the giver and the village people have mostly been at the receiving end. The assumption underlying this practice has been that the major needs and problems of the village people are well known, and that for a considerable time the Projects will have to work to provide for the recognized needs of the people. It is true that representatives of the public have been associated with the working of the projects at different levels, but so far a clear definition of the role of these bodies has not emerged. Policy making has mostly been done at the Central and State headquarters, which communicate decisions in the form of directives to the lower levels. The Project, their officers as well as representatives of the people associated with them, enter the scene to implement these policies and directives. Thus communication is mostly one-way and from top down. A close examination of the records of the various advisory bodies shows that so far there has been little effort to set up the complementary upward channel of communication. It is necessary to add here that these bodies are largely an innovation, and at the time of the present study had been in existence for only about a year. During this period very few meetings of these bodies had been held and the time involved is probably too short for their potentialities to become manifest.

5. Comment

The process of communication has been identified in one sentence as '*who* says *what* to *whom*, *how*, with *what* effect'. Between the originators of ideas, innovations, and programmes and the audience to whom they are addressed, there are significant factors of content, method, and mechanism. The ultimate outcome of the process—'what effect?'—is determined as much by certain cultural factors as by the intermediate factors of communication. In the context of societies like the one to which this study refers the factors as well as the process and results of communication are governed and influenced by the *cultural predisposition*, *cultural screens*, and *processes of cultural adaptation* in the community to which the message is addressed. An understanding of these factors is of vital significance for the successful implementation of the development programme.

There is considerable evidence to suggest that the effectiveness and acceptance of a programme of change are controlled to a very great degree by the cultural predisposition of the community towards the sponsors of change and their agents, as well as towards the media, and form and content of communication. The initial response to and the ultimate acceptance of the extension agents are both governed by this factor. The degree of effectiveness with which these extension agents can operate as opinion leaders or as agents preparing the ground for change is determined largely by the predisposition of the community in which they operate. People can grasp certain themes and symbols more easily than others, and they respond more readily to certain kinds of appeals than to others.

An innovation is rarely accepted by the community in the form in which it is presented or for the purpose it is intended by the promoters of change. It is subjected to a regular process of cultural screening at different levels, by the *élite*, the informal groups and factions, and the leaders of caste and kin groups. In passing through so many filters it often changes form and meaning. Even on the level of common villagers it is not accepted without comment and discussion. For example, construction of sanitary wells and model sanitary repairs to old wells were a part of the general programme of village sanitation and public health organized by the Project. The idea was to make provision for clean and hygienic drinking water for the people. In accepting this programme the motives of the people were different. The well-to-do people contributed towards it because they wanted to oblige the Village Level Worker and other Project officials by co-operating in a project which could be shown to visiting outsiders to impress them. The Harijans were enthusiastic about it because they wanted to enhance the prestige of their group by having something bright, new, and impressive. Construction of a well added to their sense of achievement. This is an instance of a programme accepted and set targets met, but its hygienic significance was largely lost on all sections accepting it.

An innovation may mean different things to different groups, and may be accepted at different levels for altogether different reasons. For example, in conception *shramdan* was to be a voluntary and democratic movement of village self-help in which all sections of village people contributed their labour for nation-building works. To the village *élite* it appeared simply as a programme of mobilizing labour from the village; it was voluntary only in the sense that no one was to be paid, and democratic in the sense that leader-politicians of the village were directing it. The leader-politicians found in these drives an opportunity of asserting their important position in the village. The rich and influential agriculturists also joined it. In view of their status they regarded token participation—a symbolic gesture rather than real work—as their legitimate share in it. The bulk of physical labour fell to the lot of low-income and low-status groups, i.e. sections who actually work as labourers. Under indirect pressure from officials and village leaders they did most of the work but were sorry to have lost the day's wages because of it.

Finally, these innovations are invariably adapted to the contemporary cultural norms and patterns. The revival of the *panchayats* was motivated primarily by the desire on the part of the government to create a machinery of village self-government. Ideally it was expected that this institution would work along the lines of the legendary village *panchayats* in which the democratic consensus of village people decided all issues, and village norms, caste norms and a few well-remembered precedents had the force of law. Yet the institution, democratic in conception and not foreign to village traditions, was adapted by the people as an instrument to rework the power alignments in the community. Through it the dominant families and factions attempted to stabilize their position, rival families and factions wanted to assert their claims, and the hitherto underprivileged groups sought to make a bid for gaining a position of power and influence in the community.

The Community Development Project tried to work largely with the conventional tools of democracy, and tried certain media of communication that were alien to the experience of the common village folk and had no place in their culture. Its success was most pronounced where it used the idiom, symbols, and language of the people. In the final analysis the problems of communication in rural community development are those of adapting the agents of change, the media of communication, and the form and content of communication to the culture, value system, attitudes, and world view of the community. The degree of success will depend upon the Project's ability to recognize the existing channels of communication, to anticipate the culture-directed responses of the people, and to adapt the communication programme to them.

VI

CULTURAL FACTORS IN COMMUNITY DEVELOPMENT

1. Cultural Factors in Directed Change

EXPERIMENTS IN THE FIELD of technological change and rural community development in many under-developed areas of the world have brought into sharp focus the importance of cultural factors in the acceptance or rejection of the programmes of directed change sponsored by external agencies. There has been a growing realization among rural extension experts and technical assistance workers that even some of the less involved technological or economic innovations have latent cultural and social dimensions that need careful consideration if the success of these programmes is to be assured. Detailed case studies of specific action programmes have revealed that the secondary and tertiary ramifications of given innovations are of critical significance in determining their ultimate acceptability. With this understanding planners and their staff members no longer approach an underdeveloped community with the naïve assumption that it will enthusiastically adopt superior tools and techniques when they are placed within its reach; instead, considerable emphasis is now laid on adapting modern techniques to the culture and values of the community in which the programme has to operate.

Agents of the rural development projects and of programmes of technical assistance are confronted with these factors at almost every step in their work. The acceptance of the agents of change as well as the effectiveness of the media through which they endeavour to communicate their innovations are largely governed by the cultural predispositions, attitudes, and social organization of the community in which they operate. The acceptance of the programme itself, or of its constituent parts, is determined to a considerable extent by a variety of complex cultural factors, ranging from simple habits and accepted social practices to the intricate patterns of belief, social structure, world-view, and values and attitudes.

From our study of the western U.P. Community Development Project Block in action in its different aspects, a number of points emerge that illustrate the range and effectiveness of cultural factors influencing such programmes.

2. Habits and Taste

To begin with, the habits and tastes of the people have determined the initial response of the community to a large number of innovations and programmes promoted by the Community Development Project. The improved varieties of wheat seed promoted by the Project were in the beginning not very enthusiastically received by the community because of their flat taste and also largely because of the difficulties womenfolk experienced in using flour from them to make the conventional type of unleavened bread. The superiority of the new seed in respect to its proportionately higher yield, disease- and rain-resisting qualities, and better marketability, was generally accepted, but when it came to making a choice on grounds of taste, flavour, digestibility, and general health-building qualities, the preference was unmistakably for the traditional variety. In respect to sugarcane people took to the improved varieties because they brought much higher prices from the mills as a cash crop, but the old variety was still remembered with nostalgia, for its superior taste and alleged better food value. Even when the community took to these new seeds for pressing reasons of a market economy, this acceptance was not ungrudging. A large number of minor ailments and diseases such as common colds, cough, and stomach disorders were attributed to the new products, and they were believed to be responsible for the general deterioration in the health of the people.

Considerable difficulty was experienced by the extension agents in introducing improved seed for *new purposes*. For example, the community was familiar with peas, and had been growing a degenerate local variety of it as a fodder crop, and the people, being unfamiliar with its use as food, wondered why they should spend more on buying an improved seed for a crop to be grown primarily for consumption by cattle. Also, the success of the Project in introducing new crops was hampered because the people were not sure about their utility in terms of the everyday needs of the community. Very few persons were enthusiastic about taking up vegetable growing on a reasonable scale because in their view vegetables formed a delicacy, a kind of embellishment to the diet, but were not considered a staple or a necessary part of the diet. For their novelty and prestige as an urban item of diet, some people were willing to grow vegetables on small patches of land, but, because of the commonly held views regarding the place and importance of vegetables in daily diet, the people were unwilling to extend this cultivation.

Force of habit influences the attitude toward programmes in areas other than food production also. Construction of public latrines in one of the Project villages was initially welcomed as a progressive measure in the direction of urbanization, but their use was practically abandoned after a few weeks as they were not agreeable to the habits and aesthetic sense of the people.

While there was general agreement that cow-dung was more valuable as manure than as fuel, people still continued to burn it. They did not find any other type of fuel as good for their water-pipes (hubble-bubble) or for the slow heating of milk. The use of a substitute cuts down their smoking pleasure, and slow heating of milk over a cow-dung fire is a necessary part in the traditional process of making *ghee* (clarified butter) which is regarded as one of the most essential and desirable parts of the diet.

Model sanitary repairs to wells were enthusiastically received in most Project villages, but there was a general decline in the people's enthusiasm for them after a few weeks. They liked the appearance of these wells, and could look to them with a certain sense of achievement, but it was not easy for them to adjust to the new way water had to be drawn from the reconditioned wells. For one thing, there were only two to four pulleys on each well, depending on its size, and this meant that at any one time only two to four persons could draw water from them. Others had to await their turn and many found this rather trying. Then, the high parapet wall and the rope going down the well over a pulley fixed still higher, necessitated a change in the posture as well as in the motions involved in drawing water. Most people, especially women, found this inconvenient. They claimed that the method to which they were accustomed was physically less exhausting than the one which they had to adopt in the use of the new type of well.

3. Social Practices and Tradition

When it comes down to established social practices neither appeals on scientific grounds nor logic can easily persuade the village people to give up their traditional life-ways. As a part of the rural sanitation programme the Village Level Workers got compost pits dug outside the settlements in a number of Project villages. In this they had, on the whole, understanding co-operation from the people; both for aesthetic reasons and for reasons of public health villagers thought it desirable to have pits for the deposit of manure and refuse outside the village, and co-operated willingly with the Project authorities in digging them. The local village councils passed resolutions making it obligatory for the villagers to use these pits. Depositing refuse in the village was to be punished by the council with fines. However, most of these pits remained unused. Cultural factors explain the failure on the part of the people to use them. Traditionally it is the work of women to clean the house and cattle-shed and deposit refuse and dung in one corner of the courtyard or in an open space near the house. While women of even the highest castes can do this kind of work at their homes, those belonging to the higher castes are not expected to be seen carrying loads from their houses all the way to compost pits on the outskirts of the village. Men could not do so, because *culturally* such a task is defined as 'women's work'. As very few families could afford to engage servants for this work the traditional practice was never seriously threatened and continues.

Cultural factors governing traditional work patterns determined the nature of public participation in many sectors of development activity. The government's efforts to mobilize local manpower in village reconstruction and development have received wide publicity. *Shramdan*, or 'gift of free, voluntary labour by the people', is viewed as an effective instrument for securing the people's co-operation in constructive activities. Observation and analysis of four *shramdan* drives in this Project forcefully brought to our attention how established work-patterns of a community can defeat the very essence of such movements. In the villages under the Development Project the upper caste groups traditionally assume supervisory roles, leaving the actual hard work to the poor lower caste groups. It was usual for influential men in the village to use pressure—often bordering on coercion—on the lower castes to make them undertake the hard work in all communal undertakings of the village such as repairs to roads, cleaning of wells, and construction of public buildings. The *shramdan* drives, inaugurated with great fanfare and considerable speech-making, were in practice reduced to the traditional work-patterns; the rich and influential upper caste people contributed their labour in the form of supervision, advice, and encouragement; the lower castes did all the work. As no payment was made to them for the work, the low caste labourers naturally resented it. Another related factor may also be mentioned here. While in some other parts of India women, with the exception of those from high castes, join work teams engaged in community undertakings, because of their traditional seclusion in this area, they cannot participate in such work.

Established social practices of the community appear to have affected the educational programmes of the Project materially. The value of education is recognized, and projects in this field get considerable verbal support from the people, but practical difficulties become apparent once these projects get started. The idea of an adult education class sounds excellent, but few adults want to adopt the role of a school-going child and enrol in these classes. The few who do join these classes also eventually give up because of the general amusement their position arouses. It must be remembered that we are dealing here with a population which is very sensitive concerning matters of honour and is unwilling to risk any ridicule. Classes for women meet with similar difficulties: a daughter-in-law is customarily not expected to leave the house frequently until she attains a comparatively responsible status within the family by becoming the mother of two or three children. When she is young her 'daughter-in-law' role prevents her from joining these classes, and when she has children her 'adult' role coupled with responsibilities of the household prevents her from taking advantage of them.

The ideal of ownership and management of farms by the family or close kin is so firmly established in the community that innovations seeking even slight modifications in the pattern are resisted by the people. The programme of planting community orchards sponsored by the Project was largely a failure because no one thought of it as a serious and worth-while investment. Where people yielded to pressure and agreed to plant community orchards, they thought of the venture as a gesture of compliance with the wishes of the government and not as a serious undertaking. Partly because of the impersonal nature of their ownership and also partly because of the local tradition that the owners of fruit trees, except when they take to horticulture on a commercial scale, should allow almost anyone to take some of the product, these community orchards did not receive sufficient attention from those who had planted them. The idea of co-operative ownership of tractors was received very coldly too, and no one gave any serious thought to making such a risky and uncertain investment.

4. The Area of Belief

Resistance can be expected when programmes of change touch the sensitive area of belief. The state has been actively promoting programmes to introduce better methods of cattle breeding, but without much success. The agriculturists recognize the importance of good draft cattle, and indeed invest large sums of money in buying animals of good breed. But locally they cannot do much to change the methods of cattle breeding, because of the presence in the villages of a large number of scrub bulls. The government has distributed—free or at subsidized rates—a number of pedigree bulls in the area, but they are not much help because no effective ways can be devised to dispose of the scrub bulls. Being the mount of Lord Shiva, a bull is regarded as sacred, and many of these bulls are released for religious reasons after a death or as a supplication to supernatural powers. Because of their sacred character interference with their freedom is regarded as a sin, and plans to castrate them are viewed as unthinkable by most villagers. The artificial insemination centre started by the Project appeared to be a way of countering the cultural resistance of the village people, but even this method was not without its problems. First, the villagers are not used to watching for the time when cows are ready for impregnation. Often the scrub bulls impregnate them before their condition is noticed by the owners. Then, the necessity of having to take them to a distant insemination centre interferes with other activities. Finally, some people get worried about the propriety of mechanical interference with the body of the cow, and view the denial of the satisfaction of her normal bodily cravings as a sin.

Reference has been made to the general rejection of certain new seeds on the grounds of taste; such resistance is further strengthened by the belief that older varieties have better nutritive value and greater body-building properties. Traditional practices rooted in beliefs offer obstacles to the acceptance of a wide range of programmes in the fields of rural health and hygiene, and of practices connected with maternity and child care.

The body image encouraged by the culture, views regarding essentials of good health, and theories about disease and its treatment held by the village people determine their response to modern ideas regarding sanitation and personal hygiene and the prevention and treatment of diseases. Notwithstanding compulsory vaccination, small-pox is still regarded as a 'sacred' rather than a 'secular' disease. Because they regard small-pox as the visitation of a Mother Goddess, village people give more attention to the performance of the prescribed rituals and worship than to the proper isolation and care of the patient. Certain types of ailments are attributed to supernatural causes such as the evil eye, magic, and wrath of gods and spirits. In the case of all such diseases the villagers find it hard to grasp the necessity and utility of preventive measures, and they tend to trust the traditional methods more than the modern ones.

Popular beliefs embodied in prevalent theories of disease and treatment not only determine the response of the villagers to the practitioners of modern medicine and their methods of diagnosis and treatment, but are of vital significance for the success of the programmes of preventive medicine and immunization. The common belief that medicinal treatment can commence only when the presence of a disease has definitely been established through diagnosis is largely responsible for the failure of measures in the field of preventive medicine.

Adoption of modern practices in the field of maternity and child care are also governed by some deep-seated beliefs of the people. A woman is not given any milk in the latter part of her pregnancy and for a month or so following confinement for fear that this will result in a child too big for normal delivery and will cause swelling and pus formation in the mother's fallopian tubes. For several months a new-born baby is not given any water to drink because this is believed to upset the delicate mechanism of the child's body with its 'cold' effect. The efforts of the midwives appointed by the Project had very limited success in changing the traditional practices of the community because of the strength of conventional beliefs in this area.

5. Social Structure

The interplay of factors affecting programmes of directed change in the general area of social structure is extremely complex. In this sphere it is necessary to take account of social segmentation and stratification, role differentiation in terms of age, sex, and types and levels of leadership, and vital factors of group dynamics and factionalism within the community.

The division of the society into castes, with their associated norms and expected standards of behaviour and overt and latent stresses and tensions in inter-group relations, posed a number of important problems to planners and development workers. With what particular group should they identify themselves in the village? Whose norms and standards of behaviour should they adopt? Identification with upper income and status groups, and acceptance of their norms, wins for the extension worker a certain measure of support from these influential groups. But at the same time it alienates the underprivileged groups from the programme and promoters of change. If they act in the reverse direction, the extension agents meet with coldness and even hostility from groups on the higher levels of the social hierarchy.

Where the Village Level Workers interacted mostly with the upper caste groups, the lower castes looked on them with suspicion and distrust and complained that the government was seeking to make the rich groups richer and was thereby indirectly contributing to the further economic deterioration of the lower levels. Adoption of certain improved agricultural implements such as cultivators and tractors by the upper caste agriculturists was especially criticized by the lower castes, as it reduced employment opportunities for them. These items, promoted and often subsidized by the Project, were welcomed by the upper castes because they generally reduced their dependence on the low caste groups.

Welfare measures among untouchables were adversely criticized by the upper castes as politically motivated steps for vote-getting that developed disturbing notions among the untouchables. The presence of women from the untouchable castes in the adult education classes started by the Project in an important village of the Development Block resulted in the boycott of the class by the women of the upper castes. It is generally agreed by persons working on action teams that the caste of an extension man materially affects his acceptance—both socially and as an agent of change—by the villagers. His behaviour is closely watched, and deviations from traditional norms arouse interest and comment in the society. In her enthusiasm for adoption of progressive ideas the Assistant Project Officer for Women's Welfare (an upper caste girl with university education) accepted food from untouchables. This act won for her the sympathy and support of the untouchable group, but also created a first-class sensation in the general community. The episode was widely discussed and its echoes were heard even at the district headquarters. The more traditionally-minded people started asking whether the government was out to destroy the social system of the Hindus by letting its employees set such examples.

The effects of role differentiation in terms of sex as well as kinship status and general socio-religious status have been mentioned earlier in another context. A word may here be added about age as a determinant of leadership roles. Age and experience are considered a desirable, often a necessary, attribute of positions of leadership and influence. As a consequence of this norm, measures initiated by the Project always need the blessings and support of the more tradition-bound elders. Projects initiated and run by the younger age groups are viewed as temporary developments of minor significance, and are rarely taken seriously by the community. This has to be considered in the selection of the local agents of change and the initiation of projects with long range effects.

An understanding of the levels of leadership and of the specific roles of different types of leaders is vital for development programmes. In the rural areas certain types of persons having urban contacts, especially contacts with administration and political leaders, occupy a strategic position. Yet it would be a mistake to single them out as local agents of change to the exclusion of persons on the other levels of leadership. As pointed out earlier,[1] the *élite* group and individuals occupying existing positions of power, especially in elective offices, are looked upon by the common village people as a link

[1]Chapter V.

between them and the urban world of administrators, politicians and businessmen, and consequently they come to have a somewhat specialized role in village affairs. For reasons of local prestige the *élite* group identifies itself more with the officials and with city ways than with the common village people and their traditional way of life. Because of this attitude they alienate the more traditionally minded villagers who do not accept their leadership in some spheres of life without mental reservations. For effective penetration to the grass-roots the promoters of change will have to find out the key individuals who function as decision makers on the level of organized kin groups and castes.

Village factionalism often puzzles development workers, and failure on their part to understand the group dynamics in the rural communities under their charge often leads to the ultimate failure of their desirable and technically sound projects. By narrowing down their search for 'village leaders' to function as the local agents of change and community development to the rural *élite*, the extension agents and development workers indirectly worked to restrict the appeal and benefits of their efforts to certain sections of the village population. As another outcome of this policy, in some villages of the Development Block certain sections of this favoured group developed vested interests and tended to block those aspects of community development activities which appeared to them to be helpful to their rivals and antagonists in village affairs.

6. Attitudes and Values

In the area of attitudes, values, world-view and social relations we come to grips with cultural determinants that shape the course of development projects and decide their outcome most powerfully.

In respect to attitudes, it is necessary to consider the village people's view of change. Do they consider it necessary and desirable? Then, it is useful to find out their attitude towards the promoters of change. Do the people trust them? Or do they have any misgivings about their motivations? Finally, it is necessary to determine the attitude of the people to the actual action programme and to the methods adopted for implementing it. Does the community regard the individual development projects as useful and beneficial? Do they find methods devised for their adoption by the community acceptable? As in many other parts of rural India, the villagers in this Community Development Project area tend to idealize and glorify the past, but as a concession to the necessities of the day they also admit the inevitability and desirability of change. The traditional Hindu view of time not only admits the possibility of change but also predicts its inevitability.[1] It is true that every successful stage marks a progressive decline from the high and noble standards of the idyllic past, but the dictum that values and norms of life are situational, i.e. they are determined by the context of time and geographical location, does leave enough room for acceptance of change. Apart from this deep-rooted cultural view of change the people have been sufficiently exposed to urban contacts and have known or heard enough about some of the modern amenities of life, that there has been a decided change in their level of expectation. Persistent nationalist propaganda regarding the benefits of freedom to the village people has affected the hopes and aspirations of a considerable section of the village population. The range of variation in the expectations of the different groups and levels of village population is very wide.

Indicative of this divergence are the two extremes of thought; one hoping that a free Indian Government will undo the evil influence of an alien government and will re-establish the society on its traditional foundations by recognizing and enforcing the relative statuses of different castes, and another, reflected in the thinking of the politically conscious leaders of the lower castes, that the government will take active steps to eradicate the barriers separating the high caste from the low caste and the rich from the poor. The first group interprets the Gandhian concept of *Rama-rajya* (or 'the return of the reign of Rama') to include the revival of the ancient social order in all aspects; the other group often quotes the opinions of national leaders on socio-economic matters in support of its stand. Thus, there is expectancy of change among significant sections of village people, although there is general uncertainty about its nature and outcome.

However, regarding the promoters of change and their motivations there are considerable misgivings. Indeed very few people have grasped the all-India scope and national significance of the development plans. Some people read in these plans hidden political motives. These range from the desire on the part of the Congress party to ensure success in the next elections to the secret plan of the government first to encourage more agricultural production and then to enhance taxation. To a large number of people, however, this activity is nothing more than a passing fancy of the government,

[1]According to the classical Hindu view time is divided into four *Yuga* or Ages; beginning from the ideal Age of Truth (*Sat-yuga*) human society has passed through *Treta-yuga* and *Dwapar-yuga* and has now come to the present Age of Decline or *Kali-yuga*. The cycle will start again when divine intervention, necessitated by the chaos and confusion of the later stages of this Age, will re-establish traditional values and inaugurate the cycle with *Sat-yuga* once again.

not unlike many previous shortlived drives and campaigns which were promoted by the British Government with great initial enthusiasm but which finally languished due to lack of sustained state interest in them. The common view regarding the development workers is that they work to justify their salary, not for any higher motivation. To the average villager the aim of the development workers is to satisfy and please their official superiors, and with this understanding they always co-operate with these minor officials in the execution of 'show projects' whenever visits of political dignitaries and important officials are announced.

This view is fostered by the village people's experience with government-sponsored village welfare work under the previous régime. While there has been a great deal of talk about changing the very bases of government activities, in concrete terms people have not had enough evidence of it so far to warrant a shift in their attitude. The relations between the common village people and government officials are characterized by considerable distance, reserve, and distrust. This attitude projects itself into action situations which call for joint participation by officials and the people. The people have little share in determining the development targets for their villages. As they have practically no experience in planning and executing community undertakings on a co-operative and democratic basis, it would perhaps be expecting too much to assume that they can turn out well-formulated blueprints of village development. Externally determined targets, a rigid work schedule, and insistence on visible accomplishments by the higher levels of the development staff impose severe strain on the Project officials and leave them little inclination to employ time-consuming educational and discussion methods to enable the village people to formulate their needs and take steps to meet them. Consequently on the village level the people themselves do not have a hand either in determining development projects or in executing them, nor do they have too much opportunity to learn to do so. From among the externally determined targets they choose for adoption what appears to be beneficial to them. A few more items are taken up for a variety of diverse motives or because of official pressure. And a number of others are ignored.

Values play a major role in determining the people's attitude towards programmes offered to them by the Community Development Project. Working for the prosperity, well-being, good name, and enhancement of the prestige of the family and the immediate kin group occupies a significant place in the village people's code of family ethics. Programmes contributing towards the material prosperity of the household are therefore taken up without much resistance. Several items of the agricultural extension programme have been accepted on the basis of their possible economic rewards. However, the Project has done very little to direct the expressions of family prosperity. Additional incomes earned through adoption of modern innovations and improved techniques have often been spent in putting up expensive men's quarters, in providing impressive dowries, or in buying gold and silver ornaments, rather than in productive investments.

The rural communities place a very high value on education, and for this reason projects for building schools for children get appreciable support from the villagers. But here also we find a series of conflicting values in operation. The higher castes want their children to have modern education so that they may equip themselves to face the changing conditions of the modern world and acquire modern urban skills to help their parents in maintaining their privileged status and position. But there is also the fear that lower caste children may use their education to break away from tradition and may thus bring about a disintegration of the traditional social organization. For its novelty value women's education is supported, but fears are often expressed that as a result of this education village women may take to some undesirable traits of urban women and may become misfits for traditional domestic roles. Concern for health is a dominant theme in the village people's thoughts. This predisposes them to support public health measures. But modern ideas of health and hygiene as well as modern medicine have to compete with deep-rooted traditional beliefs, and in the absence of effective public health education programmes measures in this sphere go amiss. Preserving the 'good name of the village' is another important value held by the people. Several community undertakings have been motivated by the desire to maintain or enhance the prestige of the village rather than by felt needs.

It has been suggested earlier that the widening world of the villagers has had a marked influence on raising their level of expectation and aspiration. This has contributed towards their mental preparedness for some major changes. Some recent governmental measures such as *zamindari* abolition, creation of statutory elective village *panchayats*, and the constitutional ban on public practice of untouchability have pointed towards the inevitability of change. The impact of these events on the general pattern of social relations—interpersonal as well as intergroup—has indeed been significant. The emerging aspects of group alignments and changes in power equations in the village communities have a significant bearing on the problems and prospects of rural community development.

The social analyst attempting an evaluation of the role of cultural factors in economic development in the communities like those discussed in this study is struck by a series of paradoxes. While there is an extreme dependence on the state for welfare measures, there is a general distrust of the minor government official who represents the state on the village level. Although there is much verbal idealization of traditional patterns of village life and a general suspicion and distrust of city ways, there is an unmistakable covert desire to turn to the urban people as a model for many things and to imitate their ways. Notwithstanding the acceptance of tradition as the *ideal* in preference to uncertainties of change, there is a strong expectancy of change. An understanding and critical evaluation of the inner dynamics of these apparently paradoxical attitudes, values, and motivations can help the planners and their field agents greatly in the implementation of their plans.

7. Some Ramifications of Cultural Factors

The planners and promoters of development programmes have to take account of a number of other manifestations of cultural factors. In the first place it is not enough to look for the immediate cultural consequences of an innovation in one aspect of life; its extensions into other spheres are equally important. Then, its secondary and tertiary effects also cannot be ignored. The vital cultural linkages existing between different aspects of life in peasant communities almost immediately carry the effects of an innovation to spheres other than the one in which the change was introduced. Thus, at first sight the introduction of a new kind of seed may appear to be a simple change in traditional agricultural practices, but its effects are felt in spheres of life as diverse as food habits, beliefs about health and disease, home management, and even domestic peace. Examples of the effects of the introduction of new types of seeds on food habits and health concepts have been given earlier. Home management practices are affected by these new foods when women have to put in extra labour in grinding the grain and kneading the flour, and have to be more careful in making and storing the bread. It was repeatedly pointed out to us in the field that the new type of seed could even affect domestic relations. Unless the unleavened bread made with the flour of the new wheat seed is served hot and fresh from the oven it is not only flat and tasteless, it gets 'hard like hide' and is very difficult to chew. A farmer returning home tired after a hard day's work in his fields does not find this bread very satisfying, and his dissatisfaction often expresses itself in angry outbursts addressed to his wife and children. These new seeds also involve a change in the routine to which the agriculturists are accustomed. With the old seed the threshing of one lot took about three days; the same operation for the new seed takes about five days. The cattle find the straw and chaff of the local variety of wheat more agreeable; the 'hard and dry' straw of the new variety is not as good for fodder and is believed to be less nourishing to the animals. Thus, the introduction of a new seed also requires devising new techniques of making and storing bread, introducing a new method of threshing, and finding alternative sources of fodder supply for the cattle.

It is also essential to watch the extreme selectivity and differential acceptance of the items of change offered by the development projects at different levels of the community. Closely allied to this factor is the tendency in cultures to reinterpret the proffered innovations in terms of the dominant themes and existing needs of the society. Case studies done in connexion with this research are illustrative of the selective trends in the acceptance of projects seeking to bring about modifications and changes in the society. Certain items of the development programme are accepted for reasons totally different from those which motivated the planners. The programmes of renovation of wells, paving of village lanes, and construction of soakage and compost pits have been accepted in a number of villages, but there is as yet very little understanding of their significance for the health of the community. Their acceptance has been motivated by such diverse factors as 'they look new and good', 'with them our village will look like a town', 'we must do what the government asks us to do', 'that is all that we can show the important visitors from outside', and 'other villages are doing it and so we must also do it'. Education has come to acquire a special value to the upper castes because, among other things, it is one of the factors that can enable them to maintain their traditionally higher social position. The lower castes value it because their achievements in this field promise the breaking down of some of the harsh ascriptive aspects of the traditional social organization. Organization of democratically elected village *panchayats* was expected to provide machinery for co-operative village self-government, and these bodies were also expected to reduce internal village tensions. In many instances, the village people did not grasp the purpose for which these new *panchayats* were created. Many viewed them as modern counterparts of traditional village councils, which functioned wholly as arbitrating and mediating bodies in village disputes. Far from reducing internal tensions, in the first instance they were instrumental in creating more tensions: those in existing positions of power sought to confirm them through popular vote, and those who were aspiring to rise found in the elections an outlet to make their challenge public.

In conclusion it may be said that in devising action programmes of community development, especially in their educational aspects, it is necessary to keep in mind the cultural factors that vitally influence their acceptance or rejection by the people. Many programmes are rejected not because the people are traditionally minded, conservative, or 'primitive', but because the innovations, in all their ramifications, do not fit into the total cultural setting of the community. A balanced and critical evaluation of the motivations and mechanism of change in these societies, together with the analysis of the cultural determinants of acceptance and rejection, can provide fruitful insights toward better planning and execution of development programmes.

VII

EVALUATION AND COMMENT

1. Retrospect and Prospect

THE AIM OF THIS STUDY was to examine some of the important human factors involved in externally induced and State directed programmes of economic development and culture change in a technologically under-developed society. The analyses presented here are qualitative rather than quantitative. Although the universe of this research was a single Community Development Block, and there too, attention was focused mainly on two villages, it is hoped that the problems and conclusions emerging out of the study will have, generally speaking, some validity for similar projects elsewhere in India.

So much needs to be done in village India today that any organized effort like this is bound to earn the praise of those who are interested in human welfare. In conception the Indian rural community development programme has been bold and imaginative. The planners of the programme have shown both foresight and a critical understanding of some of the problems that are involved in the process of lifting a tradition-oriented society to increasingly higher standards of living. The fact that planners at the top have not yielded to self-complacency, and have kept their minds open and receptive to new ideas, is indeed commendable. In attempting a critical appraisal of the impact of these projects, and in evaluating their successes and failures, one has to bear in mind that they represent the first massive and systematic effort in India in the development of the rural communities. The planners and their field agents have had to work against tremendous odds, and a large number of projects have had to be set up in a remarkably short time. As a matter of principle the projects were committed to a new and dynamic approach, but because of lack of experience and timely guidance and support they often reverted to traditional patterns and stereotypes. The experience of projects under the first Five Year Plan could provide correctives for future work in this direction.

Evaluation and Comment

It is now time to attempt a sharper and clearer definition of the basic aims and objectives of the rural development programme. In the absence of a clearly defined statement of these aims, the movement appears to lack a sense of social direction. It is necessary to review the social, economic and cultural goals that the programme has sought to achieve so far, and to reformulate these goals in more precise terms to guide the future development of the movement. What type of society does it visualize? In attempting to get a clearer picture of the future it will be essential to go into the question of evolving the appropriate types of relationship between the urban and the rural sections of the country's population, and also to bring into clearer perspective the patterns of integration between agriculture and industry. The problems of population growth, of increasing pressure on land, and of widening unemployment and under-employment will also have to be kept in mind. With a clearer definition of its ends, it should be easier to orient the development programme towards them.

The projects have earned the gratitude of the village people by providing them relief and services in several spheres of rural life. These ameliorative steps are worthy of praise. However, practically no attempts have so far been made to assess the long-term consequences of these measures. Development of agriculture and increase in the productivity of land are vitally related to the wider questions of market economy. A large number of agriculturists have felt that their efforts in this regard, if successful, will be followed by increased government taxation and falling prices of agricultural produce. The planners will have to anticipate such trends, and contemplate measures to preserve incentives for progressive agricultural developments. A number of other related questions also merit the attention of the planners. Even partial mechanization of agriculture and introduction of relatively simple improved implements have led to some unemployment in the villages. For example, in western Uttar Pradesh an iron cultivator is believed to do the work of four labourers, and a tractor replaces eight to ten people. Even the use of a simple mechanical device like the chaff-cutter has taken away a part of their livelihood from the Chamar community. While it is necessary to continue all possible efforts to modernize agriculture, the possibility of any undesirable consequences resulting from such efforts should also be kept in mind. With such an awareness it will be easier to anticipate problems, and to plan steps for solving them well in advance. The increasing number of village youth going to the institutions of higher learning will also pose a problem in the near future: if they are left unemployed or under-employed in the villages they will feel resentment and frustration; alternatively they will swell the ranks of the urban unemployed. The social and political consequences of such a trend will have to be watched. It has been observed that an increase in the level of education is followed by a corresponding increase in the level of aspiration. Plans must be made in advance for the proper absorption of this increasing number of educated village youth in the emerging social and economic order of the village communities. Little thought appears to have been given so far to the problems of the 'middle groups' in the village population, i.e. to the artisans and labourers, or to the lower status groups. Under-employment, sub-nutrition, disease, and illiteracy among these groups will have to be effectively attacked, if the ideal of *community development* is to be realized in practice.

As indicated earlier, considerable care and thought have been given to evolving an administrative machine that would be equal to the challenging demands of the development programme. Not only were a large number of modifications made in the traditional structure of village administration, but a series of significant practical innovations were also made. Their results might very well now be evaluated on a national scale. Careful planning based on empirical evidence could help to eliminate factors responsible for the lack of effective team work and communication within the administration, and also help towards removing some of the barriers between the people and the government. With this aim in view, a re-examination of the structure and functioning of the administrative machinery in regard to its operational suitability and its acceptability to village people may now be attempted.

A penetrating evaluation of the selection and training of development personnel is also urgently needed. It will be extremely useful at this stage to review the policy of recruitment to development posts, both high and low, and to devise ways and means of ensuring the selection of only those who have the requisite personality traits and aptitudes desirable in these positions.

Another related problem in this area that merits attention is that of evaluating the current training programmes for development workers. It will be useful to examine both the content and the methods of instruction at these centres. Besides generating idealism and spirit of social service in the trainees, these centres must aim at producing development workers who have adequate and sound training for their jobs. Unless they can convincingly demonstrate the superiority of their skill and techniques to the village people, they are not likely to gain the acceptance of their ideas and innovations from them. Dangers of unrealistic idealism and over-optimism must be guarded against, and with this end in view the prospective extension workers should be sensitized to the realities of the Indian village scene. A suitable method of orienting the trainees to the problems likely to confront them in the course of their work would be to present to them concrete case-studies of a number of specific projects, each characterized by some special problem or problems. An effort should be made to analyse the entire range of the complex human problems involved in the ultimate success or failure of a project.

Methods of programme-planning and implementation stand in need of a close scrutiny. There is no doubt that some substantial progress has been made in this field, but a lot more still remains to be done. So far much lip service has been done to the concept of planning according to *felt needs*, but most projects have followed a somewhat inflexible, standard plan. Ways should now be devised to harmonize national policies with local needs. For a number of years in the foreseeable future the government will have to maintain its leadership, but certain sectors could now be earmarked in which the people would be left free to make experiments in village development largely on their own. Their failures may entail some cost, but the educational benefit from these efforts will probably far outweigh any financial loss they involve. The strategy of programme implementation, especially the timing of projects and their introduction to certain select groups, need the closest possible attention. Until now this area has been sadly ignored. Finally, in order to achieve the objective of *community development* more balanced programmes covering the entire community in the several diverse aspects of its life will have to be evolved. Attention has so far been focused on agricultural extension and more spectacular 'public works' projects; the emphasis has been largely on visible accomplishments. Public health problems and education have been touched only superficially. Not only have some sections of the village population been left practically untouched, but very little was done for women and the younger people. Traditionally men may be considered superior to women in the Indian society, but the psychological resistance of the women can and often does effectively block the realization of many progressive aims of the development programme. Receptivity to change is, generally speaking, greater in the younger group; therefore, with an eye to the future, more time, energy, and money should be invested in work with this group.

Communication is probably the most essential but hitherto the weakest part of the programme. A more dynamic approach, using not only the language and idiom of the people but also the themes that will stir the masses, is urgently indicated. It is desirable to choose the most effective channels of communication, and to work through the existing opinion leaders and potential carriers of change. Audio-visual aids, motion pictures, and printed literature can effectively be called into service, if their production is imaginative. The utilization of these media so far has largely been ineffective, because most efforts in this field have betrayed a woeful ignorance of the rural ways of thought and action. Use of the traditional channels and agents of communication in the rural areas can be emphatically recommended for ensuring the success of the educational aspect of the plans. Little social science research in this area has been done in India so far, and the few studies that are available are more or less exploratory in nature.

Certain social and cultural factors can be barriers to progress, but often they are not insurmountable. A realistic analysis of their nature, function, and strength would provide a way to meet most of them.

The vital question of the total impact of the projects on rural India and the implications of this for the future must also be considered. How many of the innovations promoted by a development project will outlive it? Is there any evidence of psychological change in the people? Are they acquiring the habit of co-operative action? Do they show a will to undertake responsibility? Is a new leadership, capable of carrying forward the work initiated by the projects, emerging in the villages? Modest as they may appear, these projects have introduced certain ideas that will be long-lasting. The people are slow and extremely cautious in accepting innovations, but on a limited scale they too make some experiments and watch their results carefully. Some of the project sponsored innovations in the fields of agriculture and rural health, though they appear to have been rejected or very reluctantly accepted today, may finally establish themselves in about a decade from now. Signs of a psychological change, too, are evident, although they cannot be attributed in every instance or even primarily to the projects. There is an unmistakable change in the people's level of expectation, and with the gradual removal of barriers between them and the government substantial progress can be expected. However, the Project studied here appears to have done little to further even the traditional modes of co-operation in these communities. Official leadership has often been too obvious and direct, and the inclination of administration to work with established village leaders and influential men has not been conducive to the emergence of a new and effective leadership. Being subject to the political pressure of a new democracy the officials probably could not act differently. On the whole the problems of village leadership have been in a ferment due to recent constitutional and social changes. With creative imagination and concentrated effort its evolution might be channelized to more productive purposes. The situation needs to be watched carefully.

In this context it would not be out of place to emphasize the desirability of attempting a penetrating evaluation of the social consequences of the development projects in sociological terms.

This would call for a widening and re-organization of the Programme Evaluation Organization. This Organization, associated with but independent of the Planning Commission, has indeed done a commendable job by publishing a series of objective, fearless, and often highly critical annual evaluation reports on the working of the development programme. Its scope and area of operation, however, require expansion. The outlook and approach of this Organization so far have been oriented more towards the points of view of economics and public administration than of sociology, anthropology, or social relations. The inclusion of the methodology and viewpoints of these disciplines in its approach to evaluation would undoubtedly enhance the utility of the work of this Organization. Universities and independent research organizations could also increasingly share responsibilities in this sphere.

With a view to expanding the rural community development movement and making it more effective, it would be desirable to make several controlled experiments in the various branches of development activity. These 'pilot' or 'experimental' projects should be designed with foresight and imagination, and the response of the village people to each stage of their implementation should be carefully observed and analysed. A series of such projects in carefully selected areas could provide practical insights into the feasibility of their wider application, and will ensure the avoidance of pitfalls involved in utopian projects prepared by academicians and experts in their offices.

2. Applied Social Science in Community Development

While planners and administrators must share the primary responsibility for the formulation and implementation of the rural development projects, the social scientist can give them invaluable help in the areas of social organization, human relations, culture, and values touched by the plans. In this context the role of the social scientist must essentially be viewed as that of an analyst and not that of a therapist, but the insights and leads provided by applied social science research can nevertheless contribute substantially towards developing effective programmes and also towards their successful implementation. There are obvious dangers in over-selling applied social science and anthropology, and in making high sounding but impossible claims for them as 'sciences of human engineering'. The social scientist will do well to guard against this in the best interests of his profession. However, as independent subsidiaries to planners and administrators these disciplines can indeed be very useful.

In the interest of informed planning and administration we need a series of concrete base-line studies of village communities in the different parts of the country. Studies both of a general and theoretical nature as well as those with a special focus on the day-to-day needs of the development programme should be planned. It has been observed that short-term problem-oriented researches often miss some of the vital cultural linkages and the uniformities and regularities in social processes that emerge so clearly in extended research not primarily tuned to the needs of administration. In their zest to get quick results, administrators sometimes show great impatience for the way the social scientists go about their business. The conscientious social scientist is naturally reluctant even to offer tentative hypotheses without properly testing their validity, and for developing meaningful concepts and theoretical formulations he needs a considerably longer time. The administrator, who is under pressure to implement his programme within a given period, tends to look upon this time-consuming research as a luxury. When the social scientist changes his role and offers to 'advise' the administrator on matters connected with planning, especially on problems with which he has no first-hand research acquaintance, he can at best offer some common-sense propositions. Because of his scientific sophistication many of these propositions are not without insights, but they often fail to satisfy the perceptive administrator. With his practical experience and infinitely superior training in the techniques of public administration, the administrator himself can hit upon some of these ideas. He starts doubting the utility of social science itself, when he mistakenly looks upon the opinions and personal views of the social scientist as valid scientific formulations. In his zeal to be helpful the social scientist thus unwittingly causes damage to his discipline by impairing the faith of the administrator in its utility. To avoid such confusion and misunderstanding, the aims, role and function of the social scientist must be defined in the clearest possible terms. Efforts should be made to sensitize the administrator to the nature and needs of theoretically-oriented long-term social research. In developing programmes of rural research the requirements both of theory and administration should be kept in mind. As meaningful contributions to development planning can be made only through long-term research with a theoretical bias, it should not be difficult to secure official sympathy and support for it. The social scientist, on the other hand, should also be willing to undertake research on specific problems that baffle the administrator in his day-to-day routine.

Special efforts should be made to develop methodological tools to accomplish fruitful results from such research. It would be most desirable to test the conclusions of such short-term researches within the wider framework of some of the more extended research projects. In planning the base-line studies of Indian village communities, suggested earlier, we shall do well to keep some of these considerations in mind.

The sociological studies recommended above should present integrated analyses of culture and social organization in representative village communities in the different linguistic and cultural regions of India. Besides portraying the social organization, attitudes, and values of the people, they should lay special emphasis on trends and motivations in change. An attempt should be made to discover the groups that function as agents and carriers of change in the village communities. The problem of selectivity in the acceptance of ideas and innovations offered by the outside world also deserve a fuller investigation. Another area of research, having great theoretical and practical possibilities, is that of leadership and decision-making in the village communities. In this connexion problems of group dynamics and factionalism will also have to be critically analysed. Traditional forms of co-operative activities in village India also merit a serious study.

The crucial significance of communication in a programme of rural community development has been brought out earlier in this study. This field holds out challenging possibilities of social science research. It is necessary to discover the existing channels of communication in rural India, and to assess the role and function of different categories of agents of communication. It is equally essential to find out what types of themes and appeals work effectively in these communities. The response of the different segments of village population to different modes of communication needs to be evaluated carefully. The role of school education in the communication and diffusion of modern ideas also deserves to be assessed. Empirical research in this field is very necessary for developing an adequate and effective communication programme.

Another field in which the social scientist could make a useful contribution to the rural community development movement in India is that of preparing empirical case-studies of specific projects and field situations. The importance of such studies as an instructional aid in the training programmes of village welfare workers has been emphasized time and again in this study. A good case-study, which analyses the complex attitudes, beliefs and values, and assesses clearly the role of each in a specific field situation, is one of the most satisfactory methods of introducing the prospective extension agents to the problems and complexities of his task. The hypotheses emerging from these studies could be an invaluable aid to those engaged in evaluating the programme. They could be further tested in the wider and more general evaluation studies for making meaningful formulations and generalizations.

Evaluation techniques so far employed to assess the results of the development projects could be re-examined with profit at this stage. The basic conceptual framework of evaluation needs some modification, to enable sociological and anthropological points of view to make their contribution to this field. There is also considerable scope for refining the methodological tools employed for this task. The social scientist could undertake to develop short-term and long-range evaluation techniques, both of the qualitative and quantitative type. The task of evaluation has become increasingly important now because of the increasing momentum of the development projects. Attempts will now have to be made not only to assess their outcome, but also to analyse the social, psychological and economic trends initiated by them and their implications for the future.

The participation of the social scientist in training programmes for development workers could also be encouraged. He can make a distinct contribution to the success of these programmes by offering his concrete, practical insights into the village situation and thus correct the somewhat unbalanced view of the village scene held generally by the administrator.

Finally, another important area for fruitful collaboration between planners and social scientists is that of planning, analysis, and evaluation of 'Pilot Projects' to be undertaken on an experimental basis. A carefully designed pre-project survey by the social scientist should precede the formulation and initiation of these Pilot Projects. The range of problems involved in the proposed undertaking will be brought out by these surveys. In the light of this information the details of the research-cum-action programmes could be settled, and a strategy of initiation and implementation of the project could be chalked out. The social scientist should study the response of the people through the different stages of the implementation of the project, beginning from the initiation of an idea to the intensification of its implementation. A post-project survey would also be invaluable. The data gathered in these investigations, when analysed, would give to the planners a clearer picture of the problems and possibilities of the project. It would show the areas of resistance and co-operation, and bring into sharp focus the social and cultural determinants that help or hinder the programme. In the light of this evidence it would be easier to determine how tradition, attitudes and values, and factors of social organization and group dynamics affect the programme. This naturally would lead to more realistic planning and effective implementation of the project on the wider national level. Such projects are urgently indicated in the fields of rural health, especially environmental hygiene, housing, social education, and youth welfare. Projects involving mobilization of the people for co-operative group activity could also be tried experimentally first, before launching them on a national scale, to avoid waste, failure and frustration.

3. Final Comment

The Indian community development programme is an impressive and pioneering venture. Its results may influence the developments not only in Asia but in many other technologically under-developed areas of the world as well. In the long run its success or failure may vitally affect the course of political and social evolution not only in India, but in many regions of Asia, and may even have far-reaching impact on the world situation. A beginning has been made, but so far it has not done much more than touch the surface of the complex and difficult problems of the Indian masses. There are some signs that the great masses of rural India are awakening, but their first steps towards progress have been faltering and hesitating. The awakening must be followed by determined efforts to channel the vast manpower and human resources of the country into creative and productive pursuits. The task is vast and challenging and will not admit any self-complacency or much delay. The world-wide acclaim that has greeted the Indian community development programme should not blind the planners to the many pitfalls that lie ahead. The first projects must be regarded essentially as experimental in nature. Through critical self-evaluation and innovation, efforts should be made to make them more effective.

Appendix I

THE VILLAGE LEVEL WORKER

AN EMERGING ROLE IN INDIAN VILLAGE LIFE

I

THE VILLAGE LEVEL WORKER represents a new type of public servant in the administrative organization of India. Without question he is part of the vast body of government officials who run the affairs of the state, but in his case a special effort has been made to train him in ideals and methods of work which are remarkably different from those of the traditional bureaucracy. As a multipurpose rural social worker he is given special training and orientation courses so that his general approach and methods of work in the field may be different from and superior to those of the other government officials who have operated without much success on the village level in the past. The VLW is expected to function in the village not as a minor government official, but as a friend and well-wisher, and to a certain extent as a leader, of the village people. He is expected not only to promote ready-made plans and programmes but also to help constructively in formulating them. He is expected to study the *felt needs* of the people and to strive to work for their satisfaction. More than this he should endeavour to create progressive needs in them.

In conception, his role is that of a generalist, but he cannot function effectively without adequate specialization in several branches of development activities that he sponsors and guides in the villages under his charge. He has to take the initiative in several matters, and has yet to keep himself sufficiently in the background so that he may not even inadvertently obstruct the emergence of a new leadership in the village. In fact, he is expected to work in such a way that his own services may eventually become unnecessary, and in such a manner that habits of group and co-operative action will take such firm roots in village life that development activities may become self-sustaining and self-supporting. The task is indeed challenging and demands special aptitudes and personality traits. The VLW is a new and emerging role in Indian village life. Although it has gradually defined itself in limited spheres, in part it still largely remains vague. The VLW himself is not very clear about his exact position, role, functions, and responsibilities. Notwithstanding their general training in extension methods and practices the VLW's superior officers and co-workers on the village level do not possess a clear conception of his role. Indeed, the emphasis in different VLW training centres is on different things, and as a result of this trainees come out of these centres with different views of their role. The village people also have not been able to make up their minds about this new type of government functionary. To some extent they distrust him as they distrust all minor government officials, but they are not totally unaware of his somewhat unorthodox methods of approach and work, and do not lack in appreciation when they get help and advice from him. As the key figure of development effort in Indian village life the VLW deserves a close and careful study. In this study an effort will be made to examine and understand this role with particular reference to one Community Development Project Block in one of the western districts of the State of Uttar Pradesh.

It has been mentioned earlier that this Community Development Project Block was formally inaugurated in October 1953, although preparatory work in regard to it had started a little earlier. Out of a sanctioned strength of twenty multi-purpose VLWs with training in extension methods, the Project started with only seven. Gradually, as trained people became available they were appointed to this project. At the close of the first year of project activities there were eighteen such VLWs on the staff. About this time, with a view to reducing the work load of the VLWs, the Panchayat Secretaries who had undergone extension training courses of shorter duration were taken under partial CDP control, and, in addition to their own departmental work, were assigned to multi-purpose extension work in a few villages. The Cane Supervisors too were allotted some duties of this kind. This study, however, is concerned only with regular multi-purpose VLWs; the other development officials also functioning in this capacity have been touched only in passing.

With a view to understanding the VLW's problems and difficulties and evaluating his emerging role, he was approached and studied from several angles. An effort was made to understand and analyse the VLW's own understanding of his role through participant observation and through interviews in which a loosely structured schedule-cum-interview guide was used. A record of the daily activities of two VLWs was kept in two project villages for a number of days. In order to understand their views on the subject the Project officers and the village people were interviewed both formally and informally. Ranking of project VLWs on the basis of specified criteria of success and specified aptitudes by the Project officers adds considerably to our comprehension of their view of the VLW's role, problems, and difficulties.

To begin with, we shall examine the general background of the VLWs of this Project, and will follow this by an examination of their ideas of the basic aims, methods and programmes of planning and development, their views on the relative success or failure of the different parts of their multi-purpose training, their opinions regarding intra-project and inter-departmental official relations, their criteria for the success of a VLW and the self-evaluation of their own work. The basis for the observations that follow has been provided by the response of the VLWs to different questions in the key schedule administered to them in long, private interviews.

II

Out of seventeen[1] multi-purpose VLWs working in the Project seven are in age group 31–35, six are in group 20–25, two are in group 36–40, and there is one each in group 26–30, and 41–45. By caste six of them are Brahmins, five are Jats, three are Rajputs and one each are from Kayasth, Siani, and Kurmi castes. Educationally they represent different grades: two have passed the Intermediate examination, seven have graduated from High School, one has studied up to High School, six have passed the Diploma examination in agriculture, and one has passed the secondary vernacular examination. Six VLWs have additional qualifications, four having passed some vernacular examinations and two having undergone co-operative training. All but one are married. Six live with their families in their respective headquarters, ten have to live away from them for one reason or the other. None of them is divorced or separated from his wife and one is a widower. One important reason why so many cannot have their families with them is that living arrangements for them are not satisfactory. The government has not provided them with quarters, and it is not easy to rent houses in the villages. Consequently they often have to go on leave to see their families and relatives because of family affairs and emergencies, and this involves interruption of CDP work on the one hand and considerable expense to the VLW on the other.

Out of the seventeen VLWs in the Project three are direct recruits, the rest were serving in some development department of the State government at the time of their recruitment to their present job.

[1]At the time of this research one of the eighteen VLWs was transferred to another Project, leaving seventeen subjects for this study.

Before coming to their present positions six of them were in the Co-operative Department, four in the Panchayat Raj Department, two in the Agriculture Department, and one each in Prantiya Raksha Dal,[1] and the Civil Supplies Department. All have undergone six months of multi-purpose extension training. Eight of them were trained in an institution of western U.P., run according to the teachings of Mahatma Gandhi, where the accent is on mass contact and constructive work, five in an agricultural school of western U.P. where the emphasis is more on agricultural extension, one in an Etawah training centre with a comparatively balanced training programme, and one in another Gandhian institution of eastern U.P. Nine of them had volunteered for the VLW job, while eight were nominated and sent for training by their parent departments.

The motives which actuated them to accept this job were diverse. Three candidly said that they needed some employment and applied in response to advertisements for the post of VLW, four accepted it because of the possibility of an immediate raise in salary. Others had different reasons, ranging from a desire to work for the uplift of the nation to an eagerness to contribute to India's agricultural prosperity. In leaving their parent departments most of the departmental VLWs were conscious of the fact that they were going to be a part of an important national experiment. Of the fourteen departmental selections, four held positions carrying salaries in the range of Rs50–75, five in Rs76–100, one in Rs100–25, three in Rs126–50, five in Rs151–75. In their new positions ten get salaries ranging from Rs100–10, five from Rs111–20, one from Rs121–30, and one from Rs141–50. Thus among those who were in government service before, ten received an increase in their salaries. In five cases the rise is slight and in the other five it is appreciable. In four cases people had to accept a slight loss in transferring to their present positions. In one case this loss is considerable. Where there has been a reduction in salaries the individuals have presented their case for readjustment of salary, and have been waiting a long time to learn the outcome of their representations.

All the seventeen VLWs were born and brought up in villages, but three of them have spent a considerable part of their lives in towns and cities. Four of them are from the eastern part of U.P., that is, from a rural background somewhat different from the one in which they are working at present. The rest are from western districts, four being from the district in which the project itself is located. With the exception of those from the eastern districts they speak the same dialect as the people of the project area. There is general agreement

[1]A government sponsored voluntary organization of village people for military training.

among them that the caste of a VLW, in actual practice, does influence his work materially. Some characteristic responses from them are: 'One is more successful in a village of one's own caste.' 'Thakurs respect me because I am a Brahmin.' 'Higher castes are listened to by all, while an untouchable may be able to influence only the untouchables.' 'An untouchable could not have functioned effectively in a Rajput village.'

The VLWs have a fairly clear idea of the basic aims and main objectives of the Community Development Programme. In verbalizing these aims, nine said they were 'to raise the standard of living in the village', five emphasized 'inculcating a spirit of unity and co-operation', three mentioned 'creating social equality and new values', and two laid stress on 'welfare and development of the agriculturist'. Among other objectives mentioned by them are: 'improving the moral standard of the country', 'providing jobs for the unemployed', and 'co-ordinating development activity on the village level'.

Regarding the questions of what the functions of a VLW should ideally be and what they actually are, they were less precise and definite. In response to the first, eleven pointed out that multi-purpose development activity should be their main work. Some elaborated their answers further to say that their job was to understand local *felt needs* and to get targets fixed on their basis (5), developing local initiative (2), helping the villagers (2), and changing the views of the village people (1). In regard to their actual duties they also said that they were multi-purpose extension agents and were doing many-sided development work in the villages. But at least eleven added with some bitterness that in doing so they had to carry out the orders and wishes of their officers and had to achieve targets fixed by those at the top. Two said that flattering their superiors and going out of their way to please officers had become one of their most important duties.

Their view of the VLW's role is clear. Fifteen of them said that they thought of themselves as friends of the village people offering advice to them when it was needed, and three thought that they were leaders and innovators in the village. Six of them added that notwithstanding their own view of the role they could not forget the fact that they were minor government officials who had to carry out the orders of their superior officers. In response to the question as to what the job of a VLW actually is, fourteen said that it was to achieve targets fixed at the top, one said that his job was to discover felt needs of the people and on their basis to help in the determination of CDP targets, and still another said that his job was to convey the demands of the village people to higher government officials. One thought that his job was both to discover felt needs with a view to fixing targets, and to achieve targets fixed by the higher project officials.

With regard to their general approach, fourteen thought that they were in the village to help the people to help themselves, while three phrased it in terms of helping the village people. Two out of the three who said that they were in the village to help the people were of the opinion that ultimately their job should be to help the people to help themselves.

The Village Level Workers appear to have a clear conception of what the villagers generally think of their role and what they expect them to do. Eight of them thought that village people expected help in village development work from the VLWs, three said that they were generally regarded as well-wishers and helpers of the people, two said that the people expected help from them in getting money (government loans and subsidies), and two said that they were thought of as spokesmen of the villagers before higher officials. Of the remaining two, one said that the villagers did not clearly understand what the VLW's functions were and consequently did not expect anything definite from him, while another said that villagers had fantastic expectations and wanted him to produce miracles in a short time.

In regard to their view of the expectations of higher CDP officials fourteen said that above all officials expected them to achieve the targets which they fix from time to time. Six thought that officers expected them to work hard for village development, three thought that they were expected to obey orders, and one thought that the officers expected them to popularize development work.

Almost all the VLWs claimed to have discovered a number of felt needs in the villages under their charge. The list of these felt needs is long and varied and includes the need for organizing sanitation drives, provision for more irrigation facilities, paving of village lanes, construction of school buildings, supplying of improved agricultural implements, seeds and fertilizers, consolidation of land holdings, organizing co-operative societies for promoting rural industries, making provision for grazing facilities and cattle care, making model sanitary repairs to wells, construction of roads, finding work for the unemployed, and appointing trained midwives.

On the question of their contribution to the establishment of CDP targets fifteen said that they did not contribute to it at all, one said that his contribution was meagre, while only one said that the suggestions of the VLWs were generally accepted.

All the VLWs realize that they are agents of change in the communities in which they are working. According to them the following are some of the important changes introduced by them (the figures in brackets indicate the number of VLWs who claim to have introduced them): introducing improved seeds (11), giving demonstrations of modern agricultural practices (10), introducing green manuring (8), popularizing chemical fertilizers (7), introducing the dibbler (7), organizing village sanitation drives (5), paving village lanes (5), popularizing vegetable growing (4), introducing new agricultural implements (4), constructing school buildings (3), introducing the practice of interculture (3), introducing the Japanese method of paddy cultivation (3), organizing adult education classes (2), digging compost pits (2), popularizing secondary vaccination (2), starting co-operative societies (2), organizing *shramdan* drives (2), constructing *panchayat* offices (2), planting orchards (2), digging model wells (2), organizing a community centre (1), organizing a maternity centre (1), starting a youth organization (1), organizing a centre for leather curing (1), making drinking water available for the untouchables (1), introducing inoculation of cattle (1), starting a nursery (1), organizing community singing of religious songs (1).

The VLWs have tried to evaluate the success and acceptance of the different items of development programmes sponsored by them. A good response from people was reported in respect to the following items: agricultural demonstrations (6), improved seeds (5), green manuring (5), village sanitation drives (3), paving of village lanes (3), introduction of chemical fertilizers (3), use of the dibbler and new agricultural implements (3), vegetable growing (2), construction of school buildings (2), maternity centre (1), games and sports (1), compost pits (1), co-operative societies (1), leather curing industry (1), *shramdan* (1), construction of *panchayat ghar* (1), planting orchards (1). In their view, the people's response was not enthusiastic in respect to the following items in their respective areas: Japanese method of paddy cultivation (2), vegetable growing (1), community centre (1), adult literacy class (1), paving of lanes (1), model sanitary repairs to wells (1), and nursery (1). About the following items it was reported that the village people were neither too enthusiastic nor completely cold: improved seeds (3), dibbling for seed multiplication and practice of interculture (2), vegetable growing (1), green manuring (1), games and sports (1), agricultural demonstrations (1), chemical fertilizers (1), orchards (1), Japanese method of paddy cultivation (1), and new agricultural implements (1).

Most of the VLWs reported that they did not devise any specific programmes for the non-agricultural people. These people, however, benefited from general community activities such as sanitary drives, adult education classes, and youth welfare organizations. In one centre a co-operative society of the Jatia Chamars has been organized for curing and tanning leather along modern lines. Another VLW reported some effort on his part to start a co-operative society of local weavers. The general consensus of opinion was that because of the high priority given to agricultural extension and to some other items of the development programme they did not have the time, incentive, or encouragement to devise and stimulate special programmes for the non-agricultural people. Some VLWs reported that they had contacted people with a view to persuading them to join the cottage industries and handicraft classes that are being planned and will be started at the Project headquarters under the auspices of the CDP.

Regarding the success or failure of their multi-purpose VLW training, fifteen said that they had benefited from it, while two thought that they had not. The latter were inclined to feel that there was such a wide gap between the theory they had been taught in the training centre and the realities they were experiencing in the field that their training was practically useless. In answering the question as to how they had benefited from this training some said that they 'learned new practices and techniques', while others said that it 'influenced my personality and way of thinking'. The following reported gains may be mentioned especially: widening of general knowledge (6), learning effective techniques of mass contact (4), training in extension methods (5), and developing idealism, obtaining training in improved agricultural techniques, learning dignity of labour, and obtaining training in animal husbandry and cattle-care (1 each). In regard to the relative success or failure in the presentation of different items in the training programme the following were considered particularly successful: agricultural extension methods (11), social education (6), co-operative organization (5), techniques of mass contact (4), horticulture (3), and practical work and extension methods (4). Among items in the training programmes which were regarded by some not to have been effectively and successfully taught were the following: *panchayat* organization (4), co-operative organization (3), social education (2), horticulture (1), animal husbandry (3), and handicrafts and cottage industries (2). One complained that there was no practical emphasis in the training, and another remarked that subjects other than agricultural extension were not given adequate attention.

Notwithstanding the weaknesses and drawbacks of the training programme to which they called attention, fourteen VLWs thought that it changed their outlook towards life and national affairs, and only three held a contrary view. However, in view of their practical experience most of them feel that some aspects of their training programme were unrealistic. Two complaints heard most frequently from them are about the treatment which they receive from higher CDP officials, and about the planning from top down which characterizes much of the development activity in the project. The training centres emphasized that methods of work in CDP would not follow traditional bureaucratic lines and that the relationship between VLWs and higher project officials would not be a superior-subordinate relationship. Yet their field experience has showed the VLWs that the administrative set-up of CDP is not radically different from that of other government departments, and that the APO, and DyPEO, rather than helping and guiding them were often inspecting their work. Another unrealistic aspect of their training, they think, was that it laid great emphasis on grass roots planning. Time and again in the course of their training they were told that plans will grow up from village people, whereas in reality they had the frustrating experience of finding that the plans invariably came from the top and had to be carried down by them to the village people. Other complaints voiced by the VLWs were that the timely support, supplies, and co-ordinated effort promised to them in the course of their training were seldom available to them in the field.

When asked to indicate the spheres of work in which they felt that they were well qualified and adequately trained, two said that they had the necessary equipment for all aspects of CDP work, others felt that they were well qualified in some fields and somewhat inadequately equipped in others. Agricultural extension work leads the list of subjects in which VLWs feel competent and well trained (11). The setting up of co-operatives is second on the list, six VLWs regarding themselves well versed in this branch. Other items on the list are: mass contact (3), social education (2), *panchayat* organization (3), horticulture (2), and public health and sanitation (1). In enumerating the areas of CDP work in which they did not feel confident about the adequacy of their training, nine expressed diffidence over practical work in the field of animal husbandry, especially in performing castration. Most of them felt that their training in this respect, consisting in many cases of only one demonstration of castration to a large group of trainees, was insufficient and their attempts to do such work could even be dangerous. Other items in this list are: social education (2), *panchayat* and co-operative organization (4 each), public health and sanitation (2), horticulture (1), cottage industries (1), and accounting and maintenance of records (1).

The VLWs appear to have definite ideas on the subject of the group or groups of people in the village through whom they can work most successfully. Thirteen showed an unmistakable preference for 'successful cultivators with no factional affiliations'. Two said that they had to work through 'men with official connexions and political influence' because they considered it a good policy to keep them pleased, but six regarded this group as a nuisance. Five VLWs said that they had to consult 'important village leaders'and 'leaders of factions' because their co-operation is necessary for the success of development measures. Two said that they avoided such people as much as possible, one found them unhelpful, and two thought that they were helpful. Fourteen VLWs were definite in their opinion that successful cultivators of the 'middle group', those who were neither very rich nor very poor, were most helpful to them in their development work. Others listed the following as helpful: Harijans (1), very rich and very poor people (1), economically poor agriculturists (1), educated young men and school masters (1), and influential people (2). The general consensus of opinion appeared to be that since the agricultural extension programme was the most important single item on the project schedule it was best to work mostly with the middle group of agriculturists. Among those who obstructed development work on the village level 'leaders and men with official contacts' were regarded as the worst by eleven VLWs. Other obstructionists mentioned by them are: conservative elements in the population (3), petty officials (1), and educated people (1).

When they were asked whether they thought that force should be used under certain conditions to get the CDP programme accepted, nine answered in the affirmative and eight in the negative. Two of those who supported some use of force doubted if its results could be long-lasting. One who rejected the use of force by the VLWs said that some pressure could be useful for land consolidation and village sanitation if the State made necessary enactments. Nearly all who supported use of force wanted it to be limited and as far as possible legal.

Eight VLWs said that village people had started coming to them regularly for advice, six said that people came occasionally to them but that the VLW himself had to go to them mostly, three said that they had to go to the villagers only for explaining new things but for their normal requirements the people themselves came to them, and one said that people were not approaching him for any help.

Nine VLWs said agriculturists were the ones who most frequently came to consult them, and six mentioned poor people in this connexion. Manual workers, educated people, and Harijans were among those mentioned by others as appearing quite often with requests. Once again it was pointed out that persons belonging to the same caste as the VLW tended to cluster around him in the village, and generally gave him their unqualified support.

In respect of their official relations thirteen VLWs said that their officers—APOs and DyPEOs—treated them like 'subordinate officials', three said that they were treated like 'younger brothers', and one said that they were treated like a 'combination of younger brother and subordinate official—something between the two'. Regarding their general relations with other village level development staff sixteen said that their relations were good, only one regarded them as unsatisfactory. However, the same could not be said about co-operation. Only five found the other village level officials co-operative, twelve complained of lack of co-operation. The VLWs, however, could not enumerate the points on which there was lack of co-operation between them and the other village level development staff. Much of this lack of co-operation is attributed by them to the narrow departmental outlook of the other officials, who are jealous of the VLWs because of their higher emoluments and who see in them a challenge to their established position of superiority in the village. Inactivity, red tape, and lack of effort at co-ordination from the top were mentioned as other factors responsible for lack of co-operation from other officials. The Patwaris from the Revenue Department and Cane Union officials were specifically mentioned as being unco-operative.

The frequency of visits by higher CDP officials such as APOs and the DyPEO differs from centre to centre. Some centres are visited quite often while others are left relatively untouched. The key centres are, of course, visited more than other villages and APOs have to go to different villages more often than the DyPEO. Regarding visits by APOs, one VLW said that they came nearly once a week, two said that they came 'frequently', three said that they came once a fortnight, nine said that they came once a month and one said that they came once in two or three months. Regarding the DyPEO the responses were as follows: once in fifteen days (1), frequently (2), once a month (3), once in two to three months (2), and rarely (9). Analysis of orders, instructions, suggestions, and guidance given by these officers to VLWs during three visits preceding our interviews shows that these tours are more for routine inspection and for on-the-spot inquiry than for actual field guidance. Four VLWs reported having received some practical suggestions from these officers in their tours, and only three said that they were helped by them in planning field demonstrations.

On the subject of freedom of expression in staff meetings eleven said that they were permitted practically no freedom, while six claimed that they could express themselves in these meetings without any check or hindrance. Many of those who said that they had reasonable freedom of speech appeared to be doubtful about its effectiveness. Twelve said that they could speak freely in minor advisory committees; five said they could not.

With only one exception all the VLWs said that they could not contribute effectively to the formulation of CDP targets. Some pointed out that they were discouraged from doing this when they first tried to do so and have since learned to accept targets as given by the higher officers. There were practically no spheres in which they could act on their own initiative, for they needed permission, sanctions, or orders for doing nearly everything. Only one VLW was satisfied with the measure of support and co-operation given from project headquarters, three thought that the attitude of higher officials was 'generally helpful', and thirteen complained of absence of adequate and timely support. Several concrete instances were given in making this last point. In many cases VLWs promised certain things to villagers on the basis of assurances from higher officers, but were eventually let down by the officers who went back on their assurances. Frequent delays, supplies of poor seeds (to be distributed as improved types) and charging of prices higher than prevailing market prices for seed and fertilizers were some factors which hurt the rapport of VLWs in the villages. Officials did nothing to improve matters when these deficiencies and the consequent difficulties were pointed out to them. Ten VLWs thought that they could work more efficiently if they had powers to incur limited expenditure on approved projects within their respective fields. Some expressed the view that they should become fully multi-purpose and should have the powers and functions of Panchayat Secretaries and Cane Supervisors also. Two said that they did not need any additional powers, two did not understand how VLWs could be given more authority, and one said that a VLW was a servant of the people and as such did not need any 'authority'.

On the subject of the VLW's work load fourteen thought that they were overworked; three were of opinion that their work load was reasonable. Thirteen could not say if any part of their work was unnecessary, two regarded *panchayat* work as unnecessary, and two opined that frequent census work and surveys which they were called upon to do involved a waste of their time. One suggested that there should be fewer villages and a considerably smaller population under a VLW's charge. It was pointed out that sometimes they had to do menial work such as running errands for higher officials. Their multifarious activities kept them so occupied that they did not even have time to read newspapers and books. Twelve of them thought that they had to do too much routine work; five, on the contrary, regarded the amount of routine work as normal and not unusually heavy. Of the twelve who complained about the large amount of routine work, four mentioned *panchayat* work and two mentioned census work in this connexion. It was pointed out that even printed forms were not supplied to them in sufficient quantity, and on occasions they had to buy their own paper and spend a great deal of time drawing up the additional forms required. When asked to make suggestions regarding the sharing of their work load with other village officials, eight had no suggestions to offer, six suggested that Patwaris should do the survey and census work which is at present being done by the VLWs, two suggested that Patwaris should help them in keeping records, and that Panchayat Secretaries should be called upon to share their development work. Almost all approved the multi-purpose concept of VLW, and rather than give up a part of their work to others wanted their field of operation to be limited to smaller population units in the interest of effective and efficient functioning.

When asked to indicate *their* test of a 'successful VLW', they mentioned a variety of personality traits, characteristics and achievement tests. Ten thought 'selfless dedication to service and hard work' as well as 'ability to co-ordinate social work' to be the ultimate test of a successful VLW. Other responses concerned character, good behaviour and ability to get along with villagers (4), identifying oneself with villagers and reducing their difficulties (3), gaining the confidence of villagers (4), success in changing people's outlook (2), and impartiality (2).

The question as to what type of a VLW was regarded successful in actual practice brought diverse answers, but all had one common feature, namely, that the yardstick used by the village people and by the higher CDP officers was different. According to the village people a successful VLW has one or more of the following characteristics; willingness to do hard work (5), consideration for village people and understanding of their problems (4), ability to fulfil promises (2), honesty (2), success in achieving targets (2), and impartiality, character, tactfulness, ability to speak well, simplicity, and ability to gain the villager's confidence (1 each). The officers allegedly use a different measure. Ability to achieve targets (7), flattery (6), ability to speak well (2), hard work (2), obedience (1), and tactfulness (1) are, according to the VLWs interviewed, the qualities that determine their success in the judgement of their officers.

When asked to indicate one or more qualities which in their opinion were a measure of the success of a VLW they indicated a variety of characteristics: honesty and truthfulness (10), capacity to do sustained hard work (9), humility (6), impartiality (5), consideration and understanding (4), determination (4), will for service (3), ability to gain confidence of the village people (4), ability to keep one's word (2), ability to explain project objectives (2), ability to interact well (1), and knowledge of the job (1).

In evaluating their own work twelve VLWs claimed that they were most successful in agricultural extension work. Among other areas of CDP work in which they claimed outstanding success are: village sanitation (1), mass contact and public participation (1), social education (1), sports for village youth and children (1), planting of orchards (2), formation of village co-operatives (2), stimulation of a public health programme (1), and irrigation (1). Among the areas in which they thought that they either failed or were only partially successful they mentioned the following: sanitation (8), public health (5), public works (4), animal husbandry (2), adult and social education (4), horticulture (1), *panchayat* organization (1), irrigation (1), and *shramdan* and community activities (2). All of them thought that they were benefiting the community and the country. They believed that their utility lay in their work in the fields of increasing food production, in promoting rural sanitation, in initiating welfare programmes, and in adult and social education activities. When they were asked to indicate the items on their schedule which they expect will persist for at least five years after the termination of community development projects, all VLWs, with only one exception, said that new agricultural techniques introduced by them are most likely to become a part of the people's life. According to them other achievements of lasting significance are: co-operative societies (2), tube wells and irrigation facilities (2), village sanitation (4), recreation programmes (2), school (1), methods of cattle care (1), roads (2), paving of village lanes (3), libraries and reading rooms (2), and changed outlook towards life and a general attitude of co-operation in village development (2).

When asked to indicate their worries and difficulties most of them felt that conditions under which they could operate with dignity and self-respect have still to be created. When dignitaries and important guests visit the villages, far from being accorded a place of some respect and honour, the VLWs are relegated to a humble position and have to run errands. Officers often rebuke them in public, and as a result their prestige suffers. No effort is made to build up their prestige in the village, nor are the people encouraged to look upon them as their friends and leaders in village development work. Not one of the VLWs interviewed recounted that his work was praised by high officials in public.

Then there is the question of incentives and rewards. Most VLWs have to labour at their present jobs harder than they had to work in their parent departments, and that too without a paid assistant,[1] but they are not rewarded by rises in salaries, cash awards, or even

[1]In their previous jobs they had paid assistants who carried out their instructions and did most of the hard work involving manual labour.

public and official recognition of their accomplishments. They realize that in this task of national reconstruction they will have to work hard and that they cannot expect financial rewards for every little thing that they do. Nevertheless they do want some recognition for particularly meritorious work. In one or two cases when rewards were definitely promised for achievement in specific items of project work they were never given to the winners. For instance it was pointed out that two prizes for best work in promoting the orchards plantation programme have not yet been given to the VLWs who showed outstanding success in this field. A third problem that worries the VLWs is that of in-service training. No refresher courses or training camps have been organized for them, and the supply of literature giving them latest information regarding the different aspects of their work has been very meagre. Most of the VLWs who went on sightseeing tours to other projects appeared to think that they did not benefit much from such trips. Finally there is the great question of the future before them. Departmental VLWs feel that chances of promotion were better for them in their parent departments. With the policy of making direct recruitment to the posts of APOs and ADOs, both direct and departmental VLWs feel that the chances of their promotion are very considerably reduced.

III

What do the other project officers such as the Assistant Project Officers (APOs) and the Deputy Project Executive Officer (DyPEO) think about the VLW—his role, problems, and difficulties? In answering this question we shall rely mainly on material obtained in formal and informal interviews with two DyPEOs—one formerly an officer of the co-operative department, and another a revenue official who before coming to this Project earned a reputation for himself for making success of another Project, and two APOs—one formerly an information officer and now in charge of social education and public participation, and another originally from the co-operative department and now in charge of co-operatives and *panchayat*. All these officers have had training in extension methods.

In regard to the relative merits of direct recruitment compared to nominations from other development departments to the VLW posts, the general consensus of opinion appears to be that direct recruitment could be useful if it was made through fair and open competition on the basis of desirable personality traits and aptitudes and could be followed by intensive job training for an adequate period, say eighteen months or two years. It was felt that in the recruitment of VLWs factors other than those of merit and aptitude were beginning to play some part, and that this tendency led to the selection of persons who had neither the temperament nor the personality for the kind of work which they were called upon to do.

For direct recruits a training of six months is not regarded as adequate. It is felt that in several branches of CDP work they therefore come rather ill equipped. Another characteristic of a number of young direct recruits to the job is that they enter it with somewhat impractical idealism and have a tendency to become frustrated when they find that things do not necessarily develop as they wish them to. On the whole they are weak in maintenance of accounts and routine official records.

The departmental VLWs, on the other hand, are more seasoned and practical, but often lack the idealism, sense of dedication, and higher motivation demanded by the job. Their values and attitudes are influenced to a certain extent by the orientation courses and extension training that they get, but in a large number of cases the old methods of work and norms of thought which they acquired in their parent departments either persist or are easily revived. They are good in routine work, but some tend to concentrate more on 'show projects' than on substantial work. In point of honesty some may not be above reproach as they cannot easily give up the habits acquired by them in previous government service. When nominating persons for VLW jobs departments have in many cases suggested people whom they wanted to be rid of, without any consideration of their suitability for the new assignment. It was the opinion of those interviewed that policy and methods of recruitment need revision, that from both sources individuals should be taken only after proper screening, and should be given more effective training.

Among departmental personnel selected for VLW jobs, those from agriculture and co-operative departments have proved most successful. On the whole university graduates have not proved a success as VLWs. Their superior ways, manner of speech and dress, and constant desire for promotion to a higher post befitting their academic qualifications, stand in the way of their applying themselves whole-heartedly to the job. Persons having passed the matriculation or an equivalent examination, preferably with training in agriculture, are generally best suited for this work. All of these officers expressed an unmistakable preference for workers with a village background. Present salaries of the VLWs were considered adequate, although it was felt that there was great disparity in the gain to personnel recruited from different departments, Panchayat Secretaries jumping up from a salary of Rs60 a month to Rs110, but senior agriculture and co-operative people receiving no proportionate gain. It was felt that there were unreasonable delays in making legitimate salary adjustments, and that some system was needed under which especially meritorious services could be rewarded with enhanced salaries. As a general rule people work best in the section of the country from which they come, where they do not differ from the rest of the people in dress, speech and food. And it was recognized that a VLW could function more efficiently in a village which was predominantly populated by persons of his own caste.

There is general agreement that the concept of a multi-purpose VLW is useful, but the officers interviewed feel that it may not be expedient to saddle him with the work of a Patwari or Lekhpal also. As an experimental measure VLWs have been given Panchayat Secretary's work for a limited area, while Panchayat Secretaries have been given VLW's development work for one or more villages under their charge. Project officials are watching the results of this experiment. They favour withdrawal of all other village level development staff from the Project villages. They feel that there is fair understanding among the VLWs of the basic aims and objectives of the community development projects, and also of their own functions and responsibilities. They understand the VLW's role as that of 'a friend who offers advice when it is needed' but emphasize that initially the VLWs will have to think of themselves as leaders and innovators. It is realized that the ideal would be for the VLW to discover local felt needs and for the Project to formulate plans accordingly. Yet out of concession to the realities of the day it is felt necessary for the VLWs to achieve targets fixed from above. The officers point out that individual projects have very limited autonomy, the budget structure and directions from state headquarters determine their time schedule and main lines of activity to a very great extent. Under these conditions a VLW can have relatively little freedom of action and is often under pressure to achieve the targets given to him. As regards the general approach of the VLW the higher officials feel that he must endeavour to help the people to help themselves, but they argue that today they may have to use persuasion bordering almost on pressure. They expect the VLWs to work with devotion and sincerity and realize that their job involves hard labour without adequate compensation. As they are themselves under constant pressure to show concrete results to their superior officers and visiting dignitaries, they have to ensure that VLWs achieve results that can be seen.

Regarding *felt needs* of the people they think that the important ones among them are well known and that no special effort is required to bring them to light. VLWs can, of course, call attention to specific local needs and demands. There are certain areas in which people express their needs but the project can do nothing; for example, it cannot undertake consolidation of land holdings or start any major irrigation works. As there is very limited flexibility in the programme, it is difficult to have individual projects for each village, and consequently the VLWs cannot contribute materially towards determining the CDP targets. As planning so far has tended to come from the top to the bottom the autonomy of the individual projects has been considerably restricted. Regarding innovations sponsored by CDP and people's response towards them, it was pointed out that their acceptance was slow and extremely cautious, but the indications are that the tempo will increase.

About the job training programme of the VLWs the general consensus of opinion was that it has not been as successful as it ought to have been. Organization of many of the training centres leaves quite a bit to be desired; while some parts of CDP work are adequately covered in the job training, others are only superficially touched upon or are practically ignored. In general, training in improved agricultural practices is satisfactory, but the same cannot be said about animal husbandry, and public health and sanitation. Departmental VLWs are naturally strong in the work of their respective departments. It is doubtful if these training programmes succeed in changing the fundamental outlook of the trainees towards life and national affairs, or if they give them the technical knowledge of all that they are supposed to do in the villages, but they do leave the training centres with some idealism, and this in itself is a welcome addition to their mental equipment.

The officers realize that it is necessary to have a core of individuals in the villages of the project area conscious of planning developments so that people may take upon themselves an increasing share of responsibility for development work. But they frankly admit that such a leadership is at present nowhere in sight. Village councils (Gram Sabhas) are split into factions, and not many office bearers of such bodies could be described as selfless and public-minded. Men of influence often come forward with unusual requests for favours, and want certain advantages for themselves to the exclusion of others. There are certainly some individuals who are interested in development work for patriotic motives, but their number is not very large. Village Level Workers should work as far as possible with those who are interested in agricultural improvement and village development, but for practical reasons they cannot avoid 'leaders of factions' and 'men with political connexions'. It is true that some people from these classes have tended to treat the VLWs as servants, and when irregular favours were not granted to them they put obstacles in the way of community development work. Only a few people go to the VLW for advice as yet, but their number is gradually increasing. On the subject of the use of pressure and force the opinion was almost unanimous that only legal coercion should be exercised and that too after proper education of the masses.

We have pointed out earlier that the VLWs feel quite strongly that they are not treated well by some of their superior officers. The officials admitted that such complaints are not without foundation, and that some officers not properly oriented in extension methods have tended to make unnecessary displays of their authority. The VLWs are entitled to be treated well but this will not eliminate all supervision and pressure to show results. Many of the VLWs may abuse autonomy and equality if these are accorded to them. They are younger brothers, not in a western family, but in an Indian joint family. They are entitled to courtesy and consideration, but if they fail in discharging their responsibilities they cannot claim exemption from rebuke. Equality and respect have to be earned, the officers said, and added that those who work well are treated almost as equals. Those who are slow and lethargic naturally have to account for their failings, and have no right to resent criticism.

In the normal course of their duties the APOs and DyPEO have to do some inspection and to make on-the-spot inquiries. It is a fact that they have not been able to give much field guidance to the Village Level Workers, but this can be explained partly by their preoccupation with other activities in the initial period of the project.

With regard to the co-operation of the VLWs with the staff of other departments it was pointed out that initially they could not get along well with Panchayat Secretaries and Cane Supervisors. The former got less salary and were consequently jealous of the VLWs. As they could manipulate village politics they sometimes put obstacles in the way of a VLW's work. Where there was friction the VLW could not utilize the *Gaon Sabha* for his purposes for want of support from the Panchayat Secretary. The Cane Supervisors regarded themselves as more important than the VLWs, and as they could oblige people during the cane season they favoured key figures in the village in order to build up their own position and prestige as against that of the VLW.[1] Patwaris and Lekhpals lacked development consciousness, followed traditional bureaucratic methods, and refused to do even minor things without specific orders from superior revenue officials. This involved delays and caused resentment among the VLWs who could not make headway in any ventures connected with land unless they got copies of land records from the Patwari or Lekhpal. These officials have considerable local influence, are aware of the trends and developments in village politics, but are paid very

[1]They did so by allowing influential people larger quotas at shorter intervals for the sale of their sugarcane to the mills.

much less than the VLWs. As project officials can approach the Patwaris or Lekhpals only through Tahsildars of the revenue department such delays at present seem to be unavoidable.

Regarding freedom of expression in staff meetings and the VLW's contribution to over-all programme planning and setting of targets, it was pointed out that they had reasonable but limited freedom to express themselves but could not contribute much to over-all programme planning because the project was under pressure from above to undertake specific lines of action decided at the State level. In explaining why freedom of expression in staff meetings must be limited it was pointed out that they almost always had a very heavy agenda. The meetings started at 10 a.m. and continued till 5 or 6 p.m. often with only a short break. This necessitated imposing time limits on the VLWs when they started explaining their problems and points of view at length. It was true that VLWs were sometimes handicapped by lack of timely support and supplies, but this was not always the fault of the project officers. Financial regulations were very rigid, parts of the CDP programme were inflexible, and the project staff itself had very little control over the quality and even the quantity of materials supplied by State headquarters. It was a vicious circle; when the officers were disappointed in some request or expectation by their superior officers, they had to disappoint those who were working under them. It was not always wise or practical to protest against decisions and actions of State headquarters. Because of this it is necessary that careful checks be employed by State headquarters when sending improved varieties of seeds and equipment to the project. The officers consider it impractical to give any drawing and spending powers to the VLWs even for approved projects in the villages under their charge. For many more years to come supervision of their work and strict financial scrutiny and control cannot be avoided.

With regard to the work load of the VLW it is felt that he certainly has to work hard, but his work load cannot be described as excessive. By giving some development work to the Panchayat Secretaries efforts have already been made to reduce the VLW's area of operation. It is realized that the VLWs have to attend a number of staff meetings and also have to do considerable routine work, but almost all of it is necessary and cannot be eliminated. At the present stage it may create administrative and practical problems if the VLWs are asked to do the work of Patwaris or Lekhpals, and the latter are asked to do any multi-purpose development work in addition to their present duties. In the life of this project this experiment may prove undesirable.

IV

To the village people the role of the VLW is not very clear, for they have not been able to decide whether to regard him as 'a minor government functionary' operating on the village level or as 'a social worker and leader'. While these two roles are clearly understood in their separate aspects by the village people, the VLW—who appears to be a cross between the two—often puzzles them. It is generally well known that the VLW is a paid government employee and people with some education and urban contacts also know that in respect to salary and official status he occupies the lowest position in the official hierarchy of the planning and development department. However, his methods of work are somewhat unorthodox and mark him out from other village officials who still follow the traditional methods of work. The VLW is definitely much less authoritarian than other officials who have hitherto operated on the village level. Unlike others who appear on the village scene periodically (and for work connected with one department only) the VLW lives in close and continuous touch with the people of the village or villages under his charge and takes interest in several branches of development activity. In his manner of dress and speech, too, he is different from other government officials, and often speaks the language of social workers. The realization that a government servant can also function as a social worker and agent of reform is emerging very slowly, and at the time of the present study the appreciation of this possibility was confined largely to the rural *élite*.

Speaking for the Project area as a whole the people may be divided into four groups on the basis of their view and understanding of the VLW's role:

- i The rural *élite*, consisting mostly of people of higher status and higher income groups, who have some education and urban contacts. Most people in this category belong to upper castes, but it also includes other educated people who are active in village and inter-village politics.
- ii The agriculturists. This group includes most of the land-owning agriculturists who are not active in village or inter-village politics. Some of the persons classed in this category are 'opinion leaders' in certain phases of village affairs but they generally keep away from village politics, which is directed by persons of group one.
- iii Artisan groups and occupational castes. This group includes a large number of castes whose economy is integrated with the general agricultural economy of the village. In traditional rating

this group occupies a middle status, neither very high, nor very low. A major part of the subsistence of its members is obtained through the practice of their traditional crafts, and they generally do not accept work commonly regarded as 'menial labour'.

iv The low status, low income groups. This class includes the 'untouchable castes, and people who earn their livelihood by humble occupations and menial labour.

It has been suggested earlier that the first group has some degree of understanding of the VLW's role. Some individuals of this group read newspapers and attend meetings where social, political, and development questions are discussed. They are the ones most exposed to the agencies that communicate modern ideas to rural areas and their urban contacts keep them generally better informed about national and regional developments than the other sections of the village population. It is from this group that most of the members of the different advisory committees associated with CDP are drawn. Thus, this is the group best acquainted with the aims and methods of the community development movement in the village population. But this also happens to be the most status conscious group. Rather than working with the VLW, whose status is the lowest in the development organization, people from this group seek to associate more with the 'officers' whose status is higher. As some of these people have contacts with or access to political leaders, officers have to be particularly careful in their dealings with this section. On the whole this group has a patronizing attitude towards the VLW, and generally has tended to dictate what he should do. Some persons of this group have openly regarded the VLW as a kind of personal servant and have used pressure to secure his services for their own advantage. Others among this group have felt that the VLW should work in consultation with them and should generally accept their approach to village problems. VLWs have found their position rather difficult when they are subjected to conflicting pressures by rival factions in the *élite* group. Too close an association with this section has alienated some VLWs from the rest of the community, and as a consequence of this has limited development activity to a fraction of the village population. In some cases VLWs made a determined effort to remain uninfluenced by this group and to work with all sections of the village people, but most of them soon found that this policy did not pay. The officers evaluated the work of the VLWs mostly on the basis of the opinions of these people, and were reluctant to resist their pressure because of the political connexions of this section. The VLWs had therefore to exercise utmost tact in handling these people.

It was necessary to keep them pleased, and at the same time to check their undue interference in development work. On the whole the VLWs have found working with this 'enlightened' group most trying.

Of the other three groups the VLWs have had most contact with the second and the fourth, and not so much with the third. As agricultural extension and Harijan welfare had definite priorities in the schedule of project activities, this was natural. To most of the agriculturists the VLW appeared to be a combination of representatives of the agriculture and co-operative departments, and they viewed him as just another official, although of a more friendly type. The under-privileged Harijan group is conscious of the fact that the State is taking certain measures for their economic and social uplift, and they have tended to view the VLW as an official specially appointed for this purpose. However, they were somewhat disillusioned to find that he was spending most of his working time with agriculturists, and that, being landless, they naturally could not benefit much from his services in this field. However, there were other areas of work in which the VLW came in contact with them. The general view of this group is that the VLW is a government official, who has, among other obligations, the duty to look after the welfare of the under-privileged section. The third group has felt the impact of the CDP activities the least. While they are aware of the presence of the VLW they do not quite understand why he is there nor do they know what possible help and advice they can get from him.

It must be emphasized here that the presence of the VLW is not known to all the people in the second, third, and the fourth groups, and their understanding of his duties and functions is comparatively restricted. In a field survey of people's reactions and general response to its activities at the close of the first year of the CDP's life, an effort was made to find out how widely the VLW and his achievements were known. For this purpose intensive inquiries were made in two villages. In Rajput Village, a large settlement with a population of over 5,000, a stratified random sample of 10 per cent of the families living in the village was drawn, and the head of the family, or, if he were not available the next oldest adult male, was interviewed. In Tyagi Village, a smaller CDP block village with a population of about 750, 50 per cent adult males were interviewed. Out of 114 persons interviewed in Rajput Village fifty-six had heard about the Project, fifty-eight had not. Among these forty-four knew M, the former VLW, who had worked in the village for about seven months, and only twenty-two knew T, who had recently taken charge and had been in the village for only about three months. Out of this sample only fifty-nine said that they had met the VLW. The VLW had sought the co-operation of only forty-eight of these people in his development activities in the village. The picture is somewhat different in Tyagi Village, the second and smaller settlement. Out of 117 persons interviewed in this village, seventy-four had heard about the Project and forty-three were not aware of its existence; here ninety-five knew the VLW, eighteen did not. In this sample the VLW had met ninety-three people although he had sought the active co-operation of only twenty-four people. In both the villages the *élite*-agriculturist group as well as the low status, low income group knew the VLW and his activities much better than the artisan group. The village population as a whole were best acquainted with his work in the spheres of organizing sanitation and *shramdan* drives, secondary vaccination, and inoculation of cattle. Knowledge of his activities in other fields was confined to limited sections only.

Lately a number of spectacular and impressive activities were concentrated in Rajput Village and they are likely to have increased the general awareness regarding the Project and its work. In the case of Tyagi Village, because of politically conscious leadership within the village, the tempo of development activity has been greater than in other villages of comparable size. But the figures above refer to the months of October and November 1954, when the project had been in operation for only one year. In villages other than the select two dozen 'key villages' where intensive work was being done, because of less concentrated nature of project activities the VLWs had probably reached a much smaller percentage of the village population at the same period.

In the final analysis the general response of the village people to a VLW depends to a large extent on his personality and individual qualities and his initial successes and failures. His understanding and tact in grasping the local situation is of considerable importance too. The general attitudes of the village people as well as the internal organization of the village, especially the pattern of its leadership, also materially govern his ultimate acceptance and success or failure. While the village people look to the government, rather than to themselves, for active measures in the direction of village development and economic reconstruction, they have an intense suspicion and distrust of the petty government official. Initially the VLW had to start with this handicap. His approach, coupled with considerable development propaganda, has modified this way of thinking on the part of the villager to a slight degree. But people are still somewhat sceptical about the whole business, and nothing frustrates the VLW more than evidences of general apathy and distrust in those among whom he works.

V

To conclude, we shall briefly examine some of the problems and considerations emerging from this study.

In order to ensure the success of the large-scale plans of rural community development it is necessary that personnel for the VLW posts should be selected on the basis of certain desirable personality traits and aptitudes. In view of the very special and diverse nature of their work, it is also essential to provide the right kind of training for the persons selected for this job. The training programme should not only orient the trainees in the principles and methods of extension work, but should be designed to give them a reasonable degree of proficiency in all the important areas of their multi-purpose activity. The training should inspire them with an urge for dedicated national service, but the VLWs should not leave their training centres with an impractical idealism, for they will need a good deal of realism in facing a multitude of perplexing problems and tangled situations in the field. Their training would remain incomplete if this sense of realism is not imparted to them.

A series of problems arise when the VLW enters his field of action. Here his success will depend upon a number of factors, many of which are outside his control. In the first place it is necessary for him to understand and accept the programme which he seeks to promote in the area under his charge. Secondly, he should be happy and well adjusted in the total official organization of the project. In the absence of understanding, sympathy, and timely support from his colleagues and official superiors, his well-intentioned programmes can be wrecked. Thirdly, the people among whom he is working should also understand and approve his programmes, for the ultimate success of the development programme as such will depend upon the final acceptance of its ideology by the village people. The success of the CDP team can be gauged by its success in devising meaningful approaches to overcome the different types of resistances offered by the people to the acceptance of the development ideology and programmes.

Those responsible for formulating the plan have generally been aware of some of these prerequisites and vital factors governing the successful implementation of the programme, and have, therefore, devised a number of measures which are calculated to ensure proper recruitment and training and to secure suitable working conditions for the VLWs. The theoretical basis of their approach could not be fully tested against the empirical experience of the field in the first phase of the life of the projects. As data emerging from the experience of individual projects are now accumulating, it is possible to make a preliminary evaluation of the emerging role of the VLW.

In view of the above considerations we may ask if the VLWs of this project are of the right type and with desirable aptitudes and personality traits? Have they been adequately equipped for their job by their training?

Development literature lists a wide range of qualities and aptitudes desirable in a VLW. For example, a Handbook of the Uttar Pradesh Government on 'Principles of Extension Work' (*Prasar Karya ke Siddhanta*) enumerates five essential, and twenty-seven desirable attributes in a VLW. The essential qualities are: honesty, self-confidence and optimism, knowledge of the different areas of his work, sympathy, and will for sustained hard work. The list of desirable aptitudes and personality traits is long and varied, and includes, besides the five essential qualities listed above, the following: desire to acquire new knowledge, an instinct for correct on-the-spot decisions, ability to communicate ideas and plans clearly, resourcefulness, foresight, capacity to draw people to him, enthusiasm, courage, organizing ability, love of physical labour, capacity to inspire others, practical common sense, friendliness, patience and tolerance, selflessness, developed sense of co-operation and team work, willingness to hear other's points of view, habit of giving only those promises that one can fulfil, simplicity, spirit of service, and physical endurance. It will indeed be futile to look for all these qualities in every VLW of all the projects. In this study an attempt was made to rank and evaluate the VLWs on the basis of ten specified aptitudes,[1] and eight specified criteria of success.

On the basis of personal observation and the people's reactions, we are inclined to agree generally with the evaluation and ranking of the VLWs of the Project by the officers. In this ranking, three of the seventeen VLWs were graded poor, twelve average to good, and two outstanding. In ranking them according to specified aptitudes, the officers found that the VLWs of the Project as a group were strong in understanding village customs and social organization, and in 'co-operativeness' (with other project staff). They were good to average in the following: 'ability to gain confidence of the villagers', 'willingness to work with all castes and economic groups', and 'knowledge of extension principles and methods'. As a group they were weak in the following: 'initiative', 'emotional attachment to village people', and 'interest in developing village initiative and leadership'. Ranking them according to specified criteria of success the officers found the group as a whole strong in 'personal acceptance by the

[1]The criteria used in this ranking were the same as those used by the programme Evaluation Organization in the ranking of VLWs all over India.

villagers' and in 'developing balanced village programmes fieldwise'. They were good to average in 'enlisting people's participation in public works', in 'bringing programmes to all groups in the village', 'in stimulating individual villagers to adopt recommended improved practices' and in 'contributing to over-all project programme planning'. They were judged to be weak in two areas—in 'educating villagers to reasons why improved practices are better than traditional ones' and in 'developing local initiative and leadership'.

While the general level of the VLWs is, on the whole, satisfactory, it appears that they were not too carefully screened at the time of their selection for this type of work. Departmental recommendations or an all too brief interview do not appear to be the most satisfactory methods of recruitment to a pivotal job like that of the VLW. Even a simple testing for desirable aptitudes and personality traits would have excluded the selection of at least two out of the three VLWs rated as 'poor' by the officers in the ranking referred to above. The tendency of departments to get rid of undesirable individuals by their transfer to CDP must be deplored, and the tendency to use official and political influence in the matter of selection to these jobs must be guarded against. Proper screening and testing of all the applicants, and their selection only on the basis of necessary qualifications and desirable traits and aptitudes is necessary. For this it is essential to devise suitable tests, and apply them vigorously. The necessity of recruiting a large staff in a very short time is often mentioned as a reason for the lack of greater care and caution in the selection. It is realized that officials were under pressure, and that the rapid expansion of development activities made unexpected demands on them. But unplanned developments in a department of planning appear to be somewhat paradoxical. A more accurate anticipation of personnel requirements can greatly help in reducing the possibility of the selection of undesirable individuals to these posts. It should be borne in mind that a wrong type of person in a VLW post can be more harmful than a failure to fill the place.

In the absence of a full and intimate knowledge of the operation of the VLW training programmes a balanced evaluation of their success cannot be attempted here. However, on the basis of the experience with the VLWs of this Project a few general observations can be made. It appears that the different training centres have somewhat different orientations, and on the whole the programmes offered by them are not as balanced as they might be. It is not suggested that a rigid uniformity should be insisted upon, but it is perhaps necessary to ensure that certain areas of work which are basic for the VLW as an action man get adequate attention in all centres. While the partial success of the training programme is not denied, especially in the field of orienting trainees in extension methods and in imparting to them a sense of idealism, it has to be noted that in certain fields the trainees leave the centres wholly unequipped or but partially equipped. It has been noted that some VLWs were extremely reluctant to perform vaccinations because they felt that their training for this work was inadequate. Performing castrations was unusually difficult for some because their training for this work consisted of one or two hurried demonstrations by a non-resident instructor. Direct recruits to the job found that their training in accounting procedure was insufficient. Other comparatively weak areas of training have been mentioned earlier. It has also been observed that the organization of some of the training centres and their programmes bore the imprint of hurried and insufficient planning. One further observation may be made here. It appears that the trainees were not sufficiently sensitized to likely field situation. For example, they were not familiarized with areas where they could expect to meet unexpected resistance from the people even in respect to things that would be apparently beneficial to them. They were not told that the established bureaucratic tradition of administration can still be a strong influence in the actual functioning of the CDP, notwithstanding the efforts on the part of the government to orient their planning officials in modern methods of extension work. Most of the VLWs were not prepared to meet with opposition and an unsympathetic attitude from the rural *élite* in general and from the politically influential sections in particular. Inclusion of suitable case studies in the training programme based on actual experience of work in the field, will perhaps give a more balanced perspective to the trainees and will prepare them better for 'the shocks' they are likely to get in the field.

Three general suggestions may be offered in this area. First, it is desirable to attempt an evaluation of past and current VLW training programmes. Secondly, on the basis of accumulated experience it is necessary to evolve more balanced training programmes, possibly of a longer duration. Thirdly, it will be useful to benefit by the experience (the success as well as failure) of the VLWs in the field. Carefully prepared case studies, based on this experience, can be helpful not only to future VLWs in training, but also to more seasoned development workers both in the field and in higher administrative positions.

From observations and materials presented in sections II and III of this study, a number of questions emerge that concern the adjustment and functioning of the VLW in the official organization of the Community Projects. Some of the minor problems, such as lack of suitable residential accommodation and unusually long delays in making salary adjustments and payments of travelling allowances, should not detain us. However, it is necessary to point out that delays in respect to the latter cause very considerable hardship to the VLWs. Since they are usually persons with modest salaries and practically no outside resources, it is difficult for them to wait endlessly for such payments. In one case a VLW did not get his transfer T.A. for eighteen months in spite of constant reminders. In another instance, a VLW got disgusted with the delay in salary adjustment, and rather than work for a smaller emolument in CDP, decided to quit it in favour of his parent department. Some cutting of red tape, elimination of routine office formalities, and tightening of general office administration are indicated.

The major problems in this area are: (*a*) the creation of atmosphere in which a VLW can function with some initiative and independence, (*b*) the building up of his 'prestige', (*c*) the provision of adequate incentives for him to work to the best of his abilities, (*d*) the arranging for his in-service training, and (*e*) the evolving of administrative practices and organization under which the VLW can get timely support and help. Most of these problems are closely interrelated.

Bound by a rigid organizational framework and fixed targets, the VLWs feel that they have very limited independence and scope for initiative, and officials concede that this indeed is so.

In respect to his 'prestige' the VLW meets with the first challenge from his own immediate official superiors. While officials generally explain their authoritarian tone as a direct consequence of the pressure on them to 'show results', it cannot be denied that most of them have an inner conflict of values in respect to this matter. Their short training in extension methods and principles does not make them sufficiently alive to the fact that their task calls for a pattern of intra-department ordering of relations different from the one in which they were nurtured. It has not been realized that the concept of team-work as accepted by development ideology, necessitates a change in the superior-subordinate relationships that largely characterize the bureaucratic structure of India. The prevailing view among officials appears to be that the new approach is too doctrinaire, theoretical, and impractical, and that in the long run only traditional methods work. Assertion of official superiority and authority at every possible point frustrates the VLW who was given to believe in his training that in the Community Development Projects the climate of work would be basically different. The officials' view of the VLW's role and position is easily taken over by the rural *élite* and influential village leaders who inter-act with officials on a basis of equality. Soon they begin to treat the VLW as a minor government official of no consequence. Little, if any, effort has so far been made to build up the position and prestige of the VLW in the villages where he operates. As a result of the operation of these two factors, within the project administration there is a regrettable tendency toward a one-way communication: higher officials fix targets and issue directives, the VLWs try their best to realize them in action.

This raises the question of incentives for more and better work. A rigid schedule, externally determined targets, and lack of opportunity for individual initiative, coupled with authoritarian supervision and general public apathy do not provide adequate incentive for originality, innovation, and dedicated work. The realization that impressive 'show projects' earn better dividends than educational efforts to change people's ways of thought, alters the perspective in which the VLW views his role. To the detriment of the basic aims of the community development movement, he consequently begins to concentrate on the spectacular in his activities. The busy officers and visiting dignitaries like to *see* things happening, and the practical, worldly-wise VLW who has a few showpieces to offer is likely to get their approval. But even then his individual work is rarely commended in public. Often, he does not want a special reward, but denial of recognition, when recognition is due, certainly frustrates him.

In their day-to-day activities the VLWs often find that they cannot get the support necessary to redeem promises and carry out plans. At the time when they are under pressure to create interest in a certain seed for which there is really not much demand, supplies of it are often not received in time and the VLW loses prestige when he cannot fulfil promises made to villagers on the strength of assurances given by his officers. In the course of our investigations we came across a number of cases which demonstrate the plight of the VLWs in situations of this kind. In trying to dispose of a certain quantity of seed, the VLWs in desperation had to make appeals directly opposed to the aims and principles of extension work. For instance, the VLWs were asked to sell a supply of improved seed of corn which had been received too late for the season's sowing. As it is there is very little demand for this seed in the area for it is not grown there on any large scale. The VLWs had to go from door to door begging people to buy the seed for domestic consumption if for nothing else. The villagers naturally did not like paying more than the prevailing market price, and since it was 'improved seed', it was considerably dearer than ordinary corn for domestic use. We know of three VLWs who were similarly under pressure to sell a certain quantity of potato seed. It was not only received too late for sowing, it was of an inferior quality (some of it being actually deteriorated) and was priced much higher than comparable or even better seed in the market. As a last resort the VLWs had to appeal to the rich villagers to help save their jobs by buying this seed even though it was not needed. Notwithstanding these appeals they could not thrust all the unwanted seed on unwilling villagers and had actually to pay the price of the unsold seed from their own salaries.

Without multiplying examples we can pass on to another but related problem. In some cases the seed received by the Project headquarters was obviously of an inferior quality. It was evident that its use would not produce the desired and promised results. Yet VLWs were asked to distribute it in the area. The VLWs took it to the villagers who, after considerable pressure, accepted it with great reluctance and scepticism. The yield justified their misgivings. In the following year the VLWs found it difficult to sell more seed, though this time it was certainly excellent in quality. There are many examples, too, of lack of fulfilment of promises, wherein the VLWs promoted items in the project schedule, but felt let down when the promised supplies and subsidies were not received in time.

In passing it should be noted that considering the area and population under the charge of a VLW his work load is rather heavy, and this results either in his working with one section of the population only or in emphasis on a few items of the project schedule and the neglect of others.

The problems delineated above require a critical re-examination of the entire range of questions in this area. If an expert in the field of public administration is called upon to devise necessary adjustments on the basis of observed facts and accumulated experience, it may not be difficult to make suitable modifications in administrative organization and procedure of the Community Development Projects.

Traditional stereotypes and attitudes of the development officials (DyPEO, APOs) have shown a persistence that cannot perhaps be altered by brief orientation courses in extension methods. Much more will probably have to be done in this respect. Under actual service conditions steps could be taken to bring home to them the realization that the content of extension training programmes is not all 'sentimental nonsense'. It has been pointed out earlier that tight schedules and fixed targets, coupled with the insistence on 'showing results', curb the autonomy of the individual projects and, while limiting the scope for initiative and innovation, tend to attach undue importance to impressive looking but often superficial achievements. While a certain degree of rigidity in the budget and work schedule of the projects cannot be avoided, it is desirable to have a sector in which the individual project, and within the project individual VLWs, can exercise initiative on the basis of specific local felt needs.

The question of investing necessary prestige in the office of the VLW needs careful attention. In the popular estimation status and salary often go together, but it would perhaps be Utopian to suggest that the salaries of the VLWs should be measurably enhanced at the present time. Fortunately there are certain intermediate roles, such as that of the school master, which carry a status far above that warranted by the salary of their post. With persistent effort there is no reason why acceptance of a VLW in a similar role cannot be secured. Some useful steps in this direction would be to accord to the VLW a place of honour in meetings attended by important officials and political leaders, to grant constant public acknowledgement of the importance of their work, to ensure less public demonstration of authority and superior status by his immediate officers, and to provide for suitable public honour to outstanding VLWs. It would not be difficult to secure the co-operation of the press in publicizing the achievements of deserving VLWs. Some of them might even be considered for exceptional recognition through a suitable award by the President of the Republic. Such honours have recently been instituted, and the inclusion of a VLW in the lists of those so honoured would emphasize in a dramatic manner the importance of his role and position in new India.

Considerable thought has been given to the problem of providing incentives for the VLWs to work better, but so far no definite principles have been formulated. It is perhaps not desirable to have too many cash awards for minor achievements, but they should not be completely ruled out as a means of recognition for exceptionally meritorious work in specific areas. Accelerated increments in salary and promotion to higher posts should be given according to set principles which take due account of exceptional achievements of the VLWs. In this sphere, it will be necessary to guard against judging the VLWs mainly on the basis of 'show projects'. In evaluating their work consideration should be given to their success in developing a balanced village programme, in carrying it to all sections of the population, and in developing local initiative and leadership.

It has been observed that facilities for in-service training of the VLWs are practically non-existent in this area. A supply of useful literature, technically sound but simply written, could with profit be made available to them regularly. Apart from a set of seven useful extension handbooks published by the U.P. Government, the VLWs of this Project got no other development literature. Even these handbooks were made available to them only after they had been in the field for more than a year. They were not familiar with the publications distributed by the Community Projects Administration in Delhi.

What was more surprising was the fact that *Grama Sevak*, a periodical publication of CPA, which is a journal of the VLWs, by the VLWs, for the VLWs, was not known to any of the VLWs of this Project. While some of these publications have been written and produced with imagination, their distribution is unsystematic and unsatisfactory. This requires organization. Refresher courses and short training camps for VLWs need to be organized, but this must be done with forethought and careful advance planning. With imaginative planning the annual sight-seeing tours of the VLWs could be turned into positive educational experiences, but the way they are handled at present makes them of very doubtful utility. According to the evaluation of the VLWs who have participated in these trips they are 'a waste of time and money'. In many instances 'people conducting them around the other projects did not know what they were showing them'.

In order to ensure that the concept of the VLW's multi-purpose functioning becomes meaningful, it is desirable also to examine the questions of his work load, his area of operation, and timely official support for his activities. This perhaps is the most important single area that calls for systematic investigation. In this sphere, however, the social analyst can only point out the need; specific recommendations call for technical competence in the field of public administration. The experience of this Project shows that if the VLW's area of operation cannot be reduced to consist of a population of about 3,000 per VLW, he should at least be given technical help in specific items of project activity. The field teachers have been associated with the VLWs in organizing social education activities; similar help from public health workers may also be considered. The VLW would still remain in over-all charge of the area, but just as he is helped by the Field Teacher in devising and executing social education programmes he could be helped by a public health man in that field of specialization.

Similarly, it would be useful to have an agency or channel through which difficulties in programme planning and execution could be transmitted to the Community Project's Administration. State authority is both necessary and desirable, but a higher authority should be able to correct it when it errs. Project officials find it hard to criticize State level decisions, and even have to yield to the point of distributing defective seeds out of season or of undertaking action plans which they know for certain are not needed in the area. A suitable mechanism to avoid such pitfalls has yet to be evolved.

Finally a word about the personal acceptance of the VLW and through him of the development aims and programme by the village people. It is in this area that the concept of a multi-purpose extension agent and social worker is undergoing its supreme test. Deep-rooted scepticism of government-sponsored welfare measures and distrust of the official are hard to eradicate, and only years of patience, perseverance, and hard work can bring about a change in this outlook. Experience shows that village people tend to magnify failures and underrate successes in experiments of community development. VLWs have often spoken to us about the icy silence of the people concerning their successful projects and of their mirthful caricatures of their small failures. A few ill-planned initial projects can cause irreparable damage to development work. It may not be true of the area to say that nothing succeeds like success but it is certainly true to say that nothing fails like failure. Choice, planning, and execution of initial projects, therefore, call for very great caution. Initial contacts of the VLW and Project officials materially affect the general response of the village people towards their work. As community development activities cover a wide and diverse range of decision-making, the policy of working with and through the so-called leaders of the village and men of influence may be fatal to the project objectives. The movement must remain broad-based, and should for its success approach the very sources where decisions of different types are made. The blessings of influential men, or even endorsement by a village body like the *Gaon Sabha*, may fail to take the programme to the people. In the area under study the agencies of decision making are diffused: problems of everyday life are discussed and opinions are formed in informal friendship groups, and in gatherings of kinsfolk. A successful VLW will penetrate these groups, and will work with heads of households and caste groups. An unusually large part of Project activities concerns individuals and their families rather than the village as a unit. The educational objectives of the projects can be best attained by this approach, for it is conducive to an intelligent acceptance both of the VLW and of his programme by the people. Co-operation and support of village leaders is necessary for larger projects requiring the participation of village as a whole, but even in such activities persuasion through the VLW is more valuable than the pressure of village leaders. Problems of communication and of the development of effective contact techniques call for deeper sociological and psychological analyses, and deserve high priority in evaluation and planning research.

The concept of a multi-purpose village level worker is indeed useful, and has to a considerable extent proved its merit and utility in the field. It is, however, an emerging role in Indian village life—one that is still evolving and being defined. The course of its evolution and its final form can still be directed and controlled, and it should be the policy of the administration to channel it in the most appropriate direction. Empirical case studies and critical evaluation of its development will point out the areas where more thinking and planning are needed to ensure its final emergence in the form which seems most desirable. As a pivotal figure in the movement for rural community development the VLW merits wider studies both from sociological and public administration viewpoints.

Appendix II

THE VILLAGE LEVEL WORKER IN ACTION

A Day to Day Record of Ten Days' Work[1]

THIS STUDY EMBODIES a day to day record of the Village Level Worker's activities for ten consecutive days in Rajput Village. The activities of the VLW were observed very closely for three weeks, and at the end of each day during this period he was interviewed to obtain a verbatim record of his activities during the course of the day. For this reason he speaks in the first person singular in the pages that follow. Participant observation by a member of our research team was simultaneously carried on to ensure substantial accuracy in the accounts given by the VLW, and to obtain the responses and reactions of the people with whom he had worked. The characteristic responses and comments of the people are appended to each day's record. Some of the problems emerging from this study are discussed in a concluding comment.

1 November 1954

Got up at 5.30 a.m. and went to the Co-operative Seed Store. Picked up dibblers. Accompanied by the Kamdar of Seed Store (an employee of the Co-operative Department, S.C.D.) I went to Bhamula Singh. I had met him last night and had arranged with him to have a dibbling demonstration in his field early in the morning today. But when we went to him at the appointed time he said that he was going to another field, and that he would not be able to have the demonstration in his field today. We arranged with him to give this demonstration day after tomorrow.

[1]The observations reported in this study were started in the fourth week of October 1954, and were continued up to 14 November 1954. For reasons of space, activities covering only ten days are described here. The VLW, who got used to being observed by us in the first week and went about his work more or less normally afterwards, has earned our gratitude by his understanding co-operation. For practical reasons he must remain anonymous.

Next we went to Kabul Singh. I had spoken to him earlier and had arranged with him to have a demonstration tomorrow. We asked him to have it today. He agreed.

Accompanied by Kabul Singh, his three sons, two servants and the Kamdar, I went to his field. This is at a distance of about a mile from his house. The dibbling demonstration was given on half a *bigha*[1] of land earmarked for this purpose. Ten to twelve other agriculturists had assembled there. These included Prithvi Singh and Bhamula Singh who occupy a position of some importance among the agriculturists of the village. Several others also came; but most of them stayed only a few minutes, and returned to their work after seeing the method of dibbling. One of the agriculturists asked: 'Do you like this method yourself? Don't you think that it is very slow?'[2] I explained to the people the advantages of the dibbler. They did not look convinced. One of them said, 'If we adopt this time-consuming method of sowing we shall require twenty times the labour and time that we normally need for our sowing. That would be the end of our agriculture! How can we afford to waste our time experimenting with your fancy ideas?' Others nodded in agreement. His argument was not new; others had expressed the same doubts many times before. I told them 'You are right. If you sow all your wheat by this method you will surely be wasting your time. This method is recommended only for seed multiplication—for improving the seed and for maintaining its quality. That is why I ask you to select healthy grains from your seed for these demonstrations. That is why I ask you to work diligently on a small piece of land. This plot is not meant to give you wheat for domestic consumption or for sale; but you will have excellent seed for next year's sowing.' They did not appear to be wholly convinced. I asked them to see the seed from the demonstration plot after it was harvested. I added, 'That alone will be a convincing proof of what I have said just now.'

After the demonstration I measured three of Kabul Singh's fields for fertilizer demonstrations. I measured one more field for a half-field demonstration (Panjab 591[3] vs. local variety of wheat). Many people still believe that the local (*desi*) variety of wheat is better and this necessitates demonstrations of this nature.

Immediately after this I went to Tara Chand's fields for selecting

[1]The local measurement of land. The size of a *bigha* differs in different parts of Uttar Pradesh. In this region a *bigha* is about one-fifth of an acre.

[2]The process is very slow. The dibbler is a simple wooden implement with several rows of pointed wooden pegs at a distance of approximately ten inches from one another. When it is pressed into freshly ploughed soil it makes small holes in the earth in which the selected seed is sown.

[3]An improved variety of wheat developed by agricultural research in India.

suitable plots for demonstration purposes. I could not select any of his fields as they all are of an irregular shape and are more than a mile and a half from the village.

Returned home at 11.30 a.m. I had an appointment with the Cotton Supervisor (an employee of the Agriculture Department, S.C.D.) at 12.30 p.m., so I had a hurried bath and lunch. At 12.30 p.m. I went with the Cotton Supervisor to Malkhan Singh. He had sown the improved variety of cotton last year and we wanted to buy some of it for seed. I explained to him our requirements and asked him to sell us at least a part of the improved variety of cotton. He refused. He said, 'We need it for making cloth.' I tried to persuade him by suggesting that we were anxious to multiply the seed of the improved variety to popularize it and that it was for this reason that we needed the cotton from him. He said, 'Our womenfolk will never agree to do so.' After some more arguments he agreed to sell it on the condition that we shall obtain for him an equal quantity of cotton of the local variety.

In the hope of buying some more cotton of the improved variety I went with the Cotton Supervisor to G.—a nearby village. This village is located two miles from R.[1]—the village where my headquarters are. We left at about 2 p.m. Met Budh Singh, Hardeva Singh and Mangat Ram in G. For the last three or four days I had been trying to persuade them to sell their improved cotton crop to us. They were reluctant at first, but later agreed to sell it because of my personal influence and pressure. Krishan, however, refused to sell it on the ground that his family needed it for making cloth. He thought that the womenfolk would not be willing to part with it under any conditions. The cotton seed itself was needed by them to feed the cattle.

Later I vaccinated thirty to thirty-five people. Parents of very young children (of six months or less) objected to their being vaccinated; vaccination of adults is now regarded as normal and necessary. Today I vaccinated only adults. This work was continued up to 5 p.m. Back in R. I saw the college nursery,[2] and gave instructions regarding watering the beds.

Returned home. Received a note from APO (Agriculture, S.C.D.). This upset me very much. It was authoritarian and aggressive in its

[1]R. refers to the village where the headquarters of the VLW are located and where this record was obtained. It is a large village with a population of more than 5,000. The Rajputs are the dominant caste and the largest landowners in this village. Earlier in this volume it has been called 'Rajput Village'.

[2]R. has a Higher Secondary School or Intermediate College. In conjunction with CDP this institution has started a nursery where vegetable seedlings and small plants of fruit-bearing trees are raised. The nursery is subsidized from CDP funds.

tone from beginning to end. It was addressed to me without the usual 'Shri'. All through he had addressed me as *tum* (used for inferiors, S.C.D.) and not with the more courteous *aap*, although I think that there is a government directive making the use of the latter compulsory in government correspondence. I was reprimanded for not being in R. when he visited. This was most annoying. Had he found me in the headquarters he would have said, 'Have you no work to do? Field-staff are supposed to be out most of the time.' Now that he did not find me here he said, 'Why does he go about wasting his time with the Cotton Supervisor? He should take more interest in his own work.' I could not be present in R. as I had no advance information regarding his visit. The letter contained his orders asking me to give fertilizer demonstrations immediately. The APO desired that seven bags of super-phosphate and twelve bags of mixture should be used in these demonstrations. This was an order from above. I was never consulted about it. I had not even been given advance information regarding it, and so I could not speak to the people and persuade them to have these demonstrations. Further, I was scolded for not giving seed-drill demonstrations. This seed drill is in a village about three and a half miles away from R. How can I bring it? I do not have a pair of bullocks. Why could the office not send the Project tractor to bring the seed-drill to R. Now I shall have to use pressure on someone to lend me his pair of bullocks. The letter ended with a severe warning that drastic action will be taken against me if I do not comply with his orders.

When I was returning from the college nursery Tara Chand shouted, 'Today —— came.' (He twisted the name of the APO in a derogatory way.) I asked, 'At what time? I did not know his programme.' Tara Chand said, 'Today he was wild. In Tikka Singh's house he said in the presence of several people that you had no business to go out with the Cotton Supervisor. He said that he will suspend you if you do not improve your ways.' What am I to do? If I had not co-operated with the Cotton Supervisor there would have been the complaint that the VLW was not functioning as a multi-purpose man and was not co-operating with other development officials; and when I did co-operate, here I am being warned that I will be sacked.

Between 6 and 6.30 p.m. I completed my office records.

At 6.30 I had my evening meal.

Between 7 and 8 p.m. I attended the *keertan*.[1]

At 8.15 p.m. I met Mulhad Singh and arranged with him to give a half-field demonstration—Panjab 591 vs. N.P. 710.[2] He has promised

[1]Community singing of religious and devotional songs organized by CDP.
[2]Another improved variety of wheat.

to take me to his fields with him at 5.30 a.m. tomorrow and to carry the seed in the bullock-cart.

Work to be done:

i Write the diary.[1]
ii Make demonstration maps in the diary.

Villagers' Comments: Kabul Singh: 'This man, the VLW, is very sincere. He works hard. He asked me to have a demonstration in my field, and I could not refuse. . . . To tell you the truth so many people come to us these days and ask us to do all kinds of things. Take this demonstration with that wooden thing—what do they call it? (He was referring to the dibbler, S.C.D.) First of all we have to select fat, healthy grain one by one. This takes a long time. Who has the time to do it? Then we have to prepare a plot specially for sowing. Then we have to use that—the dibbler—to make rows of small holes and sow each grain individually. He says that we shall get better seed next year. Maybe he is right. But is the government going to give us the money to hire the additional labour required? No. The government only wants taxes.'
Q. 'If the experiment succeeds this year will you try it next year?'
K.S. 'Yes, if the government asks us again. We cannot give all our time to these things, and the labour we hire has no patience for these methods. We cannot keep an eye on them all the time, and when left alone they will perhaps do it the way they have done so far.'
Q. 'What do you think about the other two demonstrations the VLW is planning?'
K.S. 'I do not know what he will do. He will perhaps try some new manure (chemical fertilizer). These are good for a short time; they immediately increase your yield. But they sap the fertility of the soil.'
Q. 'What about the new wheat?'
K.S. 'We have tried it for several years. It is better in appearance, and also stands rain and frost better. It brings a better price too. Some people say that its yield is larger, but my impression is that it is the same as that of the local variety. But the local variety is better in taste. From the point of view of health there is nothing like it.'

2 November 1954

Mulhad Singh kept his appointment and came to my house at 4 a.m. I went to his field located at a distance of about a mile from the village. I had arranged to give three demonstrations there.

The first one was to be a half-field demonstration. A field of about six *bighas* was divided into two equal halves; in one part we have

[1]The VLW is required to maintain a diary of his activities.

sown Panjab 591 and in another the local variety of wheat. The second one was a manure demonstration. For this a field with an area of approximately five *bighas* has been divided into three parts. In one part we have put super-phosphate today. For the time being the other two parts have been left as they are. A further supply of fertilizer is awaited which will probably include the other manure to be used for the demonstration. The third one was a varietal demonstration. The area of the field in which this demonstration has been given is approximately four *bighas*. This has been divided into four parts. In one part we have sown Panjab 591, in another N.P. 710, in the third the local variety, and the fourth part has been reserved for a dibbling demonstration (seed to be sown is Panjab 591). This will be given tomorrow. These three demonstrations took more than three hours. No other agriculturists were present when these demonstrations were given.

At about 8 a.m. I came home and left immediately for G. on my bicycle. I reached there a little after 8.30. Here I had an appointment with Budh Singh. I had promised to meet him at dawn in his fields but was late. However, he was waiting for me. For the dibbling demonstration we needed the assistance of about five boys. As they were not present near the field we had to go to the village to fetch the boys. We came back to the field at 9 a.m. With the help of a standard dibbler, in half a *bigha* of land specially selected seeds of Panjab 591 wheat were sown. The following agriculturists were present to observe the demonstration—Buddhu, Surat, Manohar, Chandarbhan, and Loti. The boys assisting in the demonstration were supposed to be receiving training in the technique of dibbling. The demonstration continued up to 1 p.m. I returned to R. at about 1.30 p.m.

After taking my midday meal I vaccinated twenty students of the primary school. I left R. at 3 p.m. with a bullock cart borrowed from Shyam Singh (student). This was in response to the 'most urgent' orders of the APO. The project seed drill was at B-N, a village situated at a distance of about four miles from R. I met the APO for Social Education and Public Participation on the way. I told him that I was going to B-N to bring the seed drill. He asked me to proceed. I reached B-N at 5.15 p.m. The VLW was not present. The seed drill was in charge of an agriculturist who at first refused to hand it over to me. I was disappointed. I pleaded with him to give me the machine. He wanted a letter of authority. I showed him the APO's letter. He wanted to keep it. This I did not allow him to do. In the end he gave the seed drill to me after obtaining a receipt to that effect from me. I returned to R. at 7.30 p.m. Then I went to the *keertan*, spent a few minutes there and returned home to take my meal. After resting for a few minutes I went to meet the APO (Social Education) at the residence of the Principal of the local Intermediate College. I looked up the Extension Teacher (Agriculture) later, and asked him to accompany me for the seed drill demonstration tomorrow. I left the APO at 9 p.m.

Work to be done:

i Write the diary.
ii Enter in the register the names of persons vaccinated.

Villagers' Comments: Mulhad Singh: 'Government is taking keen interest in our welfare these days. The VLW is different from other officials. He is humble, and wants to improve things in the village.'
Q. 'What do you think of the new seed?'
M.S. 'What can I think? If the government thinks that it is good, it must be good.'
Q. 'Do you think that it is better than the local variety?'
M.S. 'Yes. It resists disease much better. It can stand frost and rain, and there is more demand for it in the market.'
Q. 'What about yield?'
M.S. 'I cannot say. Some people say it is more, others say it is not.'
Q. 'Some people say it is not as good in taste.'
M.S. 'They are right. It is not half as good. If the *roti* is served hot it is more or less the same, but if we keep it for an hour or so it gets as tough as hide. No, it is not as good in taste. People say that we all become very weak if we eat this wheat.'
Q. 'What is your experience?'
M.S. 'Many more people suffer from digestive disorders these days. Our children have cough and cold. Perhaps it is because of the new seed and sugarcane. It may be that the air has been spoilt by the wars.'
Q. 'And what about the new fertilizer?'
M.S. 'They increase the yield; there is no doubt about it. But they probably destroy the vitality of the land and also of the grain.'

3 November 1954

I got up at 5 a.m. and went to the college building to meet the Extension Teacher (Agriculture). I had to chalk out a programme with him to go to Tikka Singh's field situated at a distance of about a mile. Accompanied by Tikka Singh, his two sons and two servants, I reached there at 6 a.m. The Extension Teacher tried to start the seed drill, but the machine was not in order. It was releasing more seed than was necessary for the operation in hand. The machine had to be stopped. No one other than Tikka Singh, his sons, and his servants were present on the spot. We had to return to the college building to arrange for a bullock-cart to bring back the machine. I went along with the bullock-cart to the field and brought it back at 7.30 a.m.

Accompanied by Tara Chand and six students I went to the fields of Mulhad Singh for a dibbling demonstration. These fields are about a mile and a half away from the village. There I gave the dibbling demonstration. Five other agriculturists were present at that time; three from R. and two from Gs.—another nearby village. Before starting the demonstration I explained to them the advantages of dibbling. One of the persons present on the spot raised the point that this method was not suitable for fields of more than two *bighas*. I explained to them that this method was to be adopted only for improving the seed and for increasing the supply of the improved seed. The demonstration was given on one *bigha* of land and was completed at 11.15 a.m.

After this I came back to the college building with a view to meeting the Extension Teacher who unfortunately was out. Then I returned to my house for the midday meal.

After the meal I went to the midwife and told her that the APO, Social Education, wanted to see her. Then I went to this APO and discussed with him the possibility of visiting T-D, a nearby hamlet, but this could not be done as he had to see the midwife.

At about 2.30 p.m. I went to the Seed Store to obtain twenty-seven seers of superphosphate for Isam Singh. He accompanied me. Then we went to his field which is at a distance of about a mile and a half from the Seed Store. There we measured the field and divided it into three equal parts. In one part we put superphosphate and left the other two parts unmanured for the time being. In the second part we shall put another fertilizer when the field is about to be irrigated. The third part will go without any chemical fertilizer. Two agriculturists, Surjeet and Roddha, were present there. They were asked to take advantage of this plan. They expressed their willingness to do so and assured me that they will see me after preparing their fields.

After finishing this demonstration I returned to the tube well at about 5.30 p.m. and spoke to the operator about completion of *pucca* channels. I requested him to expedite the work and suggested that papaya trees should be planted around the tube well.

Then I went to see the vegetable plots of Gaje Singh. I noticed that he had planted his vegetables very close together. I asked him to do some thinning and he agreed. After this I went to the fields of Isam Singh and saw his nursery. I found that the leaves of most of the plants had fallen off and only the bare stems were left. I told him that it would be no use keeping the plants any longer in the field.

Returned home at about 5.45 p.m. Took my meal, and accompanied by the APO went to the Pradhan at 8 p.m. to seek his help in finding a suitable house for the midwife. As the Pradhan was indisposed this had to be postponed till the next morning.

After this we went to see the girls' primary school teacher who was ill and sat with her for about fifteen minutes. On our way back we met the new Ayurvedic doctor and inquired from him about the *hawan*[1] to be performed tomorrow. Then we returned home.

Work to be done:

Write the diary.

Villagers' Comments:

The seed drill—

Tikka Singh: 'They ask us to buy all kinds of new machines. Everyone said that this machine was very good. You saw how good it was? It refused to work from the very start. It is always like this with these machines. You know Prithvi Singh, the man who owns that big tractor. To buy the tractor they had to sell their bullocks. It gave them no end of trouble. They had to spend a lot of money on its repairs, and all their field operations were delayed. And finally they had to hire bullocks to complete their work. These machines are not dependable.'

Dibbler—

Mulhad Singh's comments are largely the same as those of Kabul Singh (see record of the first day).

Chemical fertilizers—

Isam Singh: 'Why will it (i.e. the chemical fertilizer) not be useful? A well-fed man is always stronger than one who is half-starved. It is the same with the soil.'

Vegetables—

Gaje Singh: 'We do not grow vegetables. This man (the VLW) wanted us to grow them this year, so we have sown some. A goldsmith takes minute care of everything when he is making ornaments. Do you expect us to do the same in agriculture? The government wants us to grow vegetables, and we accept what they say. But now they expect that lines should be straight (i.e. sowing should be done in straight lines) and plants should not be too close together. Perhaps they will order us to water the plants every two hours. We have other work too.'

[1]Burning incense and making sacrificial offerings. This doctor had just moved in from a neighbouring village and had planned this ritual to inaugurate his practice in the village.

Appendix II

4 NOVEMBER 1954

I got up at 5 a.m., and met Isam Singh. I had arranged to give a dibbling demonstration in his field. This had been fixed up yesterday, but today he told me that as they planned to do their sowing in another field it would not be possible for them to go out for the demonstration in the morning. He wanted me to give the demonstration in the evening, but I thought that it should be done the next morning as soil is humid only during that part of the day. I arranged with him to give a varietal demonstration in the evening.

After this I came to the Seed Store accompanied by the APO (Social Education). It was decided earlier that we should go together to the Project headquarters where I would inform the APO (Agriculture) that the seed drill was out of order. But the APO (Social Education) now assured me that he would send the APO (Agriculture) to R. to attend to the machine. So I dropped the idea of going to the headquarters and instead went to the field of Kabul Singh. It was 6.30 a.m. The field is at a distance of about a mile from the village. I had to give a superphosphate demonstration. The field was kept ready. I divided it into three equal parts. As in other demonstrations, superphosphate was put in one part and the other two parts were left as they were for the time being. The area under this demonstration is three *bighas*. The demonstration ended at 8 a.m.

Then I went to see the Extension Teacher of the local college. I saw the fields in which he has sown improved varieties of wheat. He has sown Panjab 591 in one plot and N.P. 710 in the other. He got the improved seeds from the Co-operative Seed Store.

Accompanied by the Extension Teacher I came to the college. We saw the seed drill and found that its chain was out of order. The machine was releasing more than the required quantity of seed. We waited for the APO (Agriculture) but he did not turn up. The Extension Teacher asked me to get the chain repaired at the Project headquarters. As suggested by him I went there on my bicycle. I went to the house of the APO (Agriculture) to inform him about the machine and to get further instructions from him about the necessary repairs. To my disappointment I learned that he had left the place on an inspection tour yesterday. Then I went to the shop of Natthu Mistri, got six joints of the chain replaced and returned to R.

While coming back to R. I met the Field Teacher (Social Education) to whom I handed over a note for the APO (Agriculture) about the break-down and repair of the machine.

I reached R. at about 3 p.m. I missed my midday meal. I handed over the repaired chain to the Extension Teacher to fit to the machine.

At about 4 p.m. I left to meet some of the Jatia Chamars living in one part of the village. On my way I met Kanhaiyya Julaha[1] who wanted to know about the help the Project could possibly render to his caste. I told him that they could get improved machines for weaving and could also obtain necessary raw material on the fulfilment of certain conditions. I suggested to him that the Julahas should have a Co-operative Society of their own.

I reached the quarters of the Jatia Chamars at 4.30 p.m. and convened a small meeting. I explained to them the facilities given to the Harijans by the CDP. I told them that if they were willing to pave the lanes the Project would grant them 50 per cent of the amount needed as a government subsidy. They could also construct model houses, dig new wells, and repair old wells, on the same condition. Then I told them that medicines were being distributed by me free and that they could see me whenever they needed them. They were also informed that there was a midwife in the village and that they could avail themselves of her services free of charge when required. Further, I explained to Baru, who happened to be an agriculturist, that he could get a loan for agricultural improvement and extension of irrigation.

They were glad to meet me and expressed their interest in the Project activities. I was assured co-operation in all the activities. About twenty-five people were present in the meeting. I was told that they have already applied for financial help towards the repairs of their wells. I informed them that money had been sanctioned for this purpose and that they could now start the work. I assured them that the CDP share of the expenses will be given to them very soon.

They demanded that they should be allowed to acquire the premises near the community well. This had been used by them for holding the meetings of their caste *panchayat*[2] for a very long time, but had now been taken possession of by Rajput Zamindars[3] (Chakhu and Kashmira). They expressed their desire to construct a *chaupal*[4] for community purposes. They told me that they had done much work in connection with the cleaning and paving of lanes when the Chief Minister of U.P. had visited the village.

Some of the Jatia Chamars wanted credit facilities. I suggested to them that they form a Co-operative Society and explained its many advantages. They promised that they would meet together and think this over. I returned with the impression that they will take keen interest in community development work and co-operate in it.

I returned to my house at 6.30 p.m. to get some agregene. I gave

[1]The Julahas are the Hindu caste of weavers who work the traditional handloom.

[2]Traditional council of elders.

[3]Landlords.

[4]The place where men sit, smoke, and usually sleep at night.

some of it to Kabul Singh and Tikka Singh. I explained to them that this disease resistant drug was to be mixed with the seed. At about 7 p.m. I went home to have my evening meal. Later I joined the *keertan* group[1] for an hour or so.

Work to be done:

Write the diary.

Villagers' Comments:

Chemical fertilizer—

Kabul Singh: 'The VLW said that the government is giving some *English manure* (*angrezi khad*, i.e. chemical fertilizer) free. I agreed to take it. He has given me very little. He has put it in only one part of the field, not in the whole field. If the government distributes fertilizer why does it not give it in sufficient quantity?'

Help to weavers—

Kanhaiyya: 'We hear that the government wants to help the village people. What has it done for us? He (the VLW) asked us to form a Co-operative Society. We are very few and are illiterate. Even if some of us can read and write that is not enough. We shall never know the rules and regulations of the Society. If we have a *babu*[2] (manager or clerk) he will eat away all our profits.'

Q. 'What about getting machines and raw materials?'

K. 'Who will give us machines? And who will give us raw materials? The government wants us to satisfy so many difficult conditions. Unless we have influence we cannot get anything.'

Help to Jatia Chamars—

Kirpa: 'The government comes to us only when it wants us to do some work for them; otherwise never. We do not have enough to eat and they ask us to build new houses. Why can they not give us land? Why can they not lend us money to build houses?'

Nakli: 'Everything is for the moneyed people. Will the *doctorni* (lady doctor, reference was to the midwife) come to us without money?'

Q. 'Did she ever refuse?'

Another person (name not recorded): 'We shall not say that. She comes to our quarters. But will she give us the same services she gives to the moneyed people? Can we buy her expensive medicines?'

Q. 'What about forming a Society?'

Laughter.

Kirpa: 'We do not have even parched gram and you want us to wear gold ornaments.'

[1]This group has been organized as a part of the social education programme of the CDP. It meets after the adult education class for community singing of devotional songs.

[2]Clerk. This term is also used for educated people who hold minor government positions.

5 November 1954

Last night I had been to the *chaupal* of Bharat Singh. Kalu Singh, Malkhan Singh, Shyam Singh and Bharat Singh were present there. I had taken some agregene with me for Kabul Singh. As he was not there, I handed it over to Bharat Singh to be given to Kabul Singh on his return and explained its uses and advantages to all the people present there. It was decided that a demonstration will be given in one of the fields of Isam Singh and that agregene mixed seed will be sown in a part of a field belonging to Shyam Singh. A varietal demonstration was also fixed for today in the fields of Tikka Singh.

I got up at 4 a.m., and went to Shyam Singh's field at a distance of about a mile from the village. I was accompanied by several agriculturists. First I measured the field. Its area is about four *bighas*. I divided it into four equal parts, and sowed the agregene mixed wheat seed in one part.

After this I measured the nearby field of Tikka Singh. Dividing it into two equal parts I gave a varietal demonstration of Panjab 591 and local wheat. Among those present at the time were Baru, Buddhu, Bhagirath, and Sadhal. I tried to persuade them to have a free trial of chemical fertilizer in their fields. Their response was not encouraging.

One-third of one of the fields of Isam Singh was prepared for a dibbling demonstration. Sarjeet Singh, Tirlok Chand, Tikka Singh and Isam Singh were present. We selected healthy grains from the seed and the demonstration was started. This continued up to 12.30 p.m. In the course of this demonstration one of the agriculturists suggested that in his opinion it might be better to have an iron dibbler instead of the wooden one now in use. I explained to him that the dibbler had been evolved after very careful research by the Director of Research, U.P., and that the wooden dibbler was inexpensive and easy to make.

I came back to the village and contacted the Tube Well Operator in connexion with the question of providing water to the fields above the channel level. He said that this will have to wait until the next year. He appeared to be helpless in the matter and could not make a definite promise.

I reached home at 1 p.m., and took my midday meal. Soon after, Bharat Singh, Kallan Singh, Malkhan Singh and Shyam Singh came to me to take fertilizer from the Seed Store. Two of them went to get bullock-carts from their houses, and Bharat Singh accompanied me to the Seed Store. A Jatia Chamar met me on the way and told me that he had a complaint to make and that he would like to speak to me privately. He told me that his brother had been malhandled and beaten by Malkhan Singh (a Rajput Zamindar). I consoled him and asked him to suggest politely to Malkhan Singh not to repeat this thing in future. I told him not to tell anyone that he had met me in connexion with this dispute. I requested Bharat Singh to use his good offices in this matter. He assured me that he would speak to Malkhan Singh.

Fertilizer and agregene were supplied to the agriculturists from the store and they left. Bharat Singh and Syham Singh told me that they were going to their fields and that they would like me to go with them. They proceeded with the bullock-cart. As I had to go to the school, I promised to join them later.

I returned to the school at about 3.30 p.m. and got the vegetable plots irrigated. Then I saw the experimental plot of Balbeer Singh who teaches Agriculture in the local college. I suggested to him that they should put dung manure in the beds, and that in some of the beds they should sow Panjab 591. I also suggested that some improved barley could be sown by the method of dibbling. He agreed to do so. I then met the Extension Teacher in connexion with the seed drill. He informed me that he had fixed the repaired chain on the machine but it had broken again. This made it impossible for us to give a seed drill demonstration. Then I went to the fields of Shyam Singh and Bharat Singh at about 4.30 p.m. These fields are about a mile and a half from the village. There I measured two fields of Bharat Singh and divided them into three parts. Fertilizer was applied in one of the parts in my presence. Later I explained to Bharat Singh and five or six other agriculturists present on the spot the method of preparing good dung manure. I told them the advantages of green manuring, and advised them to grow *sanai*, *moong* (type 1) and *dhencha*. Then I divided a three *bigha* field, belonging to Shyam Singh, into three parts and put super-phosphate into one part. I divided another one *bigha* plot into four parts, and handed over some agregene to Shyam Singh and asked him to mix it with the seed and then sow the seed into one of these parts.

It was already dark. I returned home at about 7 p.m. I had my meal. I went to the *keertan*, and then met Tirath Singh with a view to arranging a varietal demonstration of barley in his field tomorrow.

Work to be done:

i Write the diary.
ii Make diagrams of the field demonstrations given in the course of the day.

Villagers' Comments:
Agregene—
Kabul Singh: 'He (the VLW) has sent some medicine. It is to be mixed with the wheat seed.'

Q. 'Why?'
K.S. 'I don't know.'
Shyam Singh: 'We have sown some seed mixed with a new medicine.'
Q. 'Why?'
S.S. 'Because the VLW asked us.'
Q. 'In what way is the medicine useful?'
S.S. 'I do not know. Perhaps it protects the crops from disease.'

6 November 1954

Getting up at 5 a.m., I went to Tirath Singh and Kabul Singh. I took them to the Seed Store and got for them barley K.12 and barley C.251. Then I went to their fields situated at a distance of about two furlongs from the village. In area these fields are six and one and one-half *bighas*. I got both these fields divided into three equal parts for giving a varietal demonstration of the improved varieties of barley along with the local variety. Tirath Singh, Ramchandra, Jagmal, Mamraj Singh, Kabul Singh, and Naseeb Singh were also present there. After the demonstration I explained to them the advantages of sowing *berseem* which makes an excellent fodder crop. I also did some propaganda in favour of planting papaya and banana.

From there at about 9.30 a.m., I went to the school and handed over some barley seeds, C.251 and K.12, to the agriculture teacher. These were meant for a dibbling demonstration. In the nursery I saw the beds of lemon, *karonda* and *galgal.* The *karonda* seeds had sprouted, but the other two did not show any signs of life. I instructed the gardener to water the beds with a sprinkling can.

I went to the Seed Store again at 10.30 and met the Co-operative Supervisor to obtain the receipts of fertilizer distributed to cultivators so that I could enter their names in the register. There I met the VLW of Gs. and had a talk with him regarding the work in progress in his village. I returned to the village in half an hour and met Fateh Singh in connexion with the repairs to his well. He promised that he will get model sanitary repairs done to his well. Then I came home to have my midday meal.

At about 12.30 p.m., I went to Kabul Singh for completing the *sawai*[1] bonds. There I examined his buffalo which was suffering from a disease locally known as *nakkassa.* I suggested to him a local treatment consisting of boiled *tira* and pieces of raw bottle-gourd to be given to the animal at regular intervals. I asked him to inform me about the condition of the buffalo in the evening.

Then I went to the Seed Store. It was 1.30 p.m., and I was thinking of distributing fertilizer to some of the agriculturists. As the Co-

[1]Bonds pledging return with 25 per cent interest.

operative Supervisor had gone on tour I could not do this. The APO (Co-operatives and Village Organization) arrived from the Project headquarters in the meantime. I told him that the seed drill was out of order again and that no further demonstrations were now possible.

After the APO had left I went to a meeting of the weavers at 5.30 p.m. When I went there about twenty persons were present. Some more joined a little later. I explained to them the aims and objectives of CDP and the duties of the VLW. I told them that they could get free medicines from me. Then I spoke to them about the advantages of co-operative organization. I told them that CDP would be willing to give them subsidies and technical advice for improving rural sanitation, for paving village lanes, for repairs to wells, and also for installing community hand pumps.

I told them that financial help could be given to their caste (weavers) for buying improved implements and looms. The weavers put forward their difficulties and demanded a cheap and adequate supply of yarn and improved handlooms. They were asked to form a Co-operative Society so that these facilities could be made available to them. They told me that they were having great difficulty because of the pond (*johad*) near their living quarter. This pond generally overflows in the rainy season. They promised to contribute some money towards the construction of proper drains and requested help from CDP in this respect. I told them that I would approach the Rajputs of the neighbourhood so that they may also make some contribution and thereby lessen the burden of the weavers. I promised them that I shall try to obtain a one-third subsidy from CDP funds for this purpose. They assured me that they will contribute substantially in the form of *shramdan*. Next, they told me that they were experiencing great difficulty in obtaining good drinking water as the Rajputs did not allow them to use the nearby well. They said that the water in their own well was brackish. I suggested to them that either they could get a community hand-pump installed in their locality, or I would try to persuade the Rajputs to let them use their well. This well needs some sanitary repairs, and I have obtained an assurance from the weavers that they will contribute reasonably towards it if the Rajputs allow them to draw water from it. The meeting came to an end at about 6.30 p.m.

After the meeting I was taken to a child said to be suffering from enlarged spleen and fever. When I saw him he had no fever. I assured the parents that I shall get the child examined by the Co-operative Society doctor.

Next, I went to the *chaupal* of Teja Singh. Mangat Singh, Dhoom Singh, Bishan Singh and Manchand were present there. I asked them if they had sown *berseem* and planted papaya trees. They said that they were not thinking of sowing any *berseem*. I explained to them its advantages. One or two people hesitatingly said that they may try it this year. Teja Singh expressed his willingness to plant bananas near his fields adjoining the village.

I returned home at 8 p.m. and had my evening meal.

Work to be done:

i Write the diary.
ii Complete the demonstration register.

Villagers' Comments:
Improved barley seed—
Tirath Singh: 'I am trying this new barley for the first time. We have tried new wheat and sugarcane before. The VLW says that this type is better than the local variety.'
Q. 'Do you think it will be better?'
T.S. 'How can I say anything now. We must first see the results.'
Berseem—
Tirath Singh: 'We have heard about it, but have not grown it so far. If I get any seed from the government I will try it.'
Help to weavers—
Kanhaiyya: 'He (the VLW) came again. He talked about our forming a Society. I do not think we shall ever form one. Even if we do, I am sure it will fail. We are not used to working that way. We asked him to do something about the pond. He wants us to contribute money, and to work ourselves. What is the government doing?'

7 November 1954

I got up at 5 a.m., went to Kallu Singh, and accompanied him to his field situated at a distance of about four furlongs from the village. After measuring the two plots of four and five *bighas* earmarked for this demonstration, I divided each of them into three equal parts. In the five *bigha* plot I gave a mixed fertilizer trial. I applied forty-two seers of mixed fertilizer in one part and sixty-three seers in the other, and left the third part as it was. In the other plot of four *bighas*, I applied twenty-one seers of superphosphate in one part, leaving the other two parts as they were. Part 1 and 2 will get a dressing of chemical fertilizer when they are ready for irrigation. In the third part only the usual manure will be used. Kartar Singh, Kallu Singh, Bishambhar Singh, Chamela Singh and others were present on the spot to watch this demonstration. The purpose of the trial was explained to them. One of them inquired as to why the ratio of fertilizer in different fields was different. I told them that it was being done to determine the quantity most effective for the soil of R. Their attention was especially drawn towards the great utility of dung manure. They were told that if one member of the family attended exclusively to the collection and proper preparation of this manure, he would be doing a real service to the family by adding greatly to the yield of the fields. I then suggested to them that they should plant papaya and sow *berseem*. They promised to do so.

I returned to the village at about 9 a.m. Accompanied by Kallu Singh, I went to the *chaupal* of Prithvi Singh. Pratap and Lakshman were also sitting there. I asked them if they were planting any papaya trees. Prithvi Singh and Lakshman Singh promised to plant fifty each within three or four days. They were also advised to sow *berseem*. They replied that they would sow *rij* and not *berseem* as the latter is believed to be 'cold'.[1] I told them that *rij* was good for horses, and that *berseem* was to be preferred for milch cattle. They said 'yes' to me, but did not look convinced. I told them of those who had benefited from this experiment. On this they agreed to grow some *berseem*.

After this I went to the Pradhan[2] at about 11 a.m., to seek his help in finding a house for the midwife. He promised to take me in the afternoon to the house which he had already suggested to the APO (Social Education). Then I returned home for lunch. Soon after the meal I went again to the Pradhan. He asked me to call the midwife also so that she too could see the house. The Pradhan informed me that the accommodation he had in view was an independent house and not a part of another house. I went to the midwife and informed her about this house. She did not like the idea of living in a separate house. So we decided to put a tin partition in the room in which she is living at present, to separate the cattle-shed from the portion used by her.

Then I went to the Dhunias (an occupational caste which cards cotton) and called a meeting. This was at 1.30 p.m. About ten persons were present. Prominent among them were Baru Singh, Keshao, Umrao, and Majeed. I explained to them the aims and objectives of the CDP and asked them to take advantage of it. They were also informed about the medicine chest, containing medicines for most common ailments and ordinary diseases which has been supplied to me by the Project. These medicines, I assured them, could be had free of charge, and they could unhesitatingly approach me for them whenever they needed some.

[1]It is common to describe foods as 'cold' or 'hot', i.e. as cold-producing or heat-producing.

[2]Literally 'head' or 'chief'. He is the presiding officer of the elected village council, and its chief executive officer.

I explained to them that they could get carding and jinning machines if they formed a Co-operative Society. This could facilitate, accelerate, and economize their work as well as costs. They assured me that they would give careful thought to the proposal and see what they could do in the matter.

Five families wanted to have a community hand-pump. They requested financial assistance for this. I promised them that I would discuss this matter with the DyPEO, and if possible they will get the assistance. The meeting concluded at about 4.30 p.m.

Some of the Dhunia leaders said that they would hold another meeting to discuss their needs and problems and would like me to attend it. I assured them that I shall always be available for consultation and for working out the details of any plans they may have in mind.

While returning from the meeting Latour Singh met me at the *chaupal* of Fattu Singh. He informed me that his bullock was ailing, and suggested that I should examine it. I accompanied him to his house and examined the bullock. Latour Singh and Amar Singh were also present. The bullock looked very weak. It was not eating anything and was having loose motions (bowel movements). Both were symptoms of indigestion. I wrote down the following indigenous prescription: *Chiraeta*—2 *chhataks*,[1] *Sounth*—2 *chhataks*, plain salt—2 *chhataks*, Ajwain—1 *chhatak*, *Kali Jeeri*—2 *tolas*, *Hara Kasees*—2 *tolas*, *Kattha* (burnt)—2 *tolas*—to be pounded and mixed, and given in one ounce doses twice a day. I explained to the people the symptoms of several diseases of the cattle and also the methods of their treatment.

Then I called on the Co-operative Society doctor and took him to Kanhaiyya Julaha whose boy seemed to be suffering from enlarged spleen. The doctor declared him all right. The doctor also examined the daughter of Fattu Julaha. She was suffering from enlarged spleen. He asked them to get medicines from the dispensary.

At about 6.30 p.m. I returned home. After my meal I met Mula Singh regarding the irrigation of fields above the channel level.

Work to be done:

Write the diary.

Villagers' Comments:

Fertilizer and manure—

Kalla Singh: 'He has put some manure in the fields: one part has been left as it is, in another part a small quantity of fertilizer has been applied, and in the third part a still larger quantity has been applied.

Q. 'Why this difference?'

[1]Local measure of weight. Sixteen *chhataks* make one seer.

K.S. 'He wants to prove that by putting in more manure we can get a better yield.'
Another person present, 'As if we do not know!'
Q. 'What about cow dung?'
K.S. 'We know its utility and have been using it. But how to collect it? Our womenfolk cannot go about collecting it. No Rajput will send his daughter-in-law with a basket to collect cow dung.'
Papaya and *berseem*—
Prithvi Singh: 'He has asked us to grow papayas. I think I will plant a few. We do not eat them very much—they do not taste good. And women think that they are inauspicious. . . . *Beerseem* is believed to be cold, it does not give strength to the cattle. But we can try. Maybe it is as good as the VLW says.'

8 November 1954

Getting up at 5 a.m., I went to the fields near the tube well and examined the germination of wheat. In many fields it appears to be promising. I also examined the fields in which fertilizer demonstrations have been given. The germination in these fields was found to be excellent.

Returned home at 6.30 a.m. Had bath. Went to the college to meet the DPO. As he was busy I went to the school nursery. I directed Mangal, the gardener, to apply chemical fertilizer to some of the plots. In the meantime Mula Singh and Umrao Singh came there. I advised them to take some vegetable seedlings from the nursery and plant them in their backyards. They were shown the papaya seedlings that were ready, and were advised to plant them in the backyards or in the fields. They promised to do so.

At about 8.30 a.m. I returned to the village. On my way I met Sakat Singh. He told us that he wanted pea and gram seeds. I immediately took him to the Seed Store and got him the required seeds. There I found that about twenty-seven pounds of potato seed was still lying unsold. I persuaded Sakat Singh to buy that seed, and gave him detailed instructions regarding the correct method of sowing and manuring it.

Returned home at 10.30 a.m. Did some routine writing work which took about an hour. After finishing this I had my lunch.

At 1 p.m. I went to a nearby hamlet to give a fertilizer demonstration in the fields of Mussaddi Singh. This took two hours.

Then I returned to R. and went to the locality of Jatia Chamars. I took with me the medicine chest. On the way I inquired from the Julāhas if they needed any medicines. Fifteen persons took medicine for cough, two for ringworm, two for boils, and one each for constipation and fever.

After distributing the medicines I spoke to them. I asked them to attend the *keertan* and the adult education classes at the Panchayat Ghar. They were advised to start work on the two wells for their locality, money for which had been sanctioned by the CDP. They promised to start work on the wells soon. They assured me that they will send four or five persons from their locality to the Panchayat Ghar for learning to perform the *keertan*, and will then start a *keertan* centre in their quarter.

I returned home at 7 p.m., and went after a while to the Principal to inquire about his health. After half an hour I came home and had my evening meal. Then I went to the *keertan*, and there listened to the story of a greedy and untruthful person who wanted to amass wealth by unfair means and who met a deserving end.

From the *keertan* I returned home and did some routine work.

Work to be done:

Write the diary.

Villagers' Comments:
Medicines—
A Jatia Chamar: 'He came to us with medicines for the first time. It will be a great help if he can give us free medicines whenever we need them.'
Q. 'What medicines did he give?—*desi* (indigenous) or English (western)?'
J.C. 'We do not know. As he (the VLW) is a government official the medicines must be English.' (In point of fact most of the medicines in the medicine chest supplied to the VLW are Ayurvedic.[1])
Q. 'What medicines do you like?'
J.C. 'What we can get. We are too poor to be able to afford a doctor's fee. English medicines give quick relief.'
Keertan—
Ramma: 'They ask us to join the *keertan*. Will the Rajputs ever allow us to sit with them?'
Interviewer, 'They say they will.'
R. 'There is a saying. An elephant has two sets of teeth—one that he shows, another that he uses. They may say whatever they like, but they will never let us sit with them.'

9 November 1954

I got up at 4.30 a.m. today and went to the half-field demonstration plot near the Seed Store. In this field G.P. 25 and the local variety of gram had been sown some time ago. The germination was fairly good. Then I went to Ridka's field where improved variety of potato

[1]The indigenous system of Indian medicine.

seed, supplied by the CDP, has been sown. The germination was satisfactory in this field also.

Having seen these two fields I returned to my house for a bath. About twenty minutes were spent in prayer. Then I went to Malkhan Singh. He was sitting in his *chaupal* with Prithvi Singh, Kabul Singh, Shyam Singh, and some others. I asked Kabul Singh and Shyam Singh to accompany me to their fields for the demonstrations we had planned earlier. We three reached the fields at about 8.30 a.m. The distance from the village to the fields is a little more than a mile.

A fertilizer demonstration was given in the field of Shyam Singh, and then it was repeated in the field of Malkhan Singh. The distance between these fields is about a furlong. When the demonstration was being given in the field of Shyam Singh, Malkhan Singh and his servants were also present.

This is how I gave the demonstration: I divided the plot into three equal parts by measuring it with a tape. In the first part I applied supersulphate and in the second, mixed fertilizer. No fertilizer was applied to the third plot as we intended to keep it as a 'control plot'. It was decided to apply uria or more mixed fertilizer at the time of irrigating the field.

Four *bighas* of land are under the first demonstration. The second demonstration given in Malkhan Singh's plot of about three acres followed the pattern of the first.

Later, in the field of Khadak Singh, I gave a half-field demonstration. I divided a plot of two *bighas* into two equal parts. Panjab 591 was sown in one part and in the other the local variety of wheat was sown. This was done with a dibbler.

I then proceeded to the field of a Mali.[1] This field is at a distance of about six furlongs from the field of Khadak Singh. Potatoes had been sown in this field. Mixed fertilizer had been applied in two parts of this field while the third part had been left without any fertilizer. The proportion of fertilizers in the three parts of the field had been $1\frac{1}{2} : 1 : 0$. In part one, which had been given a larger dose of fertilizers, the germination was excellent. In the second part, in which only a limited quantity of fertilizer had been applied, it was better than the germination in the third plot which had no fertilizer. The third plot, being the 'control' plot, had been manured in the usual way, but without any chemical fertilizer.

At about 10 a.m. I came back to the *chaupal* of Prithvi Singh. Partap Singh (Patwari),[2] Chhanga Singh, and some others were sitting there. I spoke to them about the proper care of cattle. I also explained to them some of the modern methods of cattle breeding. I

[1] A caste of gardeners and vegetable growers.
[2] Keeper of land records, a minor government official.

also told them about the new methods of feeding the cattle. They appeared to feel that what I had told them was right and useful. I then emphasized the importance of a balanced diet for the cattle. This was very necessary if they wanted to keep their cattle healthy and free from diseases, I told them. Turning to the point of cattle breeding I asked them to improve their livestock by taking certain precautions in their village. The first thing that I asked them to do was to get all the scrub bulls castrated. There are three stud bulls in the village—one pedigree and the other two of local breed. For improving their cattle stock it was necessary for them to allow only the pedigree bull to operate.

Then I asked them to plant papaya trees in the courtyards of their houses and in their gardens. In this village I did not find anyone refusing to do so on the ground that it was inauspicious to have papaya trees near the house. In G. most people had refused to plant papaya trees on this ground. Persons present at Prithvi Singh's *chaupal* agreed to plant papaya trees. I asked Prithvi Singh to grow onions and cabbage in his field. He showed willingness and agreed to accompany me, whenever I was free, to attend to this work in his field.

I then went to J-K, a part of the village which is practically an independent hamlet, and met Nathu Singh, Isam Singh, and Musaddi Singh in the *chaupal* of Nathu Singh. I suggested to them that they have a separate primary school for their locality. Nathu Singh liked the idea but feared lack of support from the CDP officials. I asked him to write an application and hand it over to me. He said that he would consult the other elders and influential people of the locality and would let me know their final decision.

While we were talking I noticed that there were three or four heaps of cattle dung on the open ground. I explained to the people that they should cover these with earth. This was necessary if they wanted to get full advantage of the nitrogen in the dung. I told them that animal dung contains nitrogen which helps greatly in adding to the fertility of the soil, and that due to the heat of the sun most of this nitrogen escapes if the dung is left uncovered. Winds also sweep away a part of this valuable manure. In the rainy season water washes away what is left of it. In order to avoid this loss I asked them to dig pits of 8 × 6 × 4 or 12 × 8 × 4. These should be covered with earth regularly. Explaining the disadvantages of open manure heaps I told them that such manure is often responsible for crop diseases. When such manure is put in fields it is easy for the white ants to ruin the crops. I felt that they were convinced about what I had said. They promised to act on my suggestions.

I came back to my house at about 1 p.m. With about five *tolas* of agregene from my house I went to the *chaupal* of Daroga Singh. His father, Musaddi Singh, was in the house. I handed over the agregene to him and instructed him to mix it well in twenty seers of wheat. I came back to my house and had my midday meal.

After this I called on Baru Singh, Parsa, Haridwari, and Kirpa who were all present in their houses. I sat for some time with Jagdish (one of the boys who was injured in a collision between a truck and a train). I had a brief talk with him and asked him about the condition of his injuries. From his talk it was clear that he was nervous, so I consoled him. I also had a talk with Parsa. I suggested to him to sow *berseem* and explained its advantages at some length. But he was reluctant to try it. A detailed explanation was necessary to convince this man. In the end he agreed to sow *berseem* in one *bigha* as an experimental measure. Before leaving his house I told Parsa that I had medicines with me and that anyone in need could come to me.

I went to the Cornell Project House at 3 p.m. and had a talk with Dr. Dube regarding problems and difficulties of the VLW. Left Dr. Dube at 6.30 p.m.

Returned to my house, had my meal, and attended the *keertan*. After this I went out again to meet Shyam Singh. He was in his house. I asked him to be in readiness for a dibbling demonstration in his field early tomorrow morning. He agreed.

Work to be done:

i Write the diary.
ii Prepare statements for the meeting to be held in the Project headquarters tomorrow.
iii Demonstration Register to be completed.
iv Medicine Register to be completed.

The following statements are needed for tomorrow's meeting:

i Copy of the diary.
ii Survey report.
iii List of people who bought potato seed (improved).
iv List of Rabi[1] demonstrations.
v List of persons to whom fertilizer was given free.

In the preparation of all these statements at least three hours are required. It may be completed by 1.30 a.m.

Villagers' Comments:
Fertilizer demonstration—
Malkhan Singh: 'These English manures (chemical fertilizer) are good, but you have to weigh them like medicines. We are not used to it. Then you have to water the fields at regular intervals, and they

[1]Crops sown in winter.

need a lot more water. There is nothing better than cow dung, but we never have enough of it. These foreign manures are also good, if we can learn to be careful with them. They are especially good for the new varieties of sugarcane and wheat.'

Improved cattle—

Prithvi Singh: 'Who does not want improved cattle? I will be very proud if I own some. People go to the Panjab to buy them. We have contributed money to buy these large bulls. But what are we to do with the scrub bulls? Many people leave bulls[1] with a religious motive in return for a request granted by supernatural powers. You cannot castrate them. Who would go in for the sin of castrating a sacred bull?'

Compost—

Nathu Singh: 'Don't think we do not know about compost. We know its utility. We do not want manure to lie in heaps in front of our houses. But what shall we do? Our women (i.e. Rajput women) cannot carry manure to a distant pit outside the village or near our fields. Labour is difficult to get. Chamars are now swollen-headed. They do not want to serve us, and we cannot depend on them. They will carry the manure from our houses, and for a few annas throw it in the pit belonging to someone else.'

School—

Nathu Singh: 'We need one very badly. In fact we have employed a private teacher who runs a school in the *chaupal* of C.S. It is difficult to get things from the government. Officers are slow, and oblige only those who have "pull". We shall approach the government for a separate school.'

Berseem—

Parsa: 'The government is asking us to do too many things. If they give me this new seed I will grow it. We are afraid that we may be charged heavily for it, or next year they may ask us to return the seed with interest.'

10 November 1954

Got up at 5 a.m. Picked up the dibbler and went to the house of Shyam Singh. The following were present in his *chaupal*: Bharat Singh, Roopchand, Bhagmal, Chaman Singh, and Girwar Singh. I spoke to them about the importance of animal manure and told them how they could have more manure for their fields. In front of Shyam Singh's house there was a large refuse heap which was uncovered

[1]Bulls are regarded as sacred. It is believed that Shiva, a great God of Hindu Trinity, uses a bull as a mount. Calves dedicated to the gods grow into bulls and are not regarded as the property of any individual. They graze freely around the village.

and unprotected. I pointed this out to them and added that they were wasting valuable manure. I told them that the best way to protect manure is to deposit it in a properly dug manure pit and to keep it covered. I then added that the nitrogen content of the heap lying in front of the house could be preserved considerably by covering it with earth. We started work on the manure heap. In ten to fifteen minutes the heap was covered with earth. Then I spoke to them about the utility of *berseem* as a fodder crop and asked them to grow it in their fields. They told me that they have been growing *rij* or *rijka* (known locally as *lusan*) and were not particularly anxious to change from it to any other fodder crop. So I had to deal at some length with the comparative merits and demerits of *berseem* and *rijka* for milch cattle. They agreed to experiment with *berseem* on a limited scale.

We then got ready for a dibbling demonstration to be given in one of the fields of Shyam Singh. I collected six boys of the primary school and took them along with Shyam Singh and his sons to the fields. There I selected a one *bigha* plot for the demonstration. I got it ploughed. We got straight lines drawn in one plot, the distance between two lines being twenty-seven inches. Then with the aid of the dibbler, assisted by school students, I gave the demonstration.

I then hurried to the nearby field of Musaddi Singh to give a mixed fertilizer demonstration. Then I returned home and had my meal.

Today was the day of our fortnightly staff meeting. Equipped with my records and reports I left for the Project headquarters on my bicycle. On the way I gave a superphosphate trial in a three and a half *bigha* plot belonging to Fattu Singh. After this I rushed to the Project headquarters, reaching there at 11 a.m.

The meeting started punctually at 11 a.m. The new DyPEO spoke to us about the re-allocation of work. He said that it was felt that the work-load of the VLW was rather heavy and as such he was making an attempt to reduce it by relating the other development staff, such as Panchayat Secretaries and Cane Supervisors, more closely to Project activities. I was informed that from now on I shall have to look after only R. and the hamlet of T-D. G. which had so far been under my charge was now transferred to the Panchayat Secretary.

The DyPEO exhorted us to work with devotion and sincerity. It was announced that the village showing greatest enthusiasm and maximum achievement in respect of Project activity will be awarded a cash prize of Rs100. The prize money will be handed over to the Gaon Sabha. The VLW concerned will be recognized for his meritorious work by a special entry in his service roll.

Under the revised administrative set-up, groups of villages have been placed under the charge of different APOs. They will be in overall charge of all development work in these villages.

It was announced that a Refresher Training Camp was being organized at J-J. This was to be attended by all the VLWs as well as by the Panchayat Secretaries and the Cane Supervisors. The duration of the camp was to be one week. The VLWs were asked to provide two statements about the agriculture demonstrations given by them. The details regarding these statements were also given. We were asked to prepare the statements in the meeting itself but when we pointed out that the statements involved considerable work we were allowed a week's time to forward them to the office.

Plans of action for the future were discussed. The decision that amonium sulphate, groundnut cake, and bone meal could now be given as *taccavi*[1] to the agriculturists on 5½ per cent interest was announced. We were asked to prepare statements evaluating the results of *kharif* (crops sown in the rainy season) demonstrations. We were directed to enter the best agriculturists for the *rabi* (crops sown in winter) competitions. Prizes are awarded at different levels, such as, Gaon Sabha, Adalati Panchayat, Tahsil,[2] and District. We were asked to start work in connexion with the planting of community orchards. I was asked to give more attention to the college nursery. We were directed to send in our reports on kitchen gardens within a week. I was informed that agriculturists in my villages could get *taccavi* loans for Persian wheels and also for boring wells. We were asked to prepare a statement showing the area of land under cultivation, with particulars regarding land under irrigation from tube wells and from other sources. We were also informed that people could now get loans for buying good breeds of cows and buffaloes. A loan of Rs300 for a cow and Rs500 for a buffalo could be advanced; to be repaid in ten equal six-monthly instalments. All VLWs were asked to get one 'foot bath' for the cattle constructed in each village under their charge. These are to be constructed at a central place on the way the village cattle generally pass. The foot bath containing disinfectant in the water is expected to protect the cattle against hoof and mouth disease. It was clearly pointed out to us that the only subsidy CDP was willing to give for this was three bags of cement per village. Bricks and labour were to be supplied by the villagers themselves. White Leghorn eggs were to be made available at a subsidized rate of two annas per egg. If anyone wanted them to be hatched in the incubator at the Project headquarters the approximate cost of each chick would be eight to ten annas. We were asked to promote actively the programme of getting model sanitary repairs effected in the village wells, and to give priority to the paving of

[1]Loans advanced for agricultural improvement.
[2]Administrative subdivision of a district.

village lanes. We were asked to supply particulars regarding *akharas*[1] in the village. The meeting ended at about 7 p.m.

I stayed for the night at the Project headquarters.

Concluding Comment

The aim in this study has been to give an intimate picture of one Village Level Worker in action, and to bring into sharp focus some of his activities and problems. Although it is not possible to make many broad generalizations from observations extending over only ten days, some reflections and a few tentative conclusions may be hazarded.

True to the original conception of his role the VLW has been functioning as a multi-purpose extension agent. As the CDP programme centres mainly round agricultural extension most of his time and energy naturally go into this work. Nevertheless, he has given a reasonable part of his time to other items of CDP activity, such as sanitation and medical care, and care of cattle health. He has also made some effort at mass contact with a view to finding out the 'felt needs' of the people and to popularizing knowledge of the aims and objectives of the project. His success in getting items of CDP programme accepted—wholly or partially—can be attributed to his patience and perseverance in trying to educate the people to accept the plans and practices offered by the CDP. His own observations and comments by the people illustrate the degree of initial reserve, hesitation, and reluctance with which the village greets his new ideas and innovations.

The VLW understands the necessity for administrative co-ordination, and has been co-operating with the village level officials and field staff of other development departments. As the record shows he gave considerable time to the Cotton Supervisor in one of his visits. However, the fact that this gesture on his part was not well received by the APO (VLW's immediate superior) deserves to be noted.

On the whole the work-load of the VLW is rather heavy. For effective multi-purpose functioning it is necessary that he should have a much smaller area under his charge. From the record it will be clear that while he did agricultural extension work in all the villages under his charge, his other activities were confined only to R. which happens to be his place of residence. He could distribute medicines only in R. Attention to cattle health, as well as participation in youth welfare activity and CDP sponsored recreation programmes too, were possible only in this village. G. and T-D., two other villages

[1]Village wrestling pit where people take exercise and practise wrestling.

under the VLW's charge, could not receive his attention in so far as these items of CDP activity were concerned. In still another respect R. received favoured treatment. The VLW's mass contact meetings were organized only in this village. From this observation we formed the impression that while the VLW was very regular and steady in his agricultural extension and routine office work, his attention to other parts of the CDP work tended to be somewhat erratic. This is, however, not intended as a criticism of the VLW, who, to our personal knowledge, never got up later than 5 a.m. or retired before 11 p.m. At the time of this study he was preoccupied with the *rabi* operations and that is perhaps one more reason why he could not give adequate attention to some other parts of his work.

The VLW's immediate superiors do not appear to be very tactful in their dealings with him. Instead of trying to build up his prestige in the village they inadvertently help to lower it. From the record of the first day it will be seen that the APO (Agriculture) criticized the VLW publicly in his absence, and asked the village people to convey warnings to him that he would be discharged. The general tone of his letter to the VLW, mentioned in the first day's record, reveals a glaring lack of understanding of VLW's role. The denial of the elementary courtesy of addressing a co-worker with *shri* and *aap*, and the warnings and threats of dismissal are not in tune with the theory of extension work which demands utmost harmony, co-operation and team spirit for the successful execution of the programme.[1] In this particular instance the VLW does not appear to be at fault. Treatment such as this in which the VLW is dealt with as a subordinate of low status and no consequence frustrates the man in the field and kills his zest for work. It is essential that calculated effort should be made to curb this 'boss mentality' so that a healthy team-spirit may be created.

Another point elaborated further elsewhere[2] may be briefly mentioned here. From the record of the last day one will get the impression that in the staff meetings there is only a 'one-way communication'; the officers do the talking, the VLWs do the listening. To generate more life into these staff meetings and to build up the VLW's self-respect, the VLWs should be encouraged to participate more

[1]It may be added that in the traditional administrative organization of India the relations between a government employee and his official superior were generally governed by a rigid protocol, and the former had to behave as an inferior even in social matters. Political leaders viewed this as an undesirable inheritance from British rule—something quite out of tune with the aims of free India. In the orientation and training programmes for rural development workers great emphasis was laid on the necessity of discarding the out-of-date superior-subordinate mentality, and on developing a healthy co-operative team spirit.

[2]Appendix I.

actively in the deliberations and discussions of these meetings. They should be expected not only to put forward their difficulties, but also to make suggestions for improving the methods of work, something that is not being done at present.

Finally, from the general response of the people it will be evident that the community development projects are viewed largely as a sort of government 'drive' and not as a vital, democratic movement of the people themselves. People still tend to do certain things in a spirit of compliance with the directives of the State. They expect the government to do much for them, but have a deep-seated scepticism regarding its methods and motives.

BIBLIOGRAPHY

AGARWAL, S. N. *The Gandhian Plan of Economic Development for India.* Bombay, 1944.

ANSTEY, V. *Economic Development of India.* London, 1936.

BELSHAW, H., and GRANT, JOHN B. *Report of the Mission on Community Organization and Development in South and South-East Asia.* United Nations, 1953.

COMMONWEALTH CONSULTATIVE COMMITTEE ON SOUTH AND SOUTH-EAST ASIA. *The Colombo Plan.* London, 1950.

COMMUNITY PROJECTS ADMINISTRATION, GOVERNMENT OF INDIA. *Manual for Village Level Workers.* Delhi (n.d.).

Kurukshetra— A Symposium on Community Development in India. Delhi, 1955.

DUBE, S. C. *Indian Village.* Ithaca and London, 1955.

GHOSE, B. C. *Planning for India.* London, 1945.

INTERNATIONAL CO-OPERATION ADMINISTRATION. *Community Development Programmes in India, Pakistan and the Philippines.* Washington, D.C., 1955.

KUMARAPPA, B. *Capitalism, Socialism or Villagism.* Madras, 1946.

KUMARAPPA, J. C. *Gandhian Economic Thought.* Bombay, 1951.

MAJUMDAR, D. N. (ed.). *Rural Profiles.* Lucknow, 1955.

MARRIOTT, MCKIM (ed.). *Village India.* Chicago, 1955.

MEAD, M. (ed.). *Cultural Patterns and Technical Change.* Paris, 1953.

MINISTRY OF COMMUNITY DEVELOPMENT, GOVERNMENT OF INDIA. *A Guide to Community Development.* Delhi, 1957.

NAG, D. S. *A Study of Economic Plans for India.* Bombay, 1949.

NATIONAL PLANNING COMMITTEE. *National Planning—Principles and Administration.* Bombay, 1948.

OPLER, M. E. *Social Aspects of Technical Assistance in Operation.* Paris, 1954.

PAUL, B. D. (ed.). *Health, Culture and Community.* New York, 1955.

PLANNING COMMISSION, GOVERNMENT OF INDIA. *The First Five Year Plan.* Delhi, 1951.

Second Five Year Plan. Delhi, 1956.

PROGRAMME EVALUATION ORGANISATION, PLANNING COMMISSION. *Evaluation Report on First Year's Working of Community Projects*. Delhi, 1954.

Community Projects—First Reactions. Delhi, 1954.

Evaluation Report on Second Year's Working of Community Projects. Delhi, 1955.

Leadership and Groups in a South Indian Village. Delhi, 1955.

Evaluation Report on Working of Community Projects and N.E.S. Blocks. Delhi, 1956.

Evaluation Report on Working of Community Projects and N.E.S. Blocks. Delhi, 1957.

RUOPP, P. (ed.). *Approaches to Community Development*. Bandung and The Hague, 1953.

SHAH, K. T. *National Planning Committee Report*. Bombay, 1945.

Priorities in Planning. Bombay, 1946.

India's National Plan. Bombay, 1947.

SHENOY, B. R. *The Bombay Plan—A Review of Its Financial Provisions*. Bombay, 1944.

SINGH, T. *Poverty and Social Change*. London, 1945.

SOVANI, N. *Planning of Post-War Economic Development in India*. Poona, 1951.

SPICER, E. H. (ed.). *Human Problems in Technological Change*. New York, 1952.

THAKURDAS, P. and OTHERS. *A Plan of Economic Development for India*. Bombay, 1944.

WADIA, P. A. and MERCHANT, K. T. *The Bombay Plan—A Criticism*. Bombay, 1946.

WEST BENGAL GOVERNMENT PRESS. *India's Villages*. Calcutta, 1955.

INDEX

The International Library of

Sociology

and Social Reconstruction

Edited by W. J. H. SPROTT
Founded by KARL MANNHEIM

ROUTLEDGE & KEGAN PAUL
BROADWAY HOUSE, CARTER LANE, LONDON, E.C.4

CONTENTS

PRINTED IN GREAT BRITAIN BY HEADLEY BROTHERS LTD
109 KINGSWAY LONDON WC2 AND ASHFORD KENT

GENERAL SOCIOLOGY

Brown, Robert. Explanation in Social Science. *208 pp. 1963. (2nd Impression 1964.) 25s.*

Gibson, Quentin. The Logic of Social Enquiry. *240 pp. 1960. (2nd Impression* 1963.) *24s.*

Goldschmidt, Professor Walter. Understanding Human Society. *272 pp. 1959. 21s.*

Homans, George C. Sentiments and Activities: Essays in Social Science. *336 pp. 1962. 32s.*

Jarvie, I. C. The Revolution in Anthropology. *Foreword by Ernest Gellner. 272 pp. 1964. 40s.*

Johnson, Harry M. Sociology: a Systematic Introduction. *Foreword by Robert K. Merton. 710 pp. 1961. (4th Impression 1964.) 42s.*

Mannheim, Karl. Essays on Sociology and Social Psychology. *Edited by Paul Keckskemeti. With Editorial Note by Adolph Lowe. 344 pp. 1953. 30s.*

Systematic Sociology: An Introduction to the Study of Society. *Edited by J. S. Erös and Professor W. A. C. Stewart. 220 pp. 1957. (2nd Impression 1959.) 24s.*

Martindale, Don. The Nature and Types of Sociological Theory. *292 pp. 1961. 35s.*

Maus, Heinz. A Short History of Sociology. *234 pp. 1962. 28s.*

Myrdal, Gunnar. Value in Social Theory: A Collection of Essays on Methodology. *Edited by Paul Streeten. 332 pp. 1958. (2nd Impression 1962.) 32s.*

Ogburn, William F., and **Nimkoff, Meyer F.** A Handbook of Sociology. *Preface by Karl Mannheim. 656 pp. 46 figures. 38 tables. 5th edition (revised) 1964. 40s.*

Parsons, Talcott and **Smelser, Neil J.** Economy and Society: A Study in the Integration of Economic and Social Theory. *362 pp. 1956. (3rd Impression 1964.) 35s.*

Rex, John. Key Problems of Sociological Theory. *220 pp. 1961. (2nd Impression 1963.) 25s.*

Stark, Werner. The Fundamental Forms of Social Thought. *280 pp. 1962. 32s.*

FOREIGN CLASSICS OF SOCIOLOGY

Durkheim, Emile. Suicide. A Study in Sociology. *Edited and with an Introduction by George Simpson. 404 pp. 1952. (2nd Impression 1963.) 30s.*

Socialism and Saint-Simon. *Edited with an Introduction by Alvin W. Gouldner. Translated by Charlotte Sattler from the edition originally edited with an Introduction by Marcel Mauss. 286 pp. 1959. 28s.*

Professional Ethics and Civic Morals. *Translated by Cornelia Brookfield. 288 pp. 1957. 30s.*

Gerth, H. H., and **Wright Mills, C.** From Max Weber: Essays in Sociology. *502 pp. 1948. (5th Impression 1964.) 35s.*

Tönnies, Ferdinand. Community and Association. (*Gemeinschaft und Gesellschaft.*) *Translated and Supplemented by Charles P. Loomis. Foreword by Pitirim A. Sorokin. 334 pp. 1955. 28s.*

SOCIAL STRUCTURE

Andrzejewski, Stanislaw. Military Organization and Society. *With a Foreword by Professor A. R. Radcliffe-Brown. 226 pp. 1 folder. 1954. 21s.*

Cole, G. D. H. Studies in Class Structure. *220 pp. 1955. (3rd Impression 1964.) 21s.*

Coontz, Sydney H. Population Theories and the Economic Interpretation. *202 pp. 1957. (2nd Impression 1961.) 25s.*

Coser, Lewis. The Functions of Social Conflict. *204 pp. 1956. 18s.*

Glass, D. V. (Ed.). Social Mobility in Britain. *Contributions by J. Berent, T. Bottomore, R. C. Chambers, J. Floud, D. V. Glass, J. R. Hall, H. T. Himmelweit, R. K. Kelsall, F. M. Martin, C. A. Moser, R. Mukherjee, and W. Ziegel. 420 pp. 1954. (2nd Impressions 1963.) 40s.*

Kelsall, R. K. Higher Civil Servants in Britain: From 1870 to the Present Day. *268 pp. 31 tables. 1955. 25s.*

Ossowski, Stanislaw. Class Structure in the Social Consciousness. *212 pp. 1963. 25s.*

SOCIOLOGY AND POLITICS

Barbu, Zevedei. Democracy and Dictatorship: Their Psychology and Patterns of Life. *300 pp. 1956. 28s.*

Benney, Mark, Gray, A. P., and **Pear, R. H.** How People Vote: a Study of Electoral Behaviour in Greenwich. *Foreword by Professor W. A. Robson. 256 pp. 70 tables. 1956. 25s.*

Bramstedt, Dr. E. K. Dictatorship and Political Police: The Technique of Control by Fear. *286 pp. 1945. 20s.*

Crick, Bernard. The American Science of Politics: Its Origins and Conditions. *284 pp. 1959. 28s.*

Hertz, Frederick. Nationality in History and Politics: A Psychology and Sociology of National Sentiment and Nationalism. *440 pp. 1944. (4th Impression 1957.) 32s.*

Kornhauser, William. The Politics of Mass Society. *272 pp. 20 tables. 1960. 25s.*

Laidler, Harry W. Social-Economic Movements: An Historical and Comparative Survey of Socialism, Communism, Co-operation, Utopianism; and other Systems of Reform and Reconstruction. *864 pp. 16 plates. 1 figure. 1949. (3rd Impression 1960.) 50s.*

Mannheim, Karl. Freedom, Power and Democratic Planning. *Edited by Hans Gerth and Ernest K. Bramstedt. 424 pp. 1951. 35s.*

Mansur, Fatma. Process of Independence. *Foreword by A. H. Hanson. 208 pp. 1962. 25s.*

Myrdal, Gunnar. The Political Element in the Development of Economic Theory. *Translated from the German by Paul Streeten. 282 pp. 1953. (3rd Impression 1961.) 25s.*

Polanyi, Michael, F.R.S. The Logic of Liberty: Reflections and Rejoinders. *228 pp. 1951. 18s.*

Verney, Douglas V. The Analysis of Political Systems. *264 pp. 1959. (2nd Impression 1961.) 28s.*

Wootton, Graham. The Politics of Influence: British Ex-Servicemen, Cabinet Decisions and Cultural Changes, 1917 to 1957. *320 pp. 1963. 30s.*

FOREIGN AFFAIRS: THEIR SOCIAL, POLITICAL AND ECONOMIC FOUNDATIONS

Baer, Gabriel. Population and Society in the Arab East. *Translated by Hanna Szöke. 288 pp. 10 maps. 1964. 40s.*

Bonné, Alfred. The Economic Development of the Middle East: An Outline of Planned Reconstruction after the War. *192 pp. 58 tables. 1945. (3rd Impression 1953.) 16s.*

State and Economics in the Middle East: A Society in Transition. *482 pp. 2nd (revised) edition 1955. (2nd Impression 1960.) 40s.*

Studies in Economic Development: with special reference to Conditions in the Under-developed Areas of Western Asia and India. *322 pp. 84 tables. (2nd edition 1960.) 32s.*

Mayer, J. P. Political Thought in France from the Revolution to the Fifth Republic. *164 pp. 3rd edition (revised) 1961. 16s.*

Schlesinger, Rudolf. Central European Democracy and its Background: Economic and Political Group Organization. *432 pp. 1953. 40s.*

Thomson, David, Meyer, E., and **Briggs, A.** Patterns of Peacemaking. *408 pp. 1945. 25s.*

Trouton, Ruth. Peasant Renaissance in Yugoslavia, 1900-1950: A Study of the Development of Yugoslav Peasant Society as affected by Education. *370 pp. 1 map. 1952. 28s.*

SOCIOLOGY OF LAW

Gurvitch, Dr. Georges. Sociology of Law. *With a Preface by Professor Roscoe Pound. 280 pp. 1947. (2nd Impression 1953.) 24s.*

Renner, Karl. The Institutions of Private Law and Their Social Functions. *Edited, with an Introduction and Notes by O. Kahn-Freund. Translated by Agnes Schwarzschild. 336 pp. 1949. 28s.*

CRIMINOLOGY

Cloward, Richard A., and **Ohlin, Lloyd E.** Delinquency and Opportunity: A Theory of Delinquent Gangs. *248 pp. 1961. 25s.*

Friedländer, Dr. Kate. The Psycho-Analytical Approach to Juvenile Delinquency: Theory, Case Studies, Treatment. *320 pp. 1947. (5th Impression 1961.) 28s.*

Glueck, Sheldon and **Eleanor.** Family Environment and Delinquency. *With the statistical assistance of Rose W. Kneznek. 340 pp. 1962. 35s.*

Mannheim, Hermann. Group Problems in Crime and Punishment, and other Studies in Criminology and Criminal Law. *336 pp. 1955. 28s.*

Morris, Terence. The Criminal Area: A Study in Social Ecology. *Foreword by Hermann Mannheim. 232 pp. 25 tables. 4 maps. 1957. 25s.*

Morris, Terence and **Pauline,** assisted by **Barbara Barer.** Pentonville: a Sociological Study of an English Prison. *416 pp. 16 plates. 1963. 50s.*

Spencer, John C. Crime and the Services. *Foreword by Hermann Mannheim. 336 pp. 1954. 28s.*

Trasler, Gordon. The Explanation of Criminality. *144 pp. 1962. 20s.*

SOCIAL PSYCHOLOGY

Barbu, Zevedei. Problems of Historical Psychology. *248 pp. 1960. 25s.*

Blackburn, Julian. Psychology and the Social Pattern. *184 pp. 1945. (6th Impression 1961.) 16s.*

Fleming, C. M. Adolescence: Its Social Psychology: With an Introduction to recent findings from the fields of Anthropology, Physiology, Medicine, Psychometrics and Sociometry. *271 pp. 2nd edition (revised) 1963. (2nd impression 1964) 25s.*

The Social Psychology of Education: An Introduction and Guide to Its Study. *136 pp. 2nd edition (revised) 1959. 11s.*

Fleming, C. M. (Ed.). Studies in the Social Psychology of Adolescence. *Contributions by J. E. Richardson, J. F. Forrester, J. K. Shukla and P. J. Higginbotham. Foreword by the editor. 292 pp. 29 figures. 13 tables. 5 folder tables. 1951. 23s.*

Halmos, Paul. Solitude and Privacy: a Study of Social Isolation, its Causes and Therapy. *With a Foreword by Professor T. H. Marshall. 216 pp. 1952. 21s.*

Towards a Measure of Man: The Frontiers of Normal Adjustment. *276 pp. 1957. 28s.*

Homans, George C. The Human Group. *Foreword by Bernard DeVoto. Introduction by Robert K. Merton. 526 pp. 1951. (4th Impression 1963.) 35s.*

Social Behaviour: its Elementary Forms. *416 pp. 1961. 30s.*

Klein, Josephine. The Study of Groups. *226 pp. 31 figures. 5 tables. 1956. (3rd Impression 1962.) 21s.*

Linton, Ralph. The Cultural Background of Personality. *132 pp. 1947. (5th Impression 1964.) 16s.*
See also Yang, M.

Mayo, Elton. The Social Problems of an Industrial Civilization. With an appendix on the Political Problem. *180 pp. 1949. (4th Impression 1961.) 18s.*

Ridder, J. C. de. The Personality of the Urban African in South Africa. A Thematic Apperception Test Study. *196 pp. 12 plates. 1961. 25s.*

Rose, Arnold M. (Ed.). Mental Health and Mental Disorder: A Sociological Approach. *Chapters by 46 contributors. 654 pp. 1956. 45s.*
Human Behavior and Social Processes: an Interactionist Approach. *Contributions by Arnold M. Ross, Ralph H. Turner, Anselm Strauss, Everett C. Hughes, E. Franklin Frazier, Howard S. Becker, et al. 696 pp. 1962. 60s.*

Smelser, Neil J. Theory of Collective Behavior. *448 pp. 1962. 45s.*

Spinley, Dr. B. M. The Deprived and the Privileged: Personality Development in English Society. *232 pp. 1953. 20s.*

Wolfenstein, Martha. Disaster: A Psychological Essay. *264 pp. 1957. 23s.*

Young, Professor Kimball. Personality and Problems of Adjustment. *742 pp. 12 figures. 9 tables. 2nd edition (revised) 1952. (2nd Impression 1959.) 40s.*
Handbook of Social Psychology. *658 pp. 16 figures. 10 tables. 2nd edition (revised) 1957. (3rd Impression 1963.) 40s.*

SOCIOLOGY OF THE FAMILY

Banks, J. A. Prosperity and Parenthood: A Study of Family Planning among the Victorian Middle Classes. *262 pp. 1954. 24s.*

Chapman, Dennis. The Home and Social Status. *336 pp. 8 plates. 3 figures. 117 tables. 1955. 35s.*

Klein, Viola. The Feminine Character: History of an Ideology. *With a Foreword by Karl Mannheim. 256 pp. 1946. 16s.*

Myrdal, Alva and **Klein, Viola.** Women's Two Roles: Home and Work. *238 pp. 27 tables. 1956. (2nd Impression 1962.) 25s.*

Parsons, Talcott and **Bales, Robert F.** Family: Socialization and Interaction Process. *In collaboration with James Olds, Morris Zelditch and Philip E. Slater. 456 pp. 50 figures and tables. 1956. 35s.*

THE SOCIAL SERVICES

Ashdown, Margaret and **Brown, S. Clement.** Social Service and Mental Health: An Essay on Psychiatric Social Workers. *280 pp. 1953. 21s.*

Hall, M. Penelope. The Social Services of Modern England. *416 pp. 6th edition (revised) 1963. 28s.*

Heywood, Jean S. Children in Care: the Development of the Service for the Deprived Child. *256 pp. 1959. (2nd Impression 1964.) 25s.*
An Introduction to teaching Casework Skills. *192 pp. 1964. 28s.*

Jones, Kathleen. Lunacy, Law and Conscience, 1744-1845: the Social History of the Care of the Insane. *268 pp. 1955. 25s.*
Mental Health and Social Policy, 1845-1959. *264 pp. 1960. 28s.*

Jones, Kathleen and **Sidebotham, Roy.** Mental Hospitals at Work. *220 pp. 1962. 30s.*

Kastell, Jean. Casework in Child Care. *Foreword by M. Brooke Willis. 320 pp. 1962. 35s.*

Rooff, Madeline. Voluntary Societies and Social Policy. *350 pp. 15 tables. 1957. 35s.*

Shenfield, B. E. Social Policies for Old Age: A Review of Social Provision for Old Age in Great Britain. *260 pp. 39 tables. 1957. 25s.*

Timms, Noel. Psychiatric Social Work in Great Britain (1939-1962). *280 pp. 1964. 32s.*

Social Casework: Principles and Practice. *256 pp. 1964, 25s.*

Trasler, Gordon. In Place of Parents: A Study in Foster Care. *272 pp. 1960. 25s.*

Young, A. F., and **Ashton, E. T.** British Social Work in the Nineteenth Century. *288 pp. 1956. (2nd Impression 1963.) 28s.*

SOCIOLOGY OF EDUCATION

Banks, Olive. Parity and Prestige in English Secondary Education: a Study in Educational Sociology. *272 pp. 1955. (2nd Impression. 1963.) 28s.*

Collier, K. G. The Social Purposes of Education: Personal and Social Values in Education. *268 pp. 1959. (2nd Impression 1962.) 21s.*

Edmonds, E. L. The School Inspector. *Foreword by Sir William Alexander. 214 pp. 1962. 28s.*

Evans, K. M. Sociometry and Education. *158 pp. 1962. 18s.*

Fraser, W. R. Education and Society in Modern France. *150 pp. 1963. 20s.*

Hans, Nicholas. New Trends in Education in the Eighteenth Century. *278 pp. 19 tables. 1951. 25s.*

Comparative Education: A Study of Educational Factors and Traditions. *360 pp. 3rd (revised) edition 1958. (4th Impression 1964.) 25s.*

Mannheim, Karl and **Stewart, W. A. C.** An Introduction to the Sociology of Education. *208 pp. 1962. 21s.*

Musgrove, F. Youth and the Social Order. *176 pp. 1964. 21s.*

Ortega y Gasset, Jose. Mission of the University. *Translated with an Introduction by Howard Lee Nostrand. 88 pp. 1946. (3rd Impression 1963.) 15s.*

Ottaway, A. K. C. Education and Society: An Introduction to the Sociology of Education. *With an Introduction by W. O. Lester Smith. 212 pp. Second edition (revised). 1962. (2nd Impression 1964.) 18s.*

Peers, Robert. Adult Education: A Comparative Study. *398 pp. 2nd edition 1959. 35s.*

Pritchard, D. G. Education and the Handicapped: 1760 to 1960. *258 pp. 1963. 28s.*

Samuel, R. H., and **Thomas, R. Hinton.** Education and Society in Modern Germany. *212 pp. 1949. 16s.*

Simon, Brian and **Joan** (Eds.). Educational Psychology in the U.S.S.R. *Introduction by Brian and Joan Simon. Translation by Joan Simon. Papers by D. N. Bogoiavlenski and N. A. Menchinskaia, D. B. Elkonin, E. A. Fleshner, Z. I. Kalmykova, G. S. Kostiuk, V. A. Krutetski, A. N. Leontiev, A. R. Luria, E. A. Milerian, R. G. Natadze, B. M. Teplov, L. S. Vygotski, L. V. Zankov. 296 pp. 1963. 40s.*

SOCIOLOGY OF CULTURE

Fromm, Erich. The Fear of Freedom. *286 pp. 1942. (8th Impression 1960.) 21s.*
The Sane Society. *400 pp. 1956. (3rd Impression 1963.) 28s.*

Mannheim, Karl. Diagnosis of Our Time: Wartime Essays of a Sociologist. *208 pp. 1943. (7th Impression 1962.) 21s.*
Essays on the Sociology of Culture. *Edited by Ernst Mannheim in co-operation with Paul Kecskemeti. Editorial Note by Adolph Lowe. 280 pp. 1956. (2nd Impression 1962.) 28s.*

Weber, Alfred. Farewell to European History: or The Conquest of Nihilism. *Translated from the German by R. F. C. Hull. 224 pp. 1947. 18s.*

SOCIOLOGY OF RELIGION

Argyle, Michael. Religious Behaviour. *224 pp. 8 figures. 41 tables. 1958. 25s.*

Knight, Frank H., and **Merriam, Thornton W.** The Economic Order and Religion. *242 pp. 1947. 18s.*

Watt, W. Montgomery. Islam and the Integration of Society. *320 pp. 1961. (2nd Impression.) 32s.*

SOCIOLOGY OF ART AND LITERATURE

Beljame, Alexandre. Men of Letters and the English Public in the Eighteenth Century: 1660-1744, Dryden, Addison, Pope. *Edited with an Introduction and Notes by Bonamy Dobree. Translated by E. O. Lorimer. 532 pp. 1948. 32s.*

Misch, Georg. A History of Autobiography in Antiquity. *Translated by E. W. Dickes. 2 Volumes. Vol. 1, 364 pp., Vol. 2, 372 pp. 1950. 45s. the set.*

Silbermann, Alphons. The Sociology of Music. *224 pp. 1963. 28s.*

SOCIOLOGY OF KNOWLEDGE

Hodges, H. A. The Philosophy of Wilhelm Dilthey. *410 pp. 1952. 30s.*

Mannheim, Karl. Essays on the Sociology of Knowledge. *Edited by Paul Kecskemeti. Editorial note by Adolph Lowe. 352 pp. 1952. (3rd Impression 1964.) 35s.*

Schlesinger, Rudolf. Marx: His Time and Ours. *464 pp. 1950. (2nd Impression 1951.) 32s.*

Stark, W. The History of Economics in its Relation to Social Development. *104 pp. 1944. (4th Impression 1957.) 12s.*

America: Ideal and Reality. The United States of 1776 in Contemporary Philosophy. *136 pp. 1947. 12s.*

The Sociology of Knowledge: An Essay in Aid of a Deeper Understanding of the History of Ideas. *384 pp. 1958. (2nd Impression 1960.) 36s.*

Montesquieu: Pioneer of the Sociology of Knowledge. *244 pp. 1960. 25s.*

URBAN SOCIOLOGY

Anderson, Nels. The Urban Community: A World Perspective. *532 pp. 1960. 35s.*

Ashworth, William. The Genesis of Modern British Town Planning: A Study in Economic and Social History of the Nineteenth and Twentieth Centuries. *288 pp. 1954. 25s.*

Bracey, Howard. Neighbours: Neighbouring and Neighbourliness on New Estates and Subdivisions in England and the U.S.A. *220 pp. 1964. 28s.*

Cullingworth, J. B. Housing Needs and Planning Policy: A Restatement of the Problems of Housing Need and "Overspill" in England and Wales. *232 pp. 44 tables. 8 maps. 1960. 28s.*

Dickinson, Robert E. City and Region: A Geographical Interpretation. *608 pp. 125 figures. 1964. 60s.*

The West European City: A Geographical Interpretation. *600 pp. 129 maps. 29 plates. 2nd edition 1962. (2nd Impression 1963.) 55s.*

Dore, R. P. City Life in Japan: A Study of a Tokyo Ward. *498 pp. 8 plates. 4 figures. 24 tables. 1958. (2nd Impression 1963.) 45s.*

Jennings, Hilda. Societies in the Making: a Study of Development and Redevelopment within a County Borough. *Foreword by D. A. Clark. 286 pp. 1962. 32s.*

Kerr, Madeline. The People of Ship Street. *240 pp. 1958. 23s.*

RURAL SOCIOLOGY

Bracey, H. E. English Rural Life: Village Activities, Organizations and Institutions. *302 pp. 1959. 30s.*

Infield, Henrik F. Co-operative Living in Palestine. *With a Foreword by General Sir Arthur Wauchope, G.C.B. 170 pp. 8 plates. 7 tables. 1946. 12s. 6d.*

Littlejohn, James. Westrigg: the Sociology of a Cheviot Parish. *172 pp. 5 figures. 1963. 25s.*

Saville, John. Rural Depopulation in England and Wales, 1851-1951. *Foreword by Leonard Elmhirst. 286 pp. 6 figures. 39 tables. 1 map. 1957. 28s.* (*Dartington Hall Studies in Rural Sociology.*)

Williams, W. M. The Country Craftsman: A Study of Some Rural Crafts and the Rural Industries Organization in England. *248 pp. 9 figures. 1958. 25s.* (*Dartington Hall Studies in Rural Sociology.*)
The Sociology of an English Village: Gosforth. *272 pp. 12 figures. 13 tables. 1956. (3rd Impression 1964.) 25s.*

SOCIOLOGY OF MIGRATION

Eisenstadt, S. N. The Absorption of Immigrants: a Comparative Study based mainly on the Jewish Community in Palestine and the State of Israel. *288 pp. 1954. 28s.*

SOCIOLOGY OF INDUSTRY AND DISTRIBUTION

Anderson, Nels. Work and Leisure. *280 pp. 1961. 28s.*

Blau, Peter M., and **Scott, W. Richard.** Formal Organizations: a Comparative approach. *Introduction and Additional Bibliography by J. H. Smith. 328 pp. 1963. (2nd impression 1964.) 28s.*

Gouldner, Alvin W. Patterns of Industrial Bureaucracy. *298 pp. 1955. 25s.*
Wildcat Strike: A Study of an Unofficial Strike. *202 pp. 10 figures. 1955. 16s.*

Jefferys, Margot, with the assistance of Winifred Moss. Mobility in the Labour Market: Employment Changes in Battersea and Dagenham. *Preface by Barbara Wootton. 186 pp. 51 tables. 1954. 15s.*

Levy, A. B. Private Corporations and Their Control. *Two Volumes. Vol. 1, 464 pp., Vol. 2, 432 pp. 1950. 80s. the set.*

Levy, Hermann. The Shops of Britain: A Study of Retail Distribution. *268 pp. 1948. (2nd Impression 1949.) 21s.*

Liepmann, Kate. The Journey to Work: Its Significance for Industrial and Community Life. *With a Foreword by A. M. Carr-Saunders. 230 pp. 40 tables. 3 folders. 1944. (2nd Impression 1945.) 18s.*
Apprenticeship: An Enquiry into its Adequacy under Modern Conditions. *Foreword by H. D. Dickinson. 232 pp. 6 tables. 1960. (2nd Impression.) 23s.*

Millerson, Geoffrey. The Qualifying Associations: a Study in Professionalization. *320 pp. 1964. 42s.*

Smelser, Neil J. Social Change in the Industrial Revolution: An Application of Theory to the Lancashire Cotton Industry, 1770-1840. *468 pp. 12 figures. 14 tables. 1959. (2nd Impression 1960.) 40s.*

Williams, Gertrude. Recruitment to Skilled Trades. *240 pp. 1957. 23s.*

Young, A. F. Industrial Injuries Insurance: an Examination of British Policy. *192 pp. 1964. 30s.*

ANTHROPOLOGY

(*Demy 8vo.*)

Crook, David and **Isabel.** Revolution in a Chinese Village: Ten Mile Inn. *230 pp. 8 plates. 1 map. 1959. 21s.*

Dube, S. C. Indian Village, *Foreword by Morris Edward Opler. 276 pp. 4 plates. 1955. (4th Impression 1961.) 25s.*

India's Changing Villages: Human Factors in Community Development. *260 pp. 8 plates. 1 map. 1958. (2nd Impression 1960.) 25s.*

Fei, Hsiao-Tung. Peasant Life in China: a Field Study of Country Life in the Yangtze Valley. *Foreword by Bronislaw Malinowski. 320 pp. 14 plates. 1939. (5th Impression 1962.) 30s.*

Gulliver, P. H. The Family Herds. A Study of Two Pastoral Tribes in East Africa, The Jie and Turkana. *304 pp. 4 plates. 19 figures. 1955. 25s.*

Social Control in an African Society: a Study of the Arusha, Agricultural Masai of Northern Tanganyika. *320 pp. 8 plates. 10 figures. 1963. 35s.*

Hogbin, Ian. Transformation Scene. The Changing Culture of a New Guinea Village. *340 pp. 22 plates. 2 maps. 1951. 30s.*

Hsu, Francis L. K. Under the Ancestors' Shadow: Chinese Culture and Personality. *346 pp. 26 figures. 1949. 21s.*

Lowie, Professor Robert H. Social Organization. *494 pp. 1950. (3rd Impression 1962.) 35s.*

Maunier, René. The Sociology of Colonies: An Introduction to the Study of Race Contact. *Edited and translated by E. O. Lorimer. 2 Volumes. Vol. 1, 430 pp., Vol. 2, 356 pp. 1949. 70s. the set.*

Mayer, Adrian C. Caste and Kinship in Central India: A Village and its Region. *328 pp. 16 plates. 15 figures. 16 tables. 1960. 35s.*

Peasants in the Pacific: A Study of Fiji Indian Rural Society. *232 pp. 16 plates. 10 figures. 14 tables. 1961. 35s.*

Osborne, Harold. Indians of the Andes: Aymaras and Quechuas. *292 pp. 8 plates. 2 maps. 1952. 25s.*

Smith, Raymond T. The Negro Family in British Guiana: Family Structure and Social Status in the Villages. *With a Foreword by Meyer Fortes. 314 pp. 8 plates. 1 figure. 4 maps. 1956. 28s.*

Yang, Martin C. A Chinese Village: Taitou, Shantung Province. *Foreword by Ralph Linton. Introduction by M. L. Wilson. 308 pp. 1947. 23s.*

DOCUMENTARY

(*Demy 8vo.*)

Belov, Fedor. The History of a Soviet Collective Farm. *250 pp. 1956. 21s.*

Meek, Dorothea L. (Ed.). Soviet Youth: Some Achievements and Problems. *Excerpts from the Soviet Press, translated by the editor. 280 pp. 1957. 28s.*

Schlesinger, Rudolf (Ed.). Changing Attitudes in Soviet Russia.

1. The Family in the U.S.S.R. *Documents and Readings, with an Introduction by the editor. 434 pp. 1949. 30s.*
2. The Nationalities Problem and Soviet Administration. Selected Readings on the Development of Soviet Nationalities Policies. *Introduced by the editor. Translated by W. W. Gottlieb. 324 pp. 1956. 30s.*

Reports of the Institute of Community Studies

(*Demy 8vo.*)

Cartwright, Ann. Human Relations and Hospital Care. *272 pp. 1964. 30s.*

Jackson, Brian and **Marsden, Dennis.** Education and the Working Class: Some General Themes raised by a Study of 88 Working-class Children in a Northern Industrial City. *268 pp. 2 folders. 1962. (2nd Impression.) 28s.*

Marris, Peter. Widows and their Families. *Foreword by Dr. John Bowlby. 184 pp. 18 tables. Statistical Summary. 1958. 18s.*

Family and Social Change in an African City. A Study of Rehousing in Lagos. *196 pp. 1 map. 4 plates. 53 tables. 1961. 25s.*

Mills, Enid. Living with Mental Illness: a Study in East London. *Foreword by Morris Carstairs. 196 pp. 1962. 28s.*

Townsend, Peter. The Family Life of Old People: An Inquiry in East London. *Foreword by J. H. Sheldon. 300 pp. 3 figures. 63 tables. 1957. (2nd Impression 1961.) 30s.*

Willmott, Peter. The Evolution of a Community: a study of Dagenham after forty years. *168 pp. 2 maps. 1963. 21s.*

Willmott, Peter and **Young, Michael.** Family and Class in a London Suburb. *202 pp. 47 tables. 1960. (2nd Impression 1961.) 21s.*

The British Journal of Sociology. *Edited by D. G. MacRae. Vol. 1, No. 1, March 1950 and Quarterly. Roy. 8vo., £2 p.a.; 12s. 6d. a number, post free. (Vols. 1-12, £3 each.)*

All prices are net and subject to alteration without notice